W9-ANV-672

FINDING THALHIMERS

By Elizabeth Thalhimer Smartt

Dementi Milestone Publishing

Author
Elizabeth Thalhimer Smartt

Publisher
Wayne Dementi
Dementi Milestone Publishing, Inc.
Manakin-Sabot, VA 23103
www.dementimilestonepublishing.com

Cataloging-in-publication data for this book is available from
The Library of Congress.
ISBN: 978-0-9827019-1-1

Cover design by:
Noah Scalin
Another Limited Rebellion
www.ALRdesign.com

Graphic design by:
Jayne E. Hushen
Hushen Design
www.HushenDesign.com

Edited by:
Erin Elizabeth Virginia Cartwright Niumata

Printed in China

FINDING
THALHIMERS

You have the

Well Wishes

of

Wm Thalhimer

Jany 10th 1878.

It would be impossible to individually thank all of the employees who made each Thalhimers store such a special place to work and shop. During the last fifty years of Thalhimers' existence, approximately one-third of store employees had devoted at least ten years of service to the company. The Thalhimer family expresses gracious thanks to all employees for their hard work, integrity, loyalty, and commitment to excellence.

Dedicated to my father, William B. Thalhimer III,
for gently, patiently, and cleverly
giving me no option but to write this book.

Everything new must have its roots in what was before.
— *Sigmund Freud*

We can't resist this rifling around in the past, sifting the untrustworthy
evidence, linking stray names and questionable dates and anecdotes
together, hanging on to threads, insisting on being joined
to dead people and therefore to life.

— *Alice Munro, <u>The View from Castle Rock</u>*

I never think that people die. They just go to department stores.

— *Andy Warhol*

TABLE OF CONTENTS

Four generations of Thalhimers' leadership (l to r) Wolff/William Thalhimer, Issac Thalhimer, William B. Thalhimer Jr., William B. Thalhimer Sr., poster created circa 1936.

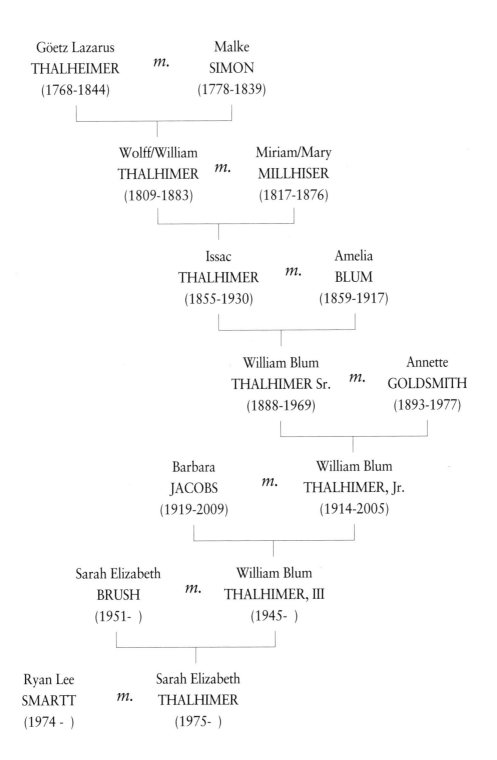

Göetz Lazarus
THALHEIMER
(1768-1844)

m.

Malke
SIMON
(1778-1839)

Wolff/William
THALHIMER
(1809-1883)

m.

Miriam/Mary
MILLHISER
(1817-1876)

Issac
THALHIMER
(1855-1930)

m.

Amelia
BLUM
(1859-1917)

William Blum
THALHIMER Sr.
(1888-1969)

m.

Annette
GOLDSMITH
(1893-1977)

Barbara
JACOBS
(1919-2009)

m.

William Blum
THALHIMER, Jr.
(1914-2005)

Sarah Elizabeth
BRUSH
(1951-)

m.

William Blum
THALHIMER, III
(1945-)

Ryan Lee
SMARTT
(1974 -)

m.

Sarah Elizabeth
THALHIMER
(1975-)

Author's direct paternal line not including siblings.

FOREWORD

John Stewart Bryan III has been chairman of Media General Inc. since 1990. He served as publisher of the Richmond Newspapers from 1978 until 2005. His family has been involved with Richmond Newspapers since the late 1880s.

Popovers with lunch in the fourth floor Richmond Room, or a hot dog from Angelo's in the basement, or a cup of navy bean soup and a sandwich at the Soup Bar on the mezzanine – one or more of these became part of the weekly ritual for many in the Richmond work force. On any day's visit to the Richmond Room, one was almost sure to encounter a Thalhimer – William Jr. or his brother Charles, or one of their sons, William III, Charlie Jr., or Harry.

I was no exception. The newspaper offices were only two blocks west of Thalhimers. That also meant that the Tea Room at Miller & Rhoads, in between the two, sometimes lured the passer-by in for lunch before he or she reached one of those Thalhimer offerings.

Clearly, though, the combination of those blocks, bounded on the north by Broad Street, the south by Grace, the east and the west by Seventh and Fifth Streets, defined the city of Richmond in the minds of many residents and visitors alike in the half century between the end of World War II and the decade of the 1990s.

Indeed, a popular saying in my youth was, "North Carolinians know the three 'Rs' as reading, writing and the road to Richmond." That was a haughty reference to the fact that our neighbors to the south, in search of high quality goods, had to come to Thalhimers and Miller & Rhoads.

If you couldn't find what you were looking for in those two blocks, either it couldn't be had or it wasn't worth purchasing. There was even a clearly marked pedestrian way across Sixth Street between the two stores, and vehicular traffic often was at a standstill while scores of folk used it in both directions.

How well I remember going with my father, freshly returned from Naval service in the Pacific, to both Thalhimers and Miller & Rhoads to be fitted with gray and dark blue suits, each with short pants and matching caps. No, I didn't like them, but that was the required uniform for church or cotillion or to visit grandmothers and great aunts.

As a child I also knew Thalhimers as people – not just a store bearing their name.

There was a close relationship between their store and my family's newspapers, *The Richmond Times-Dispatch* and *The Richmond News Leader*, and that institutional friendship carried over into personal relationships as well.

My own personal friendship with William Jr. and his wife Barbara first blossomed when I was in Florida working for *The Tampa Tribune*. In 1977, I was elected to the board of a trade association named the Newspaper Advertising Bureau (NAB).

Each year, in January, the NAB and the National Retail Merchants Association (NRMA) would take turns hosting their boards at elaborate, formal dinners in New York City.

At the first one we attended, my wife and I were seated next to Billy and Barbara; and, the next year, after 13 years in Tampa, I returned to Richmond as publisher of the *Times-Dispatch* and *News Leader*.

Billy invited me to have lunch with him and his brother Charlie at the Richmond Room during the first week I was back, and I have since counted all Thalhimers as personal friends. I am particularly gratified to have been asked by Billy's granddaughter to pen this foreword to her book about him and their forebears.

For 150 years, the people behind the stores that bore their name, the Thalhimer clan, comprised an integral thread in the tapestry of Richmond. Just as the fabrics offered in their stores gained luster and strength over the years, so, too, grew the stature and reputation of the family, in the community and in the broader world beyond.

What began as a small shop in Richmond's Shockoe Bottom in 1842 grew and expanded into a 26-store chain that blanketed the Commonwealth of Virginia and good parts of North Carolina, and had a more limited presence in South Carolina and Tennessee. Thalhimers merged with Carter, Hawley, Hale in 1978, and the family continued to manage the company until the late 1980s when it was acquired by the May Company.

The last Thalhimer, William III, left the company in early 1991, and the downtown store closed its doors in 1992.

After a century and a half in the making, Thalhimers was no more.

During those 150 years, while maintaining their strong Jewish faith and identity, the Thalhimers widened their interests and became ardent supporters of all things good in the civic arena.

Family members always remembered their roots and provided comfort to victims of anti-Semitism and, later, racial discrimination.

The author explains how, after her grandfather, William B. Thalhimer, Jr., died in 2005, chronicling the family history became an obligation, a duty that included finding the family roots in Germany.

Herein, she has provided a sensitive, fact-filled account of her family since ancestor Wolff Thalheimer, born in 1809 to Goëtz and Malke Thalheimer in Thairenbach, near Heidelberg, Germany, migrated through New Orleans, to ante-bellum Richmond.

In a well-crafted chronicle, we are transported from his original residence above the store to several sites on Broad Street and a free-standing home on Clay Street, to a handsome mansion just west of the statue of Robert E. Lee on Monument Avenue.

Simultaneously, we follow the fortunes of the retail enterprise as it grows and contracts, going through three wars, a bankruptcy, and two depressions, while changing its name from William Thalhimer to Thalhimer Brothers to Thalhimers.

Of especial interest to me is an ongoing description of the close working and personal relationships between the Thalhimers and the people of Richmond Newspapers Inc., where I had my first summer job 56 years ago and still hang my hat today. (I am happy to be able to corroborate that report from the other side of the equation.)

Elizabeth's book is required reading for anyone interested in the history of Richmond, but I recommend it to a far broader audience.

A proud and powerful family portrait, she paints it in multi-generational, sometimes surrealistic, colors. Written with love and devotion, Finding Thalhimers is, all at the same time, careful genealogical research, riveting history, and love story.

This book will grab your attention at its beginning and keep it until its ending.

– Stewart Bryan, May 30, 2010

CHAPTER ONE

ANOTHER VIRGINIA
1997

When my search begins, I'm not really looking for anything.

With my junior year at Wake Forest behind me, Dad's driving me up to New York University for a summer film program. My younger sisters, Katherine and Christie, shout, "have fun!" as we drive off in the Suburban, and Mom says, "be careful." Weaving through the merciless I-95 traffic between Richmond and New York City, Dad stays within five miles of the speed limit and maintains his composure even when another driver cuts us off. He looks in the rearview mirror every so often, just like he taught me to do when I was learning to drive. The silence between us is comfortable.

Pressing my forehead against the window, questions fly through my head as sunlight blinks through the pine trees blurring against a cloudless sky. Where is the Mason-Dixon line? Did we just cross it? Are my clothes hip enough for New York City? Will I get lost on the subway and end up in Queens? Where is Queens? Did I pack the pepper spray keychain Mom gave me? Will I meet a handsome filmmaker with five o'clock shadow and black, angular-rimmed glasses? He'll probably smoke, but that's ok. It's only for the summer. Mom and Dad will never even have to meet him.

"We're staying with Virginia Stern tonight," Dad says. "I thought it would be nice for you to meet her."

"That's cool," I mutter. "Who's Virginia Stern?"

"Your second cousin twice removed. She lives by herself on the Upper East Side and said to visit if we're ever in town."

"Neat. So you'll help me move into the dorm tomorrow?"

"We'll leave after breakfast tomorrow. It's just a short drive down to the East Village. New York isn't really that big, you know."

Dad knows the city pretty well. He used to travel there on business trips years ago when he worked at Thalhimers, the department store that bore our family name for one hundred and fifty years. Dad claims that he and a bunch of other Thalhimers buyers went to Studio 54 in its heyday, but I can't imagine him staying up that late.

My eyelids grow heavy as the tedium of the highway lulls me to sleep. The next thing I know, several hours have passed and we're parallel parking outside a fancy apartment building on Park Avenue.

Half awake, I smooth my hair into a ponytail and flip the mirror down to refresh my iridescent pink lipstick. A doorman holds the lobby door open for us, the golden buttons of his jacket catching the afternoon sunlight.

"Good afternoon," he says to us. "How can I help you?"

"We're staying with Virginia Stern on the ninth floor," Dad says. "I'm Bill Thalhimer and this is my daughter Elizabeth."

"I'll ring her right up. Here, let me help with your bags." He pulls Dad's rolling suitcase with one hand and carries my overstuffed duffle bag with the other.

I didn't know where we'd be staying the night so I packed way too much stuff. Apparently we're staying with an elderly cousin in a snooty neighborhood full of overdressed women with big sunglasses and pocketbook-dogs. I don't think I brought an outfit for that.

"Thank you so much," I say, smiling graciously as I hand the doorman my enormous bag. "I think I overpacked."

"Where are you folks visiting from?" he asks.

"Richmond, Virginia."

"That's a pretty good haul."

"It wasn't bad," I tell him with a polite smile. "I slept most of the way."

The doorman dials Virginia Stern from the house phone in the lobby. In my peripheral vision, I can see him staring at me. I pretend to search for something in my purse, perhaps the pepper-spray keychain.

"Good afternoon, Mrs. Stern," he says, continuing to study my face. "Mr. Thalhimer and his daughter are here to see you...Yes, ma'am...I'll send them right up...You're welcome."

After hanging up the phone, the doorman says to me, "Ma'am, forgive me for saying this, but you look familiar. I think I've seen your smile before."

"Really? That's weird," I stammer with a nervous laugh. "I've never been to New York before. Well, once when I was a little kid. But never, you know, here. In this building."

"The other day I found a photo album in the trash outside Mrs. Stern's apartment. I have a thing for black and white photographs. This one's got pictures of women in long dresses, on horseback, things like that. This same woman is in all the pictures. I could swear you have her smile."

"We must be cousins," I say nervously. "We're related to Mrs. Stern, right, Dad?"

Stay calm, I remind myself. This doorman is a thinly veiled psychopathic serial killer. This is New York City, where crazy stuff happens and we see it on the Nightly News and shake our heads, saying, "only in New York."

The doorman continues, "Do you want to see the album? I still have it. Give me your address and I'll mail it to you."

Not sensing my paranoia or the utter peculiarity of the situation, Dad exclaims, "That'd be great! We love family albums. Here's my business card." I cringe as he pulls his worn brown leather wallet from his back pocket and hands over his card with *William B. Thalhimer, III* and his home address embossed on it.

"No problem, Sir. I'll be right up with your bags. Keep smiling!" the killer doorman says to me as he holds the elevator door for us. I force a meek smile, nod my head politely, and gulp to keep my heartbeat from rising into my throat.

When the elevator doors slide shut, I blurt out, "Dad! Why did you give that creepy guy your card? He'll mail us a bomb."

Dad shakes his head and says nonchalantly, "Elizabeth, you are so dramatic. Let's just enjoy the day."

I inhale and hold my breath in my cheeks while staring up at the illuminated floor indicator. As it counts from one to nine, I exhale slowly to regain my composure.

"We're in New York City," Dad says. "Let's just have fun."

On the ninth floor, the bell dings and the elevator doors open to reveal a nicely dressed woman, probably in her early eighties, with a warm, dignified smile.

"Bill," she says, accepting a kiss on the cheek from Dad as she cradles his right hand with her manicured fingers. "So good to see you again. And you must be Elizabeth. Attending NYU for the summer, am I right?"

"Yes, ma'am," I respond sheepishly. "Thank you so much for having us, Ms. Stern."

"Please call me Virginia," she says, leading us the short distance down the hall to her apartment. "I hope the drive was pleasant. City traffic can be awful this time of year."

"It only took us six and a half hours," Dad says. "Really not bad at all."

Virginia turns the key and pushes the door open to reveal a well-appointed apartment with rich, crimson fabrics, lots of bookshelves, and a silver service on the sideboard. I recognize no one in the assorted photographs around the living room.

"You'll be staying in the guest room," Virginia says, ushering us into a small but comfortable Art Deco room with a queen-sized bed and green leather headboard. "I apologize there's only one bed for the two of you. Hopefully you don't mind sharing."

Dad shoots me a "yikes" glance with raised eyebrows. We both know his snoring will awaken me. If I have glazed eyes on the first day of class, I'll be so crabby and unattractive. None of the cute film-school boys will even notice me.

"I'll give you a moment to settle in," Virginia says. "Please let me know if you need anything. Let's meet back in the dining room for supper in half an hour."

The doorman delivers our bags as Dad and I take turns washing up in the guest bath. I change into a black voile skirt, a carnation pink cashmere sweater set, and strappy black wedge-heeled sandals, an outfit I'd packed in case Dad took me to The Palms. I was sort of expecting it. I can't believe he's sacrificed a father-daughter lobster dinner for this oddball Park Avenue slumber party with some distant cousin from his genealogy database.

In the dining room, a candlelit table dressed with crisp white linens awaits us. Dad pulls out my chair and slides it beneath me as Virginia's longtime housekeeper enters with plates of steaming hot turkey, roasted vegetables, and duchess potatoes. Everything about it, from the luminous chandelier to the polite decorum of the housekeeper, reminds me of Thanksgiving at Gram and Grandpa Thalhimer's house. It feels oddly familiar.

"How is your family?" Virginia asks Dad. "I hope your parents are well?"

"I told them we'd be staying with you and they send along their best. They're doing just great, still walking five miles a day and going out for dinner with friends a few nights a week. They don't go to Tahoe for the summers anymore but they're enjoying spending time with all of the children and grandchildren. We're all in Richmond now except for Elizabeth and Katherine, who are both at Wake Forest University. Elizabeth will be a senior this year."

Virginia smiles at me, saying, "Oh, that's just wonderful. They must be very proud of you."

I nod and smile as warmly as possible. I wish I knew who she was.

As Virginia tells us about her granddaughter packing her trunks to go off to sleep-away camp for the first time, I savor every bite of the home-cooked dinner. This could be my last real meal before months of pizza. Do they even have a dining hall at NYU? Will I need a meal card?

The housekeeper clears the table then returns from the kitchen with a plate of delicate butter cookies. Seeing me slide two of them off the plate, Virginia turns to me and says, "You know, if you like cookies, you're in for a real treat. New York has first-class bakeries. Practically every neighborhood has its very own."

"Mmm. Yummy," I say childishly, biting into the thin cookie.

"I remember the sweet shop at Thalhimers," Virginia says with a sentimental tilt of her head. "You could smell the butter cookies and honey buns from the street. I remember those black and white checkered bakery boxes just like it was yesterday."

The corners of her eyes crinkle like tissue paper fans, suggesting the millions of times Virginia has smiled in her life. Why does this woman remember Thalhimers? It never had any branches north of Richmond. Did she grow up in Richmond? Did her parents grow up in Richmond? I should have asked Dad more questions in the car. I'm too shy to ask now, but I'm growing more curious by the minute.

"You both outdid yourselves with this dinner," Dad says to our gracious hostess and her housekeeper. "It was just delicious."

"It's our pleasure," Virginia replies, nodding to her housekeeper who ducks back into the kitchen. "Well, shall we have a seat in the living room and take a look at the family scrapbook?"

"That's why we're here," Dad says, resting a hand on my shoulder. "We're *family*."

I nod and smile absently, trying to calculate what it means to be a second cousin twice removed. Since his career at Thalhimers ended in 1991, Dad has been searching for every cousin in our extended family tree. His database includes thousands of people, some of whom he invites to visit him and Mom at their home in Richmond. Genealogy seems like a productive use of the time and energy Dad used to spend at "The Store," as we always called it. Now he's become the Branch Manager of the family tree.

Dad, Virginia and I sit together on a delicately scaled sofa in her living room. Virginia's frail but elegant fingers lift a tattered, leather-bound album from the coffee table. She fumbles to open it, so Dad helps her open the cover to the first page. It looks like the quintessential old scrapbook from a movie, with little photo corners framing each photograph.

"Do you know who these people are, Elizabeth?" Virginia asks, pointing to two black and white images of a man and woman.

My brow furrows and the words don't seem to come as I struggle to grasp why Virginia has these pictures. Noting my inability to say anything, Dad speaks up.

"William and Mary Thalhimer," he says. "Elizabeth, those are your great-great-great grandparents."

"I know," is all I can manage to utter as I look at the photographs.

In solemn, shadowy portraits, these same faces shoot sidelong glances at us every year at our Passover Seder in Aunt Lisa and Uncle Bobby's dining room. From his portrait, William Thalhimer looks down at us from beneath an arched doorway. He wears a dark suit, a small hoop earring, and pinky rings on both hands. Why did he wear so much jewelry? Was he a pirate before he became a merchant? In his wife's portrait, Mary's angular nose, earnest expression, black dress with a crocheted collar, and jet-black hair pulled into a tight bun remind me of a Salem witch. One of her hands rests upon a red book. In what language was it written? German? English? Yiddish? I don't know anything about her aside from her name.

Another portrait of William Thalhimer, which once commanded a special spot above the center elevator at Thalhimers in downtown Richmond, now lords over the dining room table at my parents' house. William's high forehead and large ears look decidedly like Grandpa's. When we were younger, my sister Katherine told me that she saw William's ghost float out of the portrait one night when she was sneaking cereal from the kitchen. I believed her. I still do. I believe in ghosts.

As Virginia turns the next page of her scrapbook, a group of people stare back at me. Seven well-dressed adults pose stiffly in what appears to be a photographer's studio. Right away, I recognize one of the mustached gentlemen as Isaac Thalhimer, my great-great grandfather.

Isaac's darkly toned skin sets off his eyes, intense and captivating. I know those eyes. A photograph of Isaac hangs in Dad's office, and I know which one was his old brownstone house on Monument Avenue back in Richmond. We've passed it many times, but I've never been inside.

With a thin, quivering finger, Virginia points to one of Isaac's brothers and says, "This one here is Moses Thalhimer, my grandfather. He's the reason why I live in New

York even though my name is Virginia."

I begin to recall a story Grandpa told about "Uncle Mose" taking him to lunch when he lived in New York as a teenager. Why did Uncle Mose live in New York? Didn't he run Thalhimers with Isaac and the other Thalhimer brothers back in Richmond? After all, The Store was called Thalhimer Brothers; I know that much. What made the brothers split ways?

As Virginia turns the next page, a piece of notepaper tucked into the binding releases and falls to the Oriental rug beside my shoe. I pick it up, reading the handwritten script:

> Göetz Lazarus
> born February 3rd 1768
> died April 27th 1844
> at Thairenbach
> was protégé (= in German
> Schutzbuerger) and
> tradesman in wax
> and honey.
> Göetz Lazarus named
> laterly Göetz Thalheimer

"Who is 'Goats Lazarus'?" I ask Virginia, mispronouncing the unfamiliar German name.

"He was the first Thalhimer," she says, gazing proudly at the words. "My mother told me so."

The first Thalhimer? What does that mean?

⚜   ⚜   ⚜

Months later, the phone rings in my dorm room at NYU where I'm storyboarding a short film about a businessman-turned-superhero in Washington Square Park. It's not exactly original. I put my pen down and pick up the phone.

"Hello?"

"Hi, Bibbie. It's Dad." Bibbie is my nickname because that's what my sister Katherine called me before she could say Elizabeth. I wish I had a cooler nickname, like Libbie or Liza, but I didn't have much say in the matter.

"Hey, Dad. What's up?"

"I just got the package from your friend, the killer doorman. And guess what? It's not a bomb. It's a photo album that belonged to Virginia's mother, Irma Marie Thalhimer Fox. F-O-X. It's not worth mailing, but I'll leave it on your desk."

"Ok, Dad. Thanks," I say, greatly relieved. The whole doorman-mailing-us-a-trashed-family-album story seemed way too eerie to be true. I had told Dad to make sure someone else opened the suspicious package in case it was a bomb. If I'd had my way, we never would have received it in the first place, but now I'm glad we did. I'm eager to see Irma Marie's smile.

As the weeks of film classes roll by, I come to two important realizations. Number one: I have no particular talent for filmmaking. Number two: I want to live in New York City after I graduate.

There's something intangible about the city that I can't resist. Living among the bustling masses feels liberating and exciting, and hardly anyone recognizes my last name. No one can even pronounce it. I can be myself without bucking any expectations or preconceived notions of what a "Thalhimer" should look like or act like. I can walk to Ben & Jerry's in plaid pajama pants and no one even notices. I even went to the MOMA in said pajama pants. New York is the opposite of everything I've ever known.

After film classes wrap up, I return to the comfortable familiarity of my parents' house back in Richmond. I slide the hand-painted blue chair out from the desk where I clocked hundreds of hours of homework during my thirteen years of prep school. The doorman's album rests atop a stack of unopened mail.

Gently sliding my hand across the cover before opening it, the album seems fragile and abandoned. On the first page, a young woman with a mischievous, bow-shaped smile gazes up at me. Everything about the photographs seems dated and old-fashioned, but Irma Marie somehow looks contemporary. She looks nothing like my perception of myself, so I look into the mirror to study my face.

What did that doorman see in my smile? Did Virginia tell him we were relatives coming to visit? Did she tell him about Dad's genealogy research? Why does anyone steal a photo album from someone else's trash? Why did this album come to me? What am I supposed to do with it?

Seduced by the delicious strangeness of the situation, I flip from one page to the next.

A page from Irma Marie Thalhimer's scrapbook, 1910.

Irma Marie Thalhimer with her head tossed back, laughing with a friend. Irma Marie holding a parasol as she floats across a lake in a canoe. Moses Thalhimer and Irma Marie standing in a manicured garden in Ossining, New York. Irma Marie riding in an old Rambler down Monument Avenue in Richmond.

Beneath the album is a large Manila envelope full of copies Virginia made of her family scrapbook. Thumbing through them, I come across the stray note about Göetz Lazarus, the "first Thalhimer." I stare at it for a moment then carry it into the kitchen where Dad is making Tahoe Specials, open-faced turkey, cheese, and sautéed onion sandwiches. They're a Thalhimer family tradition even though practically no one in our family can cook.

"Want a Tahoe Special?" he asks, wearing an oven mitt on one hand.

"Have I ever *not* wanted a Tahoe Special?" I snag a piece of cheese from the cutting board as I re-read the note. "Dad, who is this 'Goats' guy?"

"I really don't know, Elizabeth. We're descendents of 'Gustav Thalheimer.' I think Virginia got it wrong." After removing the Tahoe Specials from the oven to cool, Dad takes off his oven mitt and reads the piece of paper. "But it's true that we came from this place: Thairenbach. That's what it says on William Thalhimer's gravestone. I'll take you over to Hebrew Cemetery whenever you want to see it. Want to go this weekend?"

"No, thanks. Maybe some other time."

He's always trying to get me to visit Hebrew Cemetery, where he's the president or something. Tahoe Specials in hand, we walk downstairs to Dad's makeshift office in the basement where his desk sits beside the ping-pong table and air hockey table.

"Have you ever been to Thairenbach?" I ask, taking a seat in one of the ubiquitous green leather chairs.

"No. Thairenbach is gone. I looked it up in an atlas at the Library of Congress. It said 'this town does not appear on a modern map.' It's just not there anymore."

"What do you mean 'not there'? Maybe it's called something else, but I'm sure the place is still there," I challenge him. "Did you check any other maps or Google it? I mean, just because it's not on a modern map doesn't mean it doesn't exist."

"Look, Elizabeth. We're not related to anyone named Lazarus and we're definitely not related to any goats." Then he laughs at his own joke, one of Dad's most charming quirks. Given his interest as Branch Manager of the family tree, I'm baffled that he doesn't seem to care about "the first Thalhimer."

I bite into my Tahoe Special as Dad slips the Goëtz Lazarus paper into a file folder in his gray metal file cabinet then slides the drawer shut with a decisive clank. There, the mysterious note will rest untouched for five years as its story unravels bit by bit, luring me closer and closer to my shared past with Virginia and Irma Marie.

Without any intention of writing a book, I set out on my quest to find the true story of my father's family.

CHAPTER TWO

THE FIRST THALHIMER
1809 - 1840

Tucked away in Germany's verdant Neckar Valley, the village of Thairenbach was home to six hundred villagers including Goëtz and Malke Thalheimer and their five daughters. The winding Tairnbächl stream sparkled with dancing sunlight as it bubbled from the forest springs just beyond the edge of town and flowed down to the Neckar River. The lush green carpeting of the forest floor and the invigorating breezes on the hillside of the Flühr Eben were enough to pacify even the most restless spirit.

On the twenty-sixth of July in 1809, Goëtz and Malke Thalheimer surely breathed easier when they heard the first precious, life-affirming cries of their newborn baby. Following five girls, they finally welcomed a baby boy into their growing family, giving him the name Wolff.

The year brought with it not only the birth of the Thalheimers' first son, but also the dawn of a new era for Jews across the Baden region. Napoleon had just granted them full, legal citizenship, allowing Jews to adopt surnames, build and own houses, cultivate farmland, and hold any occupation they chose aside from the previously mandated professions of money lending, peddling, and shopkeeping. The Jewish residents of Thairenbach were no longer second-class citizens.

Perhaps baby Wolff would be the first in the Thalheimer family to attain a higher education. Perhaps he would raise his family in a home of their own. Perhaps he would live a life of freedom apart from the institutionalized anti-Semitism his family had known for as long as they could recall. Malke could only wish these things as she held Wolff close against her chest and nuzzled the top of his head with her cheek. Goëtz dreamed that his only son might prosper beyond the life he led as a simple Jewish peddler roaming about the countryside, desperately trying to earn enough money to feed his children and pay his taxes.

Blessed with good fortune already, Wolff was the first in his family to be born with a last name. Before Napoleon's edict, he would have taken his father's name instead of a surname. He would have been "Wolff ben Goëtz," Wolff son of Goëtz. But now he was Wolff Thalheimer, a surname Goëtz and his brother Isaak chose for its picturesque meaning, "home in the valley."

When Wolff reached his eighth day of life, Malke and Goëtz held a bris, the ancient Jewish rite of circumcision, for their newborn son. Every third resident of Thairenbach was Jewish, an unusually high proportion for a rural town of only six hundred villagers, yet they lacked a resident mohel to perform the circumcision. For such occasions, the congregation summoned a rabbi from the nearby city of Heidelberg, which boasted a large Jewish community.

On the evening of the bris, Wolff's family and friends gathered in the cool, stone-walled synagogue on the banks of the flowing Tairnbächl stream just before sunset. An empty chair stood in the corner of the room, representing the throne of the Prophet Elijah. As an honored relative held squirming baby Wolff, the mohel prepared for the circumcision and recited the age-old prayers. Oftentimes after a circumcision, a few droplets of wine were placed into the baby's tiny, screaming mouth.

"Benyomin Yehudah ben Elyokum," the mohel said as he placed his hands ceremoniously on tiny Wolff, granting him his Hebrew name. The names Benyomin and Yehudah honored two of the twelve tribes of Israel. Elyokum, his father's Hebrew name, offered a permanent reminder to young Wolff that "God will establish." Wolff's Hebrew name connected him both to his ancestors and their ancient faith.

The Thalheimer family returned home to the cramped barracks of the Grundherr von Rodensteinischen Hause, a communal residence built by Thairenbach's noble family for the town's Jews. The nobles themselves lived in the comfort of the lavish Schloss, which stood like a castle in the center of town. Although the Jewish house included a mikvah ritual bath and prayer room, respecting important pillars of their faith, it mainly served to separate them from the Protestants. As a result of their living conditions, Jews formed a suffocating yet comforting kinship with their neighbors.

Not only were they physically separated, but language barriers also came between the Jewish and Protestant villagers. The Protestants spoke German while Jews spoke Judendeutsch, a form of Jewish German written with Hebrew letters. Rural Jews like the Thalheimers were literate to varying degrees. For instance, Wolff's sister Rachel could speak German but only write in Hebrew. Other less fortunate Jews could not read or write at all.

Thairenbach's Jewish children toddled about at their mothers' feet as they hung the laundry to dry and tended to their communal garden, picking ripe vegetables to prepare for dinner. Most of the town's Jews were strict religionists, adhering to traditional dietary laws.

While Malke cared for the children, prepared meals and kept house, Goëtz spent his days peddling wax and honey to the people of Thairenbach and neighboring towns. Merchants like him often traveled the countryside on weekdays and returned home for Friday night Sabbath dinners by candlelight, embraced by many Jewish families as the highlight of the week.

The Thalheimers went about their routines and lived a relatively simple existence until unexpected tragedies broke the monotony of their days. Young Treinla, said to be the most beautiful of the Thalheimer sisters, fell into the Rhine River near Mannheim and drowned. Only a few years later, the eldest sister Dina died at age twenty-two, most likely taken by an illness like cholera or pneumonia. The four remaining Thalheimer sisters, Rachel, Esther, Brendel and baby Gütel, would all survive to adulthood along with their only brother Wolff.

Goëtz's brother, Isaak Thalheimer, a merchant of second-hand goods, also lived in the communal house with his wife Kehla and their two daughters. While Kehla attended to domestic chores and Isaak peddled his wares, the young girls attended school at the synagogue with their Thalheimer cousins.

Some years, the Thalheimer brothers were too poor to pay their Judenschutzgeld, a tax due to the nobles allowing Jews the privilege of living in Thairenbach. The brothers barely eked out enough money as struggling merchants to support their families. Some years, Jewish merchants like the Thalheimers had so little money that they were forced to barter goods for grain, Sabbath wine, fruit, animal hides, and firewood.

Once Wolff reached the school-going age of six, he followed his sisters down the Judenschulweg, the "Jews' synagogue path," six mornings a week. The short path ran alongside the Thairnbächl stream, providing access from the Jewish barracks to the synagogue. Classes started at the break of dawn on summer mornings so the children could return home early enough to help their parents with chores during the daylight hours. In wintertime, the youngsters carried bundles of firewood to the synagogue to be burned in a wood stove to keep them warm during classes.

Abraham Moises Lieben, the town's cantor and teacher, lived in a small apartment inside the synagogue with his family. Herr Lieben gathered the children around his living room for their lessons. As they recited the Shema, their tiny voices offered the familiar prayer in cadence, *"Shema Yisrael Adonai Eloheinu Adonai Echad."* The children learned to read and speak Hebrew, and many of them worked on translating the five books of the Pentateuch into German.

As the years passed, Herr Liben became increasingly impressed by Wolff Thalheimer's sharp mind and perseverance. Given the opportunity, this boy seemed intellectually capable beyond the modest schooling Thairenbach had to offer. Herr Lieben suggested to Wolff's parents that they consider sending their boy away to school for a higher education.

Casting their doubts aside and accepting the financial burden of such a commitment, Goëtz and Malke made the most important decision they had perhaps ever made. They opted to send their only son Wolff thirty miles away from home to a Protestant Normal School in Karlsruhe, the bustling capital of the Baden region.

"God will establish," Wolff's Hebrew name reminded his parents.

⚜   ⚜   ⚜

Wearing brand new glasses, stocky Wolff Thalheimer made the ten-hour trek down the road from Thairenbach to Karlsruhe. Leaving the shelter and security of home for an unfamiliar school in a big city, Wolff surely felt a jumble of emotions. Liberation peppered with loneliness. Boundless optimism tempered by bouts of fear. Amazement at the possibilities in the world beyond the front door of the barracks.

Once he arrived at school, Wolff was not allowed to live in the dorms with the Protestant students. Traditionally, Jewish students stayed with Jewish families, some of them
finding room and board in the home of the local Rabbi. Wolff's maternal grandfather,
Jakob Selig, had served as a Rabbi in the town of Schreischeim for many years. He knew
Rabbis in the surrounding communities, including within the rabbinical seat of Karlsruhe,
and perhaps he found someone willing to house his grandson.

Situated in a thickly wooded forest, Karlsruhe was a decidedly modern city. Its streets
fanned out from a castle at the center of town, giving it the nickname Fächerstadt, the "fan
city." Karlsruhe had a lofty intellectual air about it; it was a place of liberal thinking and
socio-political enlightenment. These things could not have been more foreign to young Wolff.

Day after day for two years, Wolff dutifully sat behind his school desk absorbing
his lessons. Teaching seemed like an intriguing career. It allowed a young man to travel,
pursue further academic study, and inspire younger boys. The pay could support a family,
however modestly.

Upon graduating, Wolff held in his hands a letter of certification stating, "Wolff Thalheimer of Thairenbach remained two years in the Protestant Normal School of this place.
His work on the whole was satisfactory. His progress in the major subjects was adequate.
His conduct was commendable." This recommendation was the key to his future; it would
allow Wolff to seek further training as a teacher.

Wolff applied to a Protestant teachers' training college in Karlsruhe called the Evangelische Schulseminar. The school had declared plans to build a Jewish seminary in addition
to the Christian one it already had, which interested Wolff a great deal. Perhaps he would
be among the first Jewish teachers to graduate from the ranks of this Protestant institution. Perhaps a career in education was, in fact, his calling. Wolff applied to the training
school and, to his great satisfaction, was accepted.

Within the walls of the Protestant seminary school, Wolff learned the pillars of teaching from his instructor, Wilhelm Stern. Herr Stern said that a teacher should encourage each
child to cultivate and explore his individuality. A classroom shouldn't be a place for rote
memorization or rapping children's knuckles, he told Wolff, but a welcoming place, loving
and safe, much like a home. Wolff listened carefully as he subconsciously wove the threads
of Herr Stern's lessons into the fabric of his being.

To earn extra spending money, Wolff worked as a store clerk. It was almost second nature to him since he had watched his father and Uncle Isaak peddle goods for many years. Perhaps one day, should his teaching career fall short, the skills he acquired behind the cashier's desk would come in handy.

It was eventually announced that the Evangelische Schulseminar would not establish a Jewish seminary after all, as Wolff had anticipated. The school had been denied permission by the Grand Duchy of Baden due to fears that a Jewish seminary would attract too many Jews to the area, an unappealing prospect to its government.

Crestfallen, Wolff left the seminary before taking his final exam. Without earning a diploma, he only possessed the credentials to be a Jewish teacher, not a "real" teacher in a Protestant school. With his recommendation letter from the Karlsruhe school in hand, Wolff sought work as a Jewish teacher.

He travelled a few miles down the road to the village of Feudenheim, home to an ancient, deeply rooted Jewish community. At the town's only Jewish school, Wolff received his first teaching job at the age of twenty-one.

Like his old teacher Herr Lieben in the synagogue school of Thairenbach, Herr Thalheimer lived in the apartment adjoining the synagogue and taught classes to the town's Jewish children. He also assumed the role of hazan in the synagogue, leading the congregation in familiar prayers and songs. During his time in Feudenheim, he became a well-respected Talmudical scholar, writing and studying the two and a half million words of the Talmud.

After seven years of teaching, Wolff heard a rumor that the synagogue of Feudenheim might build a Jewish schoolhouse. This posed an exciting prospect for him: a new schoolhouse could provide him with a new home, a better-outfitted classroom, and, perhaps, a more secure teaching position. Surely his hopes would not be dashed again.

The Synagogenrat, the town's Jewish governing council, wrote a letter to the regional government informing them that their synagogue's schoolhouse was out of repair and they needed to replace it. The regional government politely replied that they lacked sufficient funding for such a project. The Synagogenrat responded again, this time asking for permission to collect money from Jewish congregations across the Grand Duchy of Baden in order to raise the funds for building a new schoolhouse. The terse response to their second request was this: "Such collections for Jewish school houses cannot be allowed on principle; furthermore there is no public Jewish school in Feudenheim."[1]

Not long after this definitive and gloomy announcement, Wolff Thalheimer decided to leave his job in Feudenheim. He was nearly thirty years old without a wife or children. He struggled to make money by teaching in a dilapidated Jewish schoolhouse in a rural town. Surely he could do better.

Ironically, the cornerstone for the new Jewish elementary school would be laid in Feudenheim two years after Wolff's departure, but it was no matter to him. By then, his life had taken a dramatic turn, never again to turn back.

⚜   ⚜   ⚜

Late on a spring evening in 1839, Malke, the matriarch of the Thalheimer family, passed away. Jewish burials traditionally took place the day after a person's death but the Jews of Thairenbach could not always observe this tradition as they lacked their own Rabbi or Jewish cemetery. The closest Jewish cemetery to Thairenbach was situated on the outskirts of Waibstadt, nearly ten miles away.

For two days, Wolff and his father, sisters, aunt, uncle and cousins sat Shiva, the traditional mourning period, as they awaited the travelling rabbi from Heidelberg. Only when he arrived to recite the appropriate prayers could Malke's corpse be laid into its coffin. Meanwhile, the family kept watch over her body, taking turns throughout two days and nights.

After the Rabbi arrived and administered the rites, it took more than an hour for the solemn funeral party to travel from Thairenbach to Waibstadt by horse and wagon. Along the way, Malke's lifeless body bumped down the dirt road in a rough wooden casket covered by a black blanket.

Only months after Malke's death, another shock jolted the Thalheimer family. The family received word that Uncle Isaak had died in the hospital of Hanau in the region of Hesse, perhaps while away on a peddling trip, and had been buried in a Jewish cemetery far from home. It was a difficult situation; no one in the family could be present to sit with his body before burial. A local Jewish student or Rabbi may have volunteered for the grim task of sitting with the deceased stranger.

With Uncle Isaak gone, only two Thalheimer men remained in the village of Thairenbach. Wolff knew the onness was on him. If he did not marry and have children, his surname and its legacy would disappear. As his sisters married off, the Thalheimer name became increasingly endangered. How could he disappoint his father, especially in light of their recent losses?

Precisely on the one-year anniversary of his mother's death, Wolff obtained a passport allowing him to travel through the kingdoms of Prussia, France, Wurttemberg, Bavaria and Hesse to find work. The passport declared, "All civil and military authorities of this and foreign countries are requested to let pass free and without hindrance and whenever necessary to give help and protection to the bearer of this passport, the Jewish teacher and clerk Wolff Thalheimer born and living in Thairenbach."

He also carried letters of recommendation from the schools where he had studied and taught. Feudenheim's synagogue chairman, Baruch Katze, had written a fine recommendation for Wolff, emphasizing his "faultless moral behavior" as a schoolteacher.

Wolff travelled four long months across the countryside seeking a job, but his educational record and praise from superiors were not enough. No one would hire him.

Wolff Thalheimer's passport, 1840.

Dismayed, Wolff considered his options and made a decision that would change everything. In the summer of 1840, Wolff, his younger sister Gütel, and her boyfriend Abram Schmidt decided to abandon all things familiar and travel to the enigmatic place across the sea called Neuland, known to its own residents as America.

In recent years, they'd heard stories of other Jews leaving Baden for the shores of Neuland. Letters written from these emigrants to relatives back home conveyed the unusual prospects of hope, prosperity, democracy, and religious freedom, the very things Wolff sought for himself and future Thalheimers.

Stowing their earthly belongings and meager life savings into their satchels, Wolff and Gütel bade goodbye to friends and family, including their father Goëtz, not knowing if they would ever see them again. The siblings travelled northward on a Rhine steamer to the Netherlands where they obtained travel visas in Rotterdam. From there, they sailed west to the French port of Le Havre, known as the "door to the ocean."

Wolff had saved one hundred and twenty five guildens, about a year's teaching salary, to purchase a one-way ticket on the Ship Lorena to New Orleans. Gütel and Abram followed, purchasing tickets of their own with money they and their families had saved.

Even if Abram and Gütel had wanted to marry in Baden, restrictive legislative laws prevented many Jewish couples from doing so. In some towns, a Jewish male had to wait for a vacancy on a marriage list in order to be married. In other towns, only the eldest Jewish son could marry, eliminating the possibility of marriage for his brothers. Neuland, it was said, did not enforce such stringent restrictions upon its Jewish residents.

From the docks of Le Havre, thirty-two year old Wolff, his youngest sister Gütel, and her boyfriend Abram approached the hulking Ship Lorena. The ship weighed over five hundred tons with its two decks, three masts, and majestic squared-off stern. How could this bulky vessel possibly cross the wild waves of the Atlantic Ocean carrying hundreds of men, women and children? Wolff relied upon the faith echoed by his Hebrew name Elyokum: "God will establish."

Pushing off from the docks of Le Havre on August 28, 1840, the Lorena began her precarious sail. Lice jumped from one passenger to the next, and bouts of seasickness plagued the weary travellers. Many of them slept on straw sacks and ate grub from tin plates they had to clean by hand. As the sea rolled, people vomited and slid back and forth on their chamberpots, cursing and wondering why they ever ventured to leave the comforts of home.[2]

If twenty-six-year-old Gütel seemed more miserable, seasick and irritable than the other passengers, it was with good reason. Although she remained unmarried, Gütel Thalheimer was four months pregnant with Abram's child.

Six long, queasy weeks passed onboard the Ship Lorena when a sliver of land finally graced the horizon. Its passengers knew their seaborne voyage neared its end, but few of them knew what awaited them on shore. According to some, the streets of America were

Ship Lorena en route to Le Havre, 1839. *By Edwards L. Adams. Wadsworth Atheneum Museum of Art, Hartford, CT. Bequest of Miss Kate Urquhart.*

paved with good fortune. Others said they teemed with wild panthers, bears and oxen. A few fearful passengers brought along machetes and knives to protect themselves from the unknown. [3]

"Name and age?" an official asked each immigrant prior to entry into the Port of New Orleans. His pen stood poised at the front of each blank entry box awaiting the passenger's reply, intelligible or not.

When Wolff stepped forward, the official may have heard something like, *"Mein name ist Wolff Thalheimer. Ich bin dreißig eine Jahre alt."*

The official understood enough to ink *W. Thalheimer* into the logbook followed by "21" instead of "31" for Wolff's age. How was he supposed to understand this thick foreign accent from the Old World? On the next line, he simply wrote *Gutel* and recorded her age wrong as well. Several lines down, he scribbled what appears to be *A. Schmidt.*

With a few flourishes of a pen, Wolff, Gütel, and Abram had officially arrived in America. They had little money and spoke no English, but they had hope.

CHAPTER THREE

INQUISITIVENESS TO LEARN MORE
1998

"Elizabeth," Dad shouts from the basement. "Could you come down here?"

"Sure, Dad. One minute," I yell back, grabbing a water bottle from the fridge and dashing downstairs in my gym clothes, my sneakers squeaking with each step.

"Oh! Hi, Grandpa," I say, startled to see him sitting in one of the green leather chairs by the ping-pong table. "I didn't even hear you come in."

"Please don't get up," I plead as Grandpa bears on the armrests to hoist himself up and greet me with a kiss on the cheek, a formality that is practically tradition.

"Hi, Lizaboo," he says in his distinctively deep, reverberating voice. "Good to see you."

"Good to see you too, Grandpa."

Noticing a camcorder on a tripod, I realize I'm not going to the gym after all.

"What are y'all working on?" I ask Dad.

"I'm interviewing Grandpa," he says. "This is interview number two. We're going to cover the 1800s through the Civil War and keep going until Isaac's death in 1930."

Dad thumbs through a yellow legal pad full of dozens of pages written in his illegible scribble writing.

"Could you hold the camera steady and make sure you get us both in the frame? Last time I left it in the tripod and got my head cut off," Dad says. "We don't want any decapitations in this movie." This, of course, makes him laugh, which makes me laugh.

I slide my sneakers off and sit cross-legged in one of the green leather chairs to peer through the viewfinder, pressing the zoom button to make sure I can get some good close-ups.

I zoom in on a chair. All six of the green leather chairs once surrounded the table in Thalhimers' executive boardroom. Now they're scattered around the basement, a couple of them holding boxes of dusty college textbooks. Talk about a demotion.

I zoom in on Grandpa. Wearing a thin, woolen yellow sweater over a collared shirt and a pair of gray gabardine slacks, he looks every bit the Virginia gentleman. The ever-present gold chain hangs from his belt loop to his pocket, from which dangles a shiny gold charm and key. I tip the camera downwards and zoom in on the key.

"You see this little pin right here?" Grandpa asks, fingering the charm and holding it up to the camera. "It's a miniature Beta Gamma Sigma key, which I earned because they presented me with an honorary degree at the University of Richmond back in 1973. I never even went to college."

"You're lucky," I tell him. "I have a whole year left at Wake and I'm pretty sure they won't give me a gold charm when I'm done."

I zoom in on Dad as he flips through the yellow legal pad. He puts on his glasses and clears his throat, as if preparing for an actual job interview. I hadn't noticed before, but he's wearing a suit.

"Bill, I would have worn a tie if I'd known you were wearing one," Grandpa says.

"I wore mine because I thought you'd wear one!" Grandpa responds with a snicker, revealing the charming gap between his front teeth.

"OK. Are you ready?" Dad asks Grandpa.

"Ready, Bill," he says. Dad nods to me.

"Three, two, one, ACTION!" I press the red button and point to my actors, recalling my lackluster short films from the previous summer at NYU.

"I'm William B. Thalhimer the third and this is William B. Thalhimer junior," Dad says.

"That's right," says Grandpa. "Your old man."

Dad laughs. Grandpa purses his lips and grunts. Then they both become serious, and the real interview begins. As their conversation unfolds, my mind wanders in and out of conscious listening, interweaving subtext into the conversation.

Dad tells Grandpa about their common namesake, William Thalhimer, who founded

The Store. Grandpa seems surprised with many of the details of Dad's genealogical research, never having heard them before. What would William Thalhimer have thought about a video camera recording the bare bones of his life story? What's the rest of the story – the stuff that happened between the remnants that remain?

Grandpa shares memories of his great-grandfather Isaac Thalhimer, once dubbed "The Dean of Richmond Merchants." What will that phrase mean to my kids someday? What happens to history when it isn't recorded? Does it disappear?

As the interview grows long, Grandpa becomes fidgety and impatient. The consummate Chief Executive Officer, he turns to Dad and concludes, "It's marvelous Bill, this research that you've done. Having listened to your summary, I think it's fair to say that early on the example was set by William Thalhimer of being a good father, a good businessman, an honorable man and a good citizen. These are firm grips on life itself that are bound to have passed down to Isaac Thalhimer, who passed it on to William Thalhimer Sr., and ultimately to his sons, Charles and me, and our children. That provided the spark or the guiding light for our family to go six generations being highly respected, increasingly so. Each generation carried on the tradition of love and determination to be, in our profession, the best."

What will happen to that guiding light, that tradition, now that the store is gone? How can my generation continue to carry the flame?

Before they wrap up, Dad asks one final question, "Do you have any feeling as to what it was like for William Thalhimer to run his business?"

"I really don't, Bill. Most of my thinking has come from your research, your genealogy. That has sparked all of the memory, the imagination, the inquisitiveness to learn more."

I press the red button and the camera stops recording, but my mind races, continuing to pose questions I can't answer. What can I do to make sure these stories continue to live when videocassettes become obsolete? What about the rest of the information in Grandpa's head?

When the camera rolls again two months later, Dad's behind it and I'm sitting in the green leather chair facing Grandpa with a legal pad full of questions. The transcription of our first interview fills forty typewritten pages. When August rolls around, it's time to head back to college. What a shame, I thought, that I can't stay and interview Grandpa every week. There are still so many questions to ask. Who will carry the flame?

Letter from Joshua Flegenheimer to "Wolff Thalheimer in Amerika," 1844. *Photo by Wayne Dementi, 2010.*

CHAPTER FOUR

A Store is Born
1841 - 1862

Right away, the three newcomers shed their Old World names in favor of more modern, American-sounding ones. Gütel chose Henrietta, Abram altered his name only slightly to Abraham, choosing the surname Smith, and Wolff became William.

The bustling city of New Orleans, one of America's biggest immigration ports and commercial centers, saw more than just an influx of immigrants like Henrietta, Abraham, and William. Agricultural goods from the Midwest and the South traveled down to New Orleans by way of the Mississippi River, and dry goods were sent back upriver for sale across the Northeast. New Orleans had just begun to see an explosion of Jewish residents, many of them merchants, a profession forced upon them in the Old World. The city's Jewish merchants often operated retail stores as well as wholesale houses supplying small goods for peddlers to sell from their knapsacks and wagons.

William befriended several German Jewish peddlers, and together the men peddled wares from their knapsacks as they made their way up the Mississippi River by steamboat. They intended to travel to Pittsburgh, Pennsylvania, but due to their poor grasp of English they accidentally ended up in Petersburg, Virginia. Each of them would eventually abandon their peddler's satchel to become a legitimate merchant.[4]

William Thalheimer traveled up the road a short distance to Richmond, Virginia, where, just after the year's first fragrant dogwood blossoms burst open in 1842, he laid down ten dollars for a merchant license.

No longer was William merely a student, a teacher, or a peddler. He was a proprietor of his very own store, where he intended to make a name for himself. He didn't sell much, but he had drive. He had faith. And above all, he wanted to make his father proud by giving meaning to the Thalhimer name beyond "home in the valley."

Three months after disembarking the Ship Lorena at the Port of New Orleans, Henrietta and Abraham Smith welcomed their first child, a daughter named Mary. The Smiths stayed in Louisiana until Mary was old enough for them to continue northward.

Having made their way to Richmond, Henrietta and Abraham Smith were one of the first couples to marry at synagogue K.K. Beth Shalome in 1844. Thankfully, America did not uphold any legal barriers preventing their union; it was a land where Jews could marry freely, and for love.

Abraham carried with him to Richmond a letter he had received for William, perhaps by way of a friend or relative entering the port of New Orleans. The letter was simply addressed to *Wolff Thalheimer in Richmond, Amerika.*

Written down the side of the letter in old Judendeutch handwritten script, William's cousin Joshua revealed the devastating reason for his correspondence: "Your father died the 27th of April 1844." Surely William's heart sunk upon reading Joshua's words.

By the time he received the letter, Goëtz Lazarus Thalheimer had long since been laid to rest alongside his wife Malke in the vast wooded cemetery of Waibstadt. The Rabbi from Heidelberg had come and gone, the funeral wagon had taken him down the dusty road, and his body had entered the earth for eternity. William would never have the chance to tell his father about the success of his store or starting a family to continue the legacy of the Thalheimer name he had adopted in 1809. He had no choice but to keep moving forward, committing himself to building his business and living a life that would make his father proud.

The following year, William invited his brother-in-law Abraham Smith to join him as a business partner, and Abraham readily accepted the offer. Together, the two men applied for a merchants' license to jointly manage a dry goods store at 11 East Main Street between Seventeenth Street and Shockoe Creek.

The Thalheimer and Smith store stood directly across from Richmond's lively Farmer's Market, crowded with mule-drawn wagons, slaves, and shoppers buying watermelons, corn, okra, collard greens and squash. Pigs and horses roamed freely, lending their own peculiar smells and sounds to Richmond's business district. Walking down Main Street, one could count several dozen other dry goods stores.

Only a year later, Thalheimer and Smith dissolved their short-lived partnership. Abraham announced to William that he would be starting his own business to support his growing family. He and Henrietta had just welcomed a son, Henry Clay, named after the American statesman.

Abraham would go on to hold a variety of occupations including confectioner, saloon owner, bowling alley operator, liquor distiller, and one of few Jewish slave dealers in the South. Eventually, he and Henrietta would relocate to New York City, never again to live in Richmond.

William was alone again, but he continued working away behind the counter of his fledgling business. Pulling three dollars and twenty-five cents from a cigar box, he paid a local sign painter to paint the sign hanging outside his shop. Unfamiliar with the German name Thalheimer, the painter misspelled it by eliminating the first, silent "e." William began to argue with the painter, a much larger man than he, over the cost of repainting the sign.[5] Finally, lacking enough money to repaint the sign and fearing a bigger fight, he decided to change the spelling of his name instead. That was the day he became William Thalhimer.

⚜ ⚜ ⚜

Every week, new immigrants arrived in Richmond with their satchels and trunks. One particular German Jewish girl caught William's eye. Spirited and savvy, she had captivating dark brown eyes and sleek black hair parted confidently straight down the middle of her head. Her American name was Mary Millhiser, known in the old country as Mariane Muhlhauser.

In an unusual coincidence, Mary had also come to Richmond to join her sister Henrietta who had married a man named Abraham. All four of Mary's siblings had immigrated to Richmond where the Millhiser brothers owned wholesale and dry goods businesses under their family name. Knowing the Millhisers as respectable businessmen, William pursued Mary's courtship right away.

The Millhisers came from Hagenbach, a rural German town similar to Thairenbach. As a teenager, Mary had left her family to work as a governess in Trieste, Italy.

She wrote to her parents from Trieste, "Dear parents, when I told my madam about my going [to America] she turned red with fright, but she wished my good luck. She said that over there [is] matchmaking in ten thickness in the streets. It is not everything just to get married, she said. We want to remind you that there all may go wrong, and you know what you have here. I said to her, why do you hope evil for me and not good? If I were another seven years here it would be the same, therefore it is better I take the advice of my parents than that of madam."[6]

Despite her employer's pleading, Mary heeded her parents' advice and followed her siblings to Richmond, Virginia.

In terms of matchmaking, Mary's employer had been quite right. After Mary's arrival in America, only a year passed before her marriage to the thirty-six year old German Jewish shopkeeper William Thalhimer. The couple took their vows on the sacred bimah of synagogue K.K. Beth Shalome in September of 1845. William paid a seven hundred dollar dowry and maiden payment to Mary's family for the honor of taking his new bride's hand in marriage.

With Rabbi Ellis Lyons' blessing, William turned to Mary and solemnly declared, "I faithfully promise with divine guidance that I will be a true husband unto thee. I will honor and cherish thee and will work for thee. I will protect and support thee and will provide all that is necessary for thy due sustenance even as it becomes a Jewish husband to do."[7]

Almost exactly nine months following their wedding day, the Thalhimers welcomed a baby boy. They named him Gustavus, an Americanization of Goëtz, to honor William's dearly departed father. Just down the street, Henrietta and Abraham Smith named their next-born son Gustavus as well. In this way, Goëtz Thalheimer's heritage would carry on, even when the children bearing his name no longer knew for whom they were named.[8] After all, he had been the first Thalheimer of Thairenbach.

Among Richmond's older, more established retail houses like Levy's and Christian & Lathrop, William Thalhimer's modest shop showed little promise for survival. Most of his customers were humble farm workers with little spending money. William and Mary worked tirelessly selling shirts, underwear, stockings, socks, neckwear, scarves, suspenders, and straw hats, learning English one customer at a time. Being a scholar of Hebrew and German, William picked up the language quickly. Having learned Italian in her previous job as a governess, Mary proved equally as proficient at learning English.

A Northern credit agent doing his rounds in Richmond visited William Thalhimer's dry goods stand and scratched a quick notation in his journal: "Little Jew store without any known means."[9] But the Thalhimers would not let such dismal appraisals thwart them.

Toddling downstairs from his bedroom to the store, housed in a single room measuring eighteen by sixty feet, little Gustavus watched his father cut denim for jumpers and overalls while his mother greeted customers by name, showing them to the fabrics and notions they sought. The Thalhimers often worked twelve and thirteen-hour workdays, staying open as late into the evening as customers desired to shop. The store closed only on Saturdays so the family could observe the Sabbath at home together, just as they had done in the Old Country.

As money allowed, William put advertisements for the store's wares in the local German newspaper, the *Richmond Anzeiger*. "Stop at the complete store for all seasons," it said, "clothing for farm workers, white and colorful shirts, underwear, stockings, socks, neckwear, suspenders, casual and straw hats at the lowest prices!"[10]

William began developing a reputation as a fair and trustworthy merchant in Richmond's German community and beyond. Mary handled most of the merchandise buying, a skill she learned from her brothers. Her gentle, amiable manner made it easy for her to win the business of loyal customers.

Before long, William could afford to hire domestic slaves to help out around the house, keep the store clean, and assist Mary in caring for the children. Although he was a slave owner, as were most other merchants and business people in the city, William showed some consideration and tolerance for those bound by slavery.

When one of his domestic slaves lost two infant children during a particularly cruel winter, William allowed the children to be temporarily buried in his backyard. They dug shallow graves in the snowdrifts, planning to move the small corpses for burial in Shockoe Bottom's slave cemetery when the ground thawed. However, a neighbor witnessed the illegal slave burials and turned William over to the authorities. The Mayor chastised him for allowing such an outrage against public property, especially so near the busy Farmers' Market, and fined him ten dollars. William claimed they were planning to move the bodies in the spring, but yielded to the law and paid the fee.

William and Mary had never been subjected to anything as outrageously tyrannical as slavery, but they knew the bitter sting of oppression. They understood what it meant to be members of an outcast minority. They had experienced social injustice as second-class citizens in the Old World.

⚜   ⚜   ⚜

Every two years or so, Mary's belly swelled with the next addition to the Thalhimer family. Following Gustavus came Charles, Jacob, Amelia, Isaac, Moses and Bettie. Their growing clan continued to live on the two floors above their store, its windows overlooking the constant commotion of the Farmers' Market below and Cornelius Crew's soap factory next door.

Gus, nicknamed Gussie by his playmates, earned extra money shelling peas at the Farmers' Market after school. One day he spent two hard-earned dollars on a panoramic painting done by his friend, Moses Ezekiel, who would grow up to become a world-renowned sculptor and recall the sale as his first art deal.[11]

All of the Thalhimer children, particularly the boys, gained a reputation among their playmates' parents for being perpetually tidy and well dressed. These standards of neatness and simplicity in appearance would remain deeply ingrained as they grew into distinguished young men and women representing their family's store.

Just as his parents had done for him back in Thairenbach, William ensured that each of his children received the best possible education. When Temple Beth Ahabah opened the first Jewish school in the city, The Richmond German, Hebrew and English Institute, William enrolled his children to study under the tutelage of Rabbi Michelbacher six days a week. William enhanced the children's lessons at home, eventually teaching his sons their Torah portions in preparation for their Bar Mitzvahs.

The Thalhimer boys and girls loved watching their father's hand swiftly and symmetrically produce Hebrew script so beautiful that it looked lithographed. Gussie became fluent in Hebrew by the remarkably young age of five and became known for his perfect penmanship, as did his brother Jacob.

Every Friday night at sundown, Mary lit the candles as the children gathered around the dining table. Together the family recited the familiar Hebrew prayers, the children's small faces and open-palmed hands bathing in the glow of Shabbat candlelight. William delighted in passing down the prayers and customs of his parents.

Although William had long since abandoned his teaching career, he continued to

Succession of Human Beings.

Like leaves on trees the life of man is found,
Now green in youth, now withering on the ground;
Another race the following spring supplies,
They fall successive, and successive rise :
So generations in their course decay ;
So flourish these, when those have pass'd away

Written by Isaac Thalhimer, age 14, April 1868.

serve as a lay reader and cantor in Richmond's Portuguese and German synagogues. When a Rabbi could not be present, William stood in to officiate Jewish marriage ceremonies. He even served in the pulpit of K.K. Beth Shalome for an entire year while the congregation searched for an official hazan. The synagogue thanked him for his service with a handsome sterling silver Kiddush cup engraved with his name, the year 1849 in Hebrew and English, and a message of gratitude. William treasured this silver cup as one of his most beloved possessions.

William and his sons participated in Jewish clubs and organizations like the Jefferson Literary and Social Circle, the Mercantile Club, and the Rimmon Lodge number sixty-eight – the oldest fraternal body in Richmond. They found camaraderie at charity balls and dances, intellectual stimulation through debate and literary study, and religious zeal through involvement with other Jews, many of them strict religionists like William Thalhimer.

On occasion, William volunteered in the pulpits of Christian churches needing a minister on Sunday mornings. One of them, a congregation of German Lutherans, held services in K.K. Beth Shalome's synagogue when they lacked a place to worship.[12] William easily made friends and acquaintances with Christians across the community, teaching his children firsthand the importance of tolerance for people of all races, religions, and creeds other than their own.

✤   ✤   ✤

By 1850, theatres, saloons, dance halls, bowling alleys, hotels, grocers, and over sixty different clothing and dry goods houses lined the Shockoe Bottom business district along the James River. New homes and businesses sprouted up like mushrooms along the streets of the outlying hills.

Storefront signs began to read like branches of William and Mary's growing family tree: Thalhimer, Millhiser, Hutzler, Smith, Straus, and Sycle, all of them related by blood or marriage. These families worked together by selling each other real estate, sharing resources, and dividing ownership of stores and property. When financial hardships accompanied periodic recessions and money panics, they buoyed each other. Together they endured epidemics of Yellow Fever, blizzards and fires, droughts and floods. Just like their forebears in communities across Europe, the Jews of Richmond created a compassionate network of support and sustenance.

When William Thalhimer's little clothing store finally turned a decent profit, he could treat his family to indulgences beyond the basic necessities of life. They could travel to the Warm and Hot Springs to take the healing waters, purchase jewelry, and even invest in a piano for their home. In 1859, William commissioned oil portraits to be painted of him and his wife by

Wolff/William Thalhimer. *Artist: F. Spangenberg, 1859.*

Ferdinand Spangenberg, a prominent artist passing through town.

William wanted his success
as a merchant to be evident, so he
wore an earring and rings on both
pinkies. For her portrait sitting,
Mary wore a lovely black dress
with a hand-crocheted collar, a
splendid pair of long earrings,
and her most attractive rings. She
rested one hand on a book, signifying her fine education and intellect.

A constant stream of northern
credit agents continued to flow
into Richmond from New York,
Philadelphia and Baltimore. They
began taking notice of William
Thalhimer's success as a merchant,
hesitantly extending him small
amounts of credit.

Miriam/Mary Millhiser Thalhimer. *Artist: F. Spangenberg, 1859.*

"Does a tolerable fair trade," one agent scrawled into his notebook.

"Should say good for moderate credit. Close and attentive Jew," noted another.[13]

On a rainy day in November of 1851, William stood on the wharf at Rockett's
Landing awaiting the arrival of his sister Rachel's son, William Flegenheimer, fresh from
an arduous six-week journey across the Atlantic. When the boat arrived at the docks,
Flegenheimer disembarked and embraced his uncle, whom he'd last seen ten years prior.
Together they walked through the rain back to the Thalhimers' modest house and store
on Seventeenth Street, where young William boarded for a short time. Ever loyal to their
heritage, the family stuck together.

A poised young man of nineteen, William Flegenheimer spoke no English but proved
to be a fast and able learner. The day after his arrival, his uncle set him up with a basket
of goods to sell at the Farmer's Market. Flegenheimer caught on quickly and earned a few
dollars.

"Not bad for a Greenhorn," his Uncle William remarked with a chuckle. But when Flegenheimer asked if he could buy a horse and peddler's license, his uncle refused him permission to do so. This was a good thing; Flegenheimer would prove to be a miserable peddler and dry goods clerk.

Eventually, Flegenheimer got a job as a clerk in the Treasury Department processing bank notes. One day when a twenty-dollar note came across his desk with the name *William Thalhimer* scrawled across the back, he noticed that the signature was not written in his uncle's faultless, scrolling handwriting.

Flegenheimer turned in the suspicious bank note to authorities who discovered that a slave named Robert Jones had forged William's signature. The criminal was arrested, Flegenheimer gained credibility and confidence, and William Thalhimer's store soldiered on.

CHAPTER FIVE

EVERYTHING CHANGES
2000 - 2001

According to plan, I return to New York City after graduating from college. My friend Ari finds me an apartment and roommate through his college alumni magazine, so Dad and I once again hop into the big blue Suburban, stuffed to the roof with bags of clothes, a box of kitchenware, some pillows, a comforter, and a TV with a built-in VCR.

"We'll order a mattress and bed frame when we get there," he says. "And I'll hire someone to drive up with the leather sofa and a chair from the basement."

As promised, the sofa and chair arrive a few weeks later. After placing the furniture in the living room, the man who delivered them says, "You have an awfully nice dad to send this up to you, and I really appreciate the extra money."

"I'm glad, since it's kind of a long drive. Do you make a lot of deliveries like this?"

"No. I'm a retired police officer. This may not mean anything to you, but I was the policeman that lived in your grandparents' breakfast room during the sit-ins and picket strikes at Thalhimers back in 1960. Do you know the story?"

"Vaguely," I tell him, making a mental note to ask Grandpa more questions about it. "Anyhow, thanks for bringing my stuff all the way up here."

"No problem. It's a pleasure to do anything to help your family out."

"Well, it's nice of you to say that," I tell him, immediately wishing I had asked him more questions as I shut the door.

After responding to a bunch of classifieds and getting nothing but rejections, I finally land an entry-level job at a funky animation production house near Astor Place called Curious Pictures. My stipend is one hundred dollars a week, which barely covers subway fare and lunches. I'm thrilled to have a job, especially because I have my very own telephone on my very own desk. The first time I answer, I nervously say, "Elizabeth Pictures, this is Curious," instead of "Curious Pictures, this is Elizabeth." Fortunately it's Dad.

"Hey, Bibbie," he says. "I just wanted to say hi and congratulate you on your first day."

"Thanks, Dad."

"Gramps went to Chicago to get his start, Grandpa went to New York, and now it's your turn. Go get 'em, tiger."

"Dad, I'm an intern. So far I've licked and addressed envelopes and taken a VHS tape downstairs."

"Everybody gets their start somewhere," he says.

I keep at it, working at Curious Pictures for a year and a half and eventually landing a job as Media Coordinator for an HBO Family cartoon called *A Little Curious*. When the show isn't picked up for another season, I interview for other jobs around the city at *Saturday Night Live*, a film production company, *Blues Clues*, and a host of other places, but no one will hire me.

Running down the escalator at Penn Station, breathlessly making my way onboard a train from New York back to Richmond for Thanksgiving, I search for an empty seat. The train is full, save one seat next to a man typing away on a laptop. He stops typing to help me hoist my bag up to the overhead shelf.

"Thanks," I say to him, trying to catch my breath.

"You're lucky you made it," he says.

"I'm always late. It's terrible…I know. Every time I'm late, I think of my grandfather. I don't think he's ever been late for anything."

"What business is he in?" he asks.

"Oh, it's gone," I tell him. "It was a department store."

"Here in the city?"

"No, in the south. I'm from Richmond."

"Me, too. What was the store?"

"Thalhimers."

"No kidding! One of the biggest brands in Richmond's history. My name is Mark Speece," he says.

"Nice to meet you. I'm Elizabeth Thalhimer."

We continue to talk for the entire seven-hour train ride, and my neck begins to hurt from turning my head to talk to Mark. He has the most fascinating job ever: Mark is a Naming Consultant. He names companies and products, from cars to cell phone networks to airlines.

"Here," he says, turning his laptop towards me. "I'll walk you through a naming presentation."

By the time we get to Richmond, I'm convinced. I want to be a Naming Consultant, too.

"Call me when you get back to the city," Mark says, handing me a shiny silver business card that says FutureBrand. "I'd love to get you in for an interview."

So I do, and Mark hires me. He's the best boss, encouraging my creativity and building my confidence. Plus, he's hilarious. We travel the country, naming stuff from dotcoms to mutual funds.

A year after he hires me, Mark gets a job as Naming Director at Landor Associates, one of the most respected branding agencies in the world. A few months after he leaves me to fend for myself at FutureBrand, a member of Landor's naming team announces he's leaving.

Mark invites me out for hamburgers and says, "A spot is opening up on the naming team. Are you interested?"

"Are you kidding, Mark? Of course I'm interested."

After a series of tough interviews and finally being offered the job a couple months later, I'm sitting in my new cubicle at Landor Associates. A tall, slender, dark-haired man named Ryan walks over with a hefty binder in his hands. He's the one who's leaving the naming team, and he has two weeks to train me.

"You're going to need these on the job," he says with a charming smirk. Along with the binder, Ryan places two bottles of glitter glue and a football card of a player named Elvis Grbac on my desk.

"Really?" I respond sarcastically. "I had no idea I'd get to do art projects here."

"Oh, yeah. You never know when you'll need to make a diorama."

"You know, back in Mrs. Melton's history class I made the coolest diorama on a lazy susan. It had little Confederate soldiers marching over a bridge with real water under it."

"Elvis Grbac would have liked that very much."

I laugh as I pin the Elvis Grbac card to my cubicle wall. I have no idea who he is, but I've heard of the Kansas City Chiefs.

"Go Chiefs," I say with a sarcastic smile, and Ryan smiles back.

This Ryan character seems sillier yet more grounded than anyone else I've met in New York. Too bad he's leaving in two weeks.

"You know, I'm having a Halloween party next weekend," I tell him. "I invited the whole naming team except you, since I figured you wouldn't want to hang out with us Landor people longer than you have to. But I'd love it if you could make it."

"Thanks," Ryan says. "Halloween is my birthday."

"Cool! I'll put a candle in your beer."

No one else from the office bothers to show up, but Ryan arrives at the party with his two roommates. He's dressed as Buddy Holly, wearing horn-rimmed glasses, a pale blue blazer over a button-down shirt, a thin black tie, and a handmade cardboard guitar slung over one shoulder.

The guy I've been dating for the past month, whom my girlfriends call "Rock Star" because he wears blue nail polish and Gucci sunglasses, calls at the last minute to say he can't come to the party. Ironically, he refuses to wear costumes.

Ryan and I spend most of the evening on the terrace of my seventeenth floor apartment in the freezing cold, drinking beer, chatting and laughing. I'm dressed as Christina Aguilera with a fake belly button tattoo, long blonde wig, and turquoise tube top. I'm freezing, but I pretend I'm not cold just so I can stay outside with him.

Later on, while talking to my friend Mary, I notice Ryan leaving with another girl dressed as a bumblebee, a friend of my roommate's. It hurts seeing him leave with someone who isn't me.

The following week, I call Ryan at his apartment.

"Thanks for coming to the party," I tell him. "You left your guitar."

"Really?" he asks. "Hey, if I come by to pick it up this Friday, would you want to grab a drink?"

"This Friday? Oh, I can't. I'm already booked," I lie in an uncharacteristic attempt to sound busy and popular. On Friday night, I'll probably stay home, make a cheese omelet, and play Air Supply on the piano. "But I'm free next Thursday."

"Sure," he says. "Thursday works. I'll come by your apartment."

I'm excited about the date but have few expectations that it will go well. Just a few days before, Rock Star broke up with me by email and I'm wallowing in self-pity.

When Ryan arrives, I still haven't showered. I invite him in to watch the end of *Will and Grace*, and he sits beside me on the leather sofa from Thalhimers' board room. Oddly enough, we're perfectly comfortable watching TV and laughing together.

After the credits roll, Ryan patiently allows me to check my mailbox on our way through the lobby. Walking down Eighth Avenue together, I open a manila envelope from my mother. Along with a congratulatory note written in her perfect calligraphy is an article from the Richmond paper about the gift book we just published together.

"I just wrote this little book," I tell Ryan. "My mom illustrated it." I show him the photo accompanying the article.

"That's a great picture," he says. "Nice bear suit."

"Oh, that's my dad. My dad is a bear. Should I have told you that before?"

Ryan laughs at my dumb joke, making me realize how comfortable I am with him. We sit on leather cubes by the front window at Zanzibar.

"What's your book about?" he asks.

"It's about Snow Bear. He was the holiday bear at my family's department store. Santa's 'right-arm bear.' Everyone loved Snow Bear, even the kids who were afraid of Santa."

"What's the store called?"

"Thalhimers. It's closed now."

"I've never heard of it. We didn't have it back in Kansas."

"No," I laugh, sipping my amaretto sour. "I'm pretty sure Snow Bear's never been to Kansas."

It's refreshing to meet someone who doesn't know me as a Thalhimer. To Ryan, I'm just a girl who moved to New York City after college. A co-worker who happened to throw a Halloween party with her roommate. The writer of a spiral-bound book about a pretend bear. To Ryan, I'm just me.

Walking back up Eighth Avenue in a bitterly cold drizzle, Ryan takes off his leather jacket and holds it over my head. As we say goodnight outside my apartment building, I hope he'll kiss me, but instead he embraces me in a hug. It feels strangely intimate as we hold each other at midnight on Fifty-Second Street.

About two months later, as I'm lying on the sofa with a raging sore throat and fever,

Ryan shows up at my apartment with a single, fresh orange and a small teddy bear. It's the most thoughtful, simple gesture, but it strikes me as incredibly romantic.

We take turns planning surprise dates for each other all over the city, playing skeeball at a Times Square arcade, sipping Crème de Menthes while listening to sultry jazz bands in underground clubs, circling the ice rink hand-in-hand at Rockefeller Plaza, cheering as U2 rocks Madison Square Garden, and sharing a blanket on a horse-drawn carriage ride through Central Park. As we sink our spoons into cups of frozen hot chocolate at Serendipity, I smile. I think I'm falling in love.

Over the course of the next ten months, we spend every possible moment together, emailing each other silly, romantic messages from work. When I go back to Richmond and he returns to Wichita for the holidays, we can hardly stand being apart. Without even having the "let's define our relationship" conversation, we know we are meant to be together.

⚜   ⚜   ⚜

After the dotcom bubble bursts and the economy begins to sour, I lose my job at Landor. Again, I have trouble getting anyone to hire me, so I sign on with a temp agency that places me in surreal, menial jobs around the city. Data entry for a Japanese fire and marine insurance company with secretaries who talk about making their own candles. Filing deeds in a real estate office run by a flamboyant man who makes comments like, "Ooh, girl...get your salad on!" Tearing encyclopedia entries individually from their binding with the straight edge of a ruler at a colossal publishing house.

Although my affection for Ryan grows stronger by the day, I begin to feel invisible and depressed. Then things start to get weird. I start having dizzy spells on the subway, my palms start sweating for no reason, and recurring nightmares about falling buildings haunt me even in daylight.

Naturally, I call my mom.

"I think I need to see a psychiatrist," I tell her. "I'm just not myself anymore."

"You're fine," she says reassuringly. "You just need to get out more. Go for walks. Do yoga. Go to the library. Spend more time with your girlfriends."

I try all of these things and more. I walk through Central Park, sitting on benches to breathe deeply while watching the disco roller skaters and the kids playing Frisbee. I take yoga from yogis who only speak in Sanskrit. I write essays about street performers, just for fun. I join my best girlfriends, Ashley and Mary, for brunch on the weekends.

Oddly enough, I find solace in wandering the Saks Fifth Avenue store alone on Sunday afternoons. I'm comforted by inhaling the sweet fragrances of the cosmetics department, riding escalators through the heart of the store, chatting with the friendly salespeople, and savoring a cup of crab and corn chowder in the Eighth Floor restaurant. I rarely buy anything other than a tube of lipstick, but I feel a nostalgic sense of comfort and calm within the world of the store. Back out among the chaos and noise of Fifth Avenue, I long for home.

On September 3, 2001, I wake up in the middle of the night in a sweat; shaking, dizzy, and crying so hard that I wake Ryan. Tired and confused, he strokes my hair and says gently, "Everything's ok. It was just a dream. Go back to sleep."

But I can't quiet my mind. It's too real. I step out on the terrace to inhale deep breaths of the cool city air and recount the nightmare in my head.

In my dream, a dark force had wrapped itself around the world. It was a force like gravity but stronger, making every movement feel heavy and lifeless. An evil man did a frantic dance around certain people, madly waving his arms in the air, bouncing back and forth from one leg to the other and screaming like a banshee. Everyone on earth lived in fear that the evil dancing man would find them.

In my dream, I could fly. I drifted among the clouds, looking down at the evil dancing man and his victims. I watched him encircle a helpless, pale woman who was screaming and flailing her arms too.

"Help me," she cried.

I swooped down and tried to pick her up, but the dark force was too strong. I pulled and pulled but could not lift her. Finally, I let her go, and flew alone to a small, secluded spot in the Blue Ridge Mountains, a place where we always vacationed when I was a child. When I got there, I could finally breathe. The air felt crisp and pure as the evil force released its grip, and I woke up.

Waking up on September 11, my alarm clock cuts on to the radio. I look over at the clock; it's 8:50am. The radio announcer says, "It appears that a plane has hit one of the World Trade Towers."

I lurch across the bed and turn on the television to *The Today Show*. Sure enough, an airplane has shot a hole straight through one of the towers. I shake my head in disbelief.

The phone rings.

"Hello?" I mutter, rubbing my eyes.

"Are you ok?" I immediately recognize my sister Katherine's voice.

"Yeah," I say. "Are you watching this? It's so strange. Lemme go so I can call Ryan. I'll call you back later."

I call Ryan, and as I'm giving him a play-by-play description of the scene on TV, another plane slams into the other World Trade Tower.

I'm suddenly gripped by the devastating power of the dark force from my nightmare and imagine the evil man dancing around me. I become hysterical. Inconsolable.

"My nightmare," I tell Ryan, barely able to utter the words. "It's happening."

"Elizabeth, listen to me. Turn off the TV right now and don't go anywhere," he says. "I'm on my way."

Ryan jumps into a cab outside his office, but traffic is at a standstill. Horns honk, cabbies yell, but no one moves. He hands the driver a five, then gets out and starts running. Stopping only once to catch his breath, he looks down Fifth Avenue to see the World Trade Towers burning like smokestacks.

Waiting for Ryan, I grip the phone like a lifeline with a clammy, shaking hand. I listen as Katherine and Mom gently and calmly speak to me, and try to focus on their words. Gasping for air and crying wildly, I tell them that I already know what I need to do. I need to pack my suitcase and come home. I know this, but I can't make myself move.

As if I were a young child, Mom and Katherine talk me through getting dressed and packing my suitcase.

"Put a shoe on your right foot," Katherine, a pre-kindergarten teacher, says slowly. "Now put the other on your left foot. Tie the laces. Now double knot them."

I mindlessly do as she says, trying to internalize the calm tone of her voice.

"Don't forget to pack your pajamas and underwear," Mom says as I methodically fold my clothes into a small rolling suitcase. "Be sure to put on something comfortable. Wear layers. Dress so you're ready to run if you have to."

When I hear a knock on the front door, I hang up the phone and run to open it. Ryan holds me tightly in his arms.

"I can't be here anymore," I tell him, gasping through a flood of tears. "I'm leaving. I have to go home. This isn't home."

"I know," he says, smoothing my hair. "It's ok."

Fearing what might happen next, I grasp Ryan's hand as we sit in the backseat of a slow-moving cab. Our cab driver tells us in broken English, "The towers has fallen. I seen them fall."

"What does that mean?" I turn to Ryan and ask, like a child.

"Don't worry," he says. He doesn't know any more than I do. "We're ok."

When we get out of the taxi at Penn Station, a man with bulging eyes, tattered pants and disheveled hair repeatedly shouts from a street corner, "The Israel army is attacking! The Israel army is attacking!" A man in an Oxford shirt and khakis grabs the arm of a younger woman, saying, "The Pentagon has been hit! Planes are going down everywhere!" We're surrounded by chaos.

"I don't know what to believe," I tell Ryan.

"Just keep moving and keep breathing," he says. "Don't focus on anything but breathing."

Looking up at the arrivals and departures board in the station, each train's status twirls click-click-click-click as they all flip to read CANCELLED. An unsteady voice comes over the intercom commanding, "Everyone must evacuate the station immediately. The station must be evacuated."

As people radiate towards the exits in tidal waves of bodies, I am, somehow, one of the last people to leave. I look around at Penn Station, vacant and cavernous. It seems even more nightmarish than my real nightmares.

On our slow trek back uptown to my apartment, I drag my rolling suitcase and watch the scene unfold around me. Automatic bus doors close on the arm of a desperate woman crowding into an uptown city bus. Several people walk past us covered in white ash, their ghastly faces completely expressionless.

"I need to be in Richmond now," I explain to Ryan. "I need to be where my family is. It's my real home. Will you come with me?"

The question hangs in the air. After all, we've only been dating for eleven months.

"I have a feeling we're not going anywhere anytime soon. Let's stop at the grocery store."

"Why?"

"I don't know."

A few blocks from my apartment, we stop at Food Emporium to buy grapes, bread, peanut butter, chicken, cans of Sterno, and a jug of water. Ryan grabs a six-pack of beer and puts it in the cart.

"It's the end of the world and you need beer? Really?" I ask, clearly flustered.

Ryan puts the beer back on the shelf.

Back at my apartment, I continue calling Amtrak until they finally have trains running again. I reserve a ticket on the first southbound train scheduled to leave the next morning. Ryan calls his parents back in Wichita to explain what's going on.

"Should I go with her?" I hear Ryan asking his father.

"Follow your heart," his father says.

After he hangs up, Ryan looks at me and says, "I'll take you back to the station in the morning. I'm going to the office tomorrow but I'll be on the next train I can catch. I'm coming with you."

With tears in my eyes, I throw my arms around Ryan. I don't know what I would do without him.

After a sleepless night, I hold Ryan's hand as we walk down the vacant streets of Times Square toward the subway station. I look for a *New York Times* but all of the newspaper machines are empty. Ryan buys the only paper we can find at a newsstand: the *New York Post*. I thumb through it in the empty subway car. One photograph shows a severed hand with an open palm lying on the pavement of Lower Manhattan, and I am too queasy to turn the next page.

At Penn Station, I stop by the gift shop to buy an iconic white t-shirt imprinted with "I ♥ NY" before boarding the train. Before I step on the escalator to the train platform, Ryan kisses me, looks me straight in the eyes, and says, "I'll be there soon. I love you."

"I love you too," I tell him. "I'm going to be ok now."

"We're both going to be ok," he says reassuringly, stroking my cheek. As I descend on the escalator, I watch as Ryan slowly disappears from sight.

Pressing my forehead against the window of the train, the landscape changes under a long cloud of smoke extending along the horizon like a snake slithering through a crystalline lake. As the cloud dissipates midway through New Jersey, the knot in my chest begins to loosen. The world is not right, but everything feels better. I can breathe.

Arriving at the station in Richmond seven hours later, my mother embraces me, sobbing with relief and joy. "Welcome home," she says. The following day when Ryan arrives, she does the exact same thing. "Welcome home," she tells him, hugging him tightly. Dad shakes Ryan's hand and says, "You know you're both welcome to stay with us for as long as you need to."

"Thank you," Ryan says.

And we do.

For the next three months, Ryan and I live in the recreation room above my parents' garage. Neither of us has a job, we left all of our stuff in New York, and we have no idea what will happen next. But I am home, I am with my family, and I want to be with Ryan forever.

CHAPTER SIX

THE WAR AND THE STORE
1862 – 1865

Cannons and ammunition wagons rattled their way down the cobblestone streets of Shockoe Bottom past the Old Market. The Thalhimer children listened as Confederate boots clomped in unison down Main Street in their daily battle exercises. Although Richmonders felt confident in the South's ability to defeat the Yankees, everyone feared the storm to come.

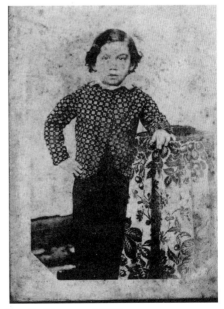

William Flegenheimer, who had arrived at the docks only a few years prior to meet his Uncle William Thalhimer, had become an acknowledged penman and calligraphic artist. On April 17, 1861, he engrossed the Virginia Ordinance of Secession and, with that, Virginia was no longer part of the United States. It was a foreign territory.

One night just after little Isaac Thalhimer had turned six years old, he saw the reflection of fire flickering in the windows of his bedroom. He went outside to see what was happening, and was surprised to see a big, rowdy crowd waving fiery torches in the air as they made their way past the Farmers' Market. He joined in, whooping and hollering, and

Isaac Thalhimer, age 4, 1859.

slung rocks into the air with the neighborhood boys. It was the Great Secession Parade, and the beginning of a national nightmare, but the Thalhimer boys thought it was as much fun as setting off firecrackers.

Shortly after the war broke out, the southern economy began to deteriorate. Northern suppliers cut off credit to southern stores. United States soldiers blockaded the James River at Fort Monroe, stopping the usual import of goods from the north. Banks withdrew notes as gold and silver disappeared from circulation. United States currency was no longer accepted in Richmond. Inflation exploded.

A case of lawns, a type of fine, light fabric that had only recently cost William Thalhimer just a few cents, became unobtainable when its cost skyrocketed to thousands of dollars. Ordinary thread now sold for ten dollars a spool.

To make do with the little resources they had, women began making dresses with cruder materials, using calico in place of silk and coarse skirt braid for ribbons. Men wore shoes with wooden soles when shoe leather became too expensive. Fat doubled for soap; potato and carrot peelings served as coffee beans. Stores began stocking increased amounts of inexpensive black fabric since so many women required mourning dresses as they received the unwelcome news of their sons, brothers, and fathers dying on the battlefields.

The northern blockade provided a major obstacle for merchants, but William somehow found ways around it. In August 1862, he took out an ad in the *Richmond Times* boasting, "New goods run the blockade!" allowing his shoppers to find "much-desired goods" at his store.

Running the blockade was no small feat. Blockade runners had to be brave, clever, and quick; their ranks included free blacks, shifty and adventurous women, and, the likes of two Jewish Richmonders, Philip Whitlock and his brother-in-law Ellis Abram. These two men may have been William's keys to running the blockade, as they were personal friends and members of his synagogue.

Whitlock and Abram stayed in New York for almost a week buying small goods. Their handbags stuffed with fine tooth combs, silk handkerchiefs, tobacco pipes, and pencils, the two men were arrested trying to cross Confederate lines and soldiers pilfered items from their bags. When the blockaders returned to Richmond, they sold their merchandise to struggling merchants like William Thalhimer. All in all, they broke even on the venture.[14]

In May 1862, seven northern warships approached Richmond by way of the James River, throwing bombs, bullets and hand grenades as they sailed. Farmers fled from the riverbanks up to Richmond, feverishly spreading the news that the Yankees were coming within a few hours.

Storeowners hurriedly closed up shop and boarded their windows. Mary's brothers, the Millhisers, published a notice in the local paper announcing that their dry goods store would be "closed for a season."[15] Although they were too old to be enlisted, the Millhiser brothers would become heavily involved with Confederate efforts, raising money for the war and housing sick and wounded soldiers in their homes.

Only a month passed before William decided to move his store and family uphill to Broad Street, away from the growing wartime pandemonium of the market district. The Thalhimers packed their belongings into horse-drawn carts and said goodbye to their old home and store beside the Farmers' Market, making their way to Broad Street between Third and Fourth. Little did William know that this would be one of many serendipitous business moves he would make over the years, saving The Store from almost certain disaster.

To keep business moving along, William began selling goods to be used in fashioning and repairing soldiers' uniforms. In 1864, he sold six spools of cotton to the Third Division of Jackson Hospital.

The Thalhimers' domestic slaves, Matilda and Lavinia, ran away with the neighbors' slavegirl, leaving the household chores to Mary. She worked tirelessly to keep domestic affairs running smoothly while supporting war efforts in any small ways she could. Rabbi Michelbacher's wife Marian gathered a group of Jewish women in the basements of the local synagogues to repair and pick lint off of Confederate uniforms and, occasionally, provide medical care for wounded soldiers. For a time, synagogue Beth Ahabah even served as a hospital.

Having received a diploma in double-entry bookkeeping at the age of thirteen, a rare and illustrious accomplishment, Gustavus worked as bookkeeper and cashier at his father's store. When the war broke out, Gus enlisted in the Army and served as a Private in the K-Regiment of the Third Light Defense. His cousin Henry Clay Smith volunteered as well, although he lied about his age to enlist. Henry Clay was only sixteen.

Gus fought with McAnerny's Batallion when they defeated Dahlgren's raid, returning home with nothing more than a few scratches and scrapes, but Henry Clay was not as fortunate. Abraham and Henrietta Smith received the horrific letter that every soldier's parent fears. The captain of their son's battery unit wrote to inform them that Henry Clay had been killed by a close-range bullet to the forehead in the Battle of Bloody Run.

"He lived only a few moments," wrote Captain Otey, "never speaking after he was shot. I had him properly buried, in a nice coffin, and his grave enclosed and marked." The Captain included with his letter Henry Clay's Bible and other personal effects.

Only days later, Captain Otey himself died from fatal wounds received in battle. Such were the gruesome everyday surprises brought by the bloodiest war ever to stain American soil.

Upon Gus Thalhimer's return to civilian life, he started his own fruit stand on Franklin Street between Sixteenth and Seventeenth. His brothers continued to help out around the store, even little Isaac, only nine years old. For fun, the children played "stone the Yankees" and climbed the big sycamore tree outside of the White House of the Confederacy with Jefferson Davis' children. One time, Moses Thalhimer fell from the tree and was roundly chastised by his mother when he returned home with torn knickerbockers and skinned knees.

Word began to travel from house to house that Richmond would soon be evacuated and surrendered to the north. Banks forced customers to remove their money. Children ran through the streets, eavesdropping to hear the latest news and report back to their parents. Entire families packed a few belongings into their carriages and left town, abandoning their homes to the shock of the slaves left standing on the front stoops.

In April 1865, four years after the war had started, the hooves of Confederate officers' horses thundered down Broad Street. Drunk and sober soldiers alike crowded filthy sidewalks littered with broken glass as merchants boarded up their stores.

Panicked shouts of "Fire! Fire!" filled the city as Richmond's streets roared and crackled with the rampant spread of flames. Ships exploded in the harbor as the Navy Yard burned. Tobacco warehouses and feed stores collapsed along with the courthouse, Post Office, War department and almost a thousand homes and businesses. The city's two fire engines were left to do what little they could to douse the fires.

The biggest ironies of Richmond's "great conflagration" were these: the fire was started by Confederate troops and put out at the command of a Yankee. Many Richmonders assumed Yankee Generals Sherman and Sheridan were responsible for igniting the fires, but Confederate troops had accidentally caused the inferno by burning bridges and warehouses as they retreated from the Federal army. In a gentlemanly gesture, General Grant's men helped put out the flames, rescuing the paltry remains of Richmond's business district.

By the time General Lee surrendered to General Grant in Appomattox, William Thalhimer had returned to the cashier's desk of his store. The Federal government demanded that merchants re-open their stores on Tuesday following the fire, so boards were removed from windows and front doors swung open for business.

After the war, William Flegenheimer served in the United States Quartermaster Department. He served for six years as deputy clerk of the United States District Court, where he wrote the bail bond for Jefferson Davis. With Flegenheimer's pen gracing documents from the beginning and the end of the struggle, the war was over.

President Lincoln and his son Thaddeus, nicknamed Tad, arrived in Richmond not long after the south's surrender. Flanked by army officers and surrounded by the cheers and celebratory songs of newly freed slaves, the President and his son walked down Main Street to the Farmers' Market at Seventeenth Street, near the original location of William Thalhimer's store.

If William had kept his store beside the Old Market, he could have lost his business, his home, his possessions, and perhaps even the lives of his wife and children. Now he and his family were safely settled on Broad Street where they would remain for the Reconstruction to come. William Thalhimer's little store stood like a Confederate soldier: injured, tired, and scarred, yet still alive.

William Thalhimer's Kiddush cup given to him in 1849. *Photo by Wayne Dementi, 2010.*

CHAPTER SEVEN

DOORS OPEN
2002 - 2003

On a crisp November morning, I'm lounging around, watching *The Today Show* in my pajamas at our rental apartment in Richmond's historic Fan District. Ryan and I have taken the day off to spend a long weekend at my parents' vacation house in the Blue Ridge Mountains, and we plan to leave after breakfast. Christina Aguilera has just started singing "Genie in a Bottle" when Ryan walks in, turns off the television, and leaves the room.

"What are you doing?" I ask, but he's already halfway down the hall. "I kind of like that song."

Ryan returns with a breakfast tray holding a plate of French toast, a small pitcher of maple syrup, a cup of coffee, and a small, black velveteen box. He forgets to get down on one knee, but I think I know what's going on.

My heart pounding, I hinge the velveteen box open, revealing the sparkling ring we designed with diamonds from two of my maternal great-grandmother's rings. Ryan slides it onto my finger.

"Will you marry me?" he asks.

"Ryan," I tell him, "You know the answer is yes."

Seven months later, our wedding takes place in the peaceful majesty of the Blue Ridge Mountains. After honeymooning on the Caribbean island of Nevis, we settle into our first home in Richmond. It's a charming yellow cottage built in 1937, the yard bursting with the perfume of camellias, hydrangeas and azaleas.

I turn the key to the front door, push it open, and Ryan lifts me over the threshold into our empty living room. That evening we sit together on the hardwood floor and watch a Kansas basketball game as we eat Mrs. Fearnow's Brunswick Stew straight out of the Crockpot with a ladle, the only utensil we can find in the boxes scattered around the kitchen.

"I've never been so happy," I tell him, leaning over the Crockpot to give him a kiss.

      ⚜   ⚜   ⚜

Now that I'm back in Richmond and only doing an occasional freelance naming project, I return to the beckoning call of Dad's gray file cabinet and afternoon interviews with Grandpa.

"Don't you know *anything* else about William Thalhimer?" I whine to Dad one afternoon, leaning against the file cabinet as he works at his desk. "Is this folder all we've got on his whole life? Just birth and death certificates and pictures of a gravestone? *I want to know his story.*"

"Why don't you join me for lunch tomorrow?" Dad asks, seeming to ignore me. "I'd like for you to meet Emily."

"Dad, are you even listening?"

"I am. Just meet us here tomorrow at noon."

The next day, I'm munching pita chips in my parents' kitchen when the doorbell rings. Behind the glass door awaits a round-faced woman of indeterminate age wearing a turtleneck sweater and a simple A-line skirt. Her Prius has vanity plates that read "Mthr E." Her cheeks look naturally ruddy and she wears her brown hair in a simple bob tucked behind her ears. When Dad opens the door, "Mthr E" leans down and gives Kacey, my parents' spoiled-rotten Bichon Frise, a treat from her pocket. Kacey licks her hand.

"Hi. I'm Elizabeth," I tell her, outstretching my hand. "Do I get a treat?"

"I'm Emily. You can have a bacon snack too, if you want," she says, jokingly reaching into her skirt pocket and handing me one.

"Hey, I've got an idea. Why don't we have tuna fish instead?" Dad interjects, laughing.

The three of us head to the sunroom and sit down to our boxed lunches, which Dad loves. They are organized, modest, and predictable. He goes to the same sandwich shop several times a week, where he loves to chat with the manager and his wife. It makes me think about how much he misses Thalhimers.

"Emily and I are on GRIVA together," Dad says. "That's G-R-I-V-A, the Genealogical Research Institite of Virginia."

Emily chimes in, "When I met your Dad and he told me about the research he's doing on his family, I just couldn't help myself. He had more questions than answers. William Thalhimer's life seemed like a mystery just waiting to be solved."

"Are you from Richmond?" I ask her, confused about why she even cares about William Thalhimer.

"No. I'm from Pennsylvania."

"So, let me get this straight. You started helping Dad with his genealogy because you were interested in the founder of a store you'd never heard of?"

"William wanted me to help," Emily says. "I'm just drawn to him."

"I think she has a crush on him!" Dad says jokingly.

I am utterly speechless. Only an hour earlier, Emily was a Hybrid-driving, turtle-necked stranger. Now she's a dream come true: a masterful researcher obsessed with finding my great-great-great grandfather who died over a century ago. She feels the gravitational pull of the quest just like I do. She feels the insatiable desire to dig up forgotten stories, one at a time. I feel an immediate bond with Emily.

"Emily has done an enormous amount of reading and research. She works for the Family History Center. She's just been up to Boston where she found some old Thalhimers' records at Harvard's Business Library. I think you should take a look at her work," Dad says.

"This is unbelievable. How can we ever thank you, Emily?"

"Don't worry about that right now," she replies. "We have work to do."

⚜   ⚜   ⚜

From the tuna fish box lunches onward, Dad, Emily and I become a quirky detective team.

Dad continues to maintain his genealogical database of thousands of our ancestors and their descendants, storing hard copies of his documentation in the grey file cabinet and contacting hundreds of distant cousins from Bacova, Virginia, to Paris, France, to ask what they know about the family's history. Fixated on building handwritten timelines on spreadsheets, he draws up pages and pages of details illustrating the chronology of each generation of the family alongside the growth of the Thalhimers store.

Armed with white gloves and a pencil, Emily tackles the tough archival research. She doesn't fear daunting archives and has a special tenacity for finding things that we've been told "don't exist." We spend countless hours at the Library of Virginia, forgetting to eat lunch as we squint to scan the tiny, newsprinted text on the microfiche readers.

I begin filling notebooks with stories and notes, meeting regularly with Emily to share our findings. She gives me piles of research in return. We find an advertisement here, a property tax there, a signature here, a letter there. Odds and ends scattered in attics, basements, libraries and archives across the country. People who know someone who knows someone who knows something.

Occasionally, I pull open the metal drawers of Dad's gray file cabinet to deposit our newest research. I return to read and re-read the files and stare at photographs, as if trying to coax out their stories. My notebooks and file folders of photocopies pile up until they fill a canvas Thalhimers tote bag, then, when the bag begins to rip, I replace it with a rolling suitcase. Wherever I go, I literally drag my past around behind me.

"Emily," I ask on one of our marathon phone calls to discuss research, "can Jews have godmothers? If so, will you be my godmother? I always wanted one."

"I don't know about Jewish godmothers," she says, "but we can look into it."

CHAPTER EIGHT

FORTUNES AMONG MISFORTUNES
1865 - 1883

With the horrors of war behind them, Mary and William opened their home to friends. They hosted festive parties and dances above The Store, where as many as sixteen people could dance the Lancers. The lighthearted fun of these gatherings helped relieve the tension of post-war life and ease Mary's suffering.

Every July, Mary took to the healing mineral waters of the Warm and Hot Springs of Bath County, Virginia, to relieve her arthritis. Friends and customers hardly knew she was ailing because of her pleasant disposition, but Mary's pain grew worse by the day. Finally, she quit working at The Store to stay home and focus on improving her health and caring for her children, the youngest of whom was only four years old.

Mary Millhiser Thalhimer, circa 1870.

Richmond continued to face numerous challenges and inconveniences. Confrontations between blacks and whites escalated into riots in the city's streets, where violent crimes, arson, and burglaries were on the rise. Cholera and small pox spread from one house to the next, especially in the oppressive summer heat. The Federal military presence continued as northern peddlers hawked their wares on the sidewalks. Confederate dollars had become worthless, and many Richmonders were homeless and destitute.

Making tough times even tougher, William Thalhimer's store was robbed by one of its very own employees, a clerk named Ellen Jones. She had slowly pilfered items from the shelves, placing an additional drain on William's deteriorating profits.

Without a doubt, William Thalhimer needed additional credit lines to keep his struggling store alive. He requested credit extensions from the New York firms of Sweetser, Pembroke & Co., C.B. Rouss, and H. B. Claflin. All three had reputations for bailing out dry goods firms, especially southern establishments, during financial panics.

Thankfully, William's Hebrew name held true: "God will establish." These firms, as well as two in Baltimore, agreed to extend credit lines to William as he had proven himself to be an honorable and reliable merchant. Without their help, his store would have most likely folded like so many of its retail brethren, including Thomas R. Price's longtime store just down the street. Mr. Price, it was said, died of heartbreak when his store could not recover from bankruptcy.

Retailers weren't the only ones suffering. One Friday night, Gus Thalhimer and a friend arrived late for Sabbath services at their synagogue, K.K. Beth Shalome. They quietly opened the big wooden doors as not to disturb the congregants and, much to their surprise, found the hazan preaching to empty pews. Without even stopping, the reader watched the two boys enter and continued delivering the service to his newfound congregation of two.

With his wife slowly dying from rheumatism in her mid-forties, his store struggling, his synagogue's congregation waning, and old age creeping up on him, William Thalhimer decided the time had come. He would usher his eldest sons, Gus and Charles, into the business.

In June 1868, William leased a small store at 1519 East Main Street from Jacob Ezekiel, a fellow dry goods merchant. He placed an ad in the *Richmond Daily Dispatch* announcing that this branch store would operate under the leadership of his son, Mr. Gus Thalhimer. It would be called William Thalhimer and Sons.

"A Pleasant Surprise," the ad boasted, "To find that Goods can be bought as cheap as before the war, and some at even LOWER PRICES THAN EVER." Gus, Charles, and four other young gentlemen managed the branch store while little brothers Isaac and Moses served as errand boys.[16] A northern credit agent observed in his notebook, "Sons are young men of good habits and character. And it is considered a careful firm now have two stores: One on Broad St. and other on Main St."[17]

But the branch store would not succeed. After only two years, William closed the Main Street store and consolidated all goods back up to the bigger store on Broad Street. Profits could not support the operation of two branches, although it had been a gutsy and hopeful attempt to grow the business.

William paid close attention to the goings-on of successful stores in other cities, including A.T. Stewart's Marble Dry Goods palace in New York City, Wanamaker's in Philadelphia, and Rowland H. Macy's stores in Massachusetts and New York. These merchants created the practice of "no-haggle" shopping, which meant that each product was identified with a marked price tag. Thalhimer & Sons adopted this system, introducing the concept of one-price shopping to Richmonders. John Wanamaker took the one-price policy ever farther, claiming "satisfaction guaranteed" on all purchases. If a customer was not satisfied, an item could be returned or exchanged. This radical practice caught on, and made its way to William Thalhimer's shop as well.

In autumn of 1870, heavy rainfall brought over twenty-four feet of water to Richmond's market district. Richmonders paddled canoes down Main Street to search for loved ones, animals, and possessions as pigs, trees, and barrels of flour floated past.

As the streets flooded, William realized he had uncannily saved his business from another disaster. Had he kept the Main Street branch store open for only a few more months, it would have been decimated by floodwaters. Instead, newspaper ads cleverly boasted, "Unprecedented occurrence: Main Street removed to Broad. Not the street itself, but the popular bargain store of William Thalhimer & Sons who have removed to their own capacious building No. 315 Broad Street between 3rd and 4th Streets." [18]

⚜   ⚜   ⚜

In the post-war years, the United States' economy seemed to be in a constant state of flux. New tax laws made it nearly impossible to run an honest, reputable house of business. The crash of a major financial firm in New York rippled out across the country causing bankruptcies everywhere and draining currency from circulation. Property taxes escalated so that they sometimes exceeded the actual property values.

"Whether the economy will get better is a big question," wrote Richmonder Johann Gottfried Lange in his diary. "Today again eleven bankruptcy petitions were filed in court. It [seems] to me as if bankruptcy had become an evil sport, he who does not go bankrupt is not a Virginia businessman. Honesty and character are walking on dark roads; big business is conducted with somebody else's money."[19]

William decided to move his store and home up a few blocks to 601 East Broad Street, right on the corner of Sixth Street near another bustling, open-air market. However he soon began to realize, affected by the burden of the recent branch store closing and multiple relocations, he had spread himself too thin.

One of his creditors, Paton & Company, filed suit in a petition against William Thalhimer & Sons. William, Gus and Charles owed Paton one thousand thirty-nine dollars and ninety-six cents and were unable to repay it.[20] Their debts to other creditors added up to a staggering eighteen thousand dollars.

On March 8, 1873, William Thalhimer surrendered. He had no choice. His beloved store, which he had kept alive for more than thirty years, officially declared bankruptcy.

William submitted to his creditors a complete inventory of all goods and possessions in his store: yards upon yards of laces, silks, and cambrics, parasols, shawls, diaper pins, spittoons, fans, pocket knives, belts, suspenders, and work boots. In order to pay off the debt to Paton, a United States Marshal would hold a public auction of all Thalhimer & Sons stock. If necessary, they would auction off personal items from the Thalhimers' residence as well, including indulgences the family had so richly earned, like the piano, sewing machine, sausage maker, clocks, and the engraved pistol William had bought to protect himself and his family. It seemed like the end of the line for the Thalhimers.

In a heroic attempt to save his brother-in-law's business, Moses Millhiser, an increasingly successful businessman, purchased the entirety of William Thalhimer's goods. He allowed William to sell the stock as his own agent, giving him the opportunity to re-establish his business and pay back his creditors.

This caused yet another problem, as Paton & Co. alleged that the public auction of goods had only raised four-thousand dollars and William was fraudulently hiding the majority of his merchandise at Millhiser's store and other locations throughout the city. On account of violating the Bankruptcy Laws of 1863, William Thalhimer and his sons Charles and Gus were issued warrants of arrest, and court orders demanded that Moses Millhiser cease the sale of goods. Millhiser claimed that he took over Thalhimer's store and stocked it with his own merchandise, and none of the sold goods belonged to Thalhimer & Sons.

Standing before District Judge John C. Underwood, Millhiser and the Thalhimers made their case, arguing against their arrest and pleading their innocence. The arrest was maintained, and William and Charles posted bail of fifteen hundred dollars each. Gus, who had somehow been let off the hook, took off for San Francisco, California, where he found a job as a clerk with M. Heller & Sons, Importers of Dry Goods. Jacob, sensing that his father's business had no future, joined his brother Gus in California months later.

Over the course of the next year, the bankruptcy ruling was overruled, the Thalhimers' paid their debts by selling goods under the watchful eye of the court, and by January 22, 1874, William Thalhimer & Sons was miraculously back in business at 601 East Broad Street.

A northern credit assessor noted in his ledger, "T has worked safely through his financial troubles and has made money since…a respectable old gentleman, bears a good character, and is very steady."[21] There was still hope for William Thalhimer & Sons, although now only three of those sons remained in Richmond.

⚜   ⚜   ⚜

Finally succumbing to the painful rheumatism that had plagued her for eleven years, Mary Thalhimer died at the age of fifty-eight in the family's home above The Store on a frigid day in the winter of 1876. She passed away surrounded by her loving husband and children, with the exceptions of Gus and Jake who could not make the journey from San Francisco in time.

Family and friends braved the cold on the hillside of Hebrew Cemetery to throw handfuls of dirt upon Mary's casket as Rabbi Michelbacher offered a final prayer. Etched on the back of Mary's headstone the Hebrew words read, "Rest in Peace. A glorious woman our teacher Miriam…May her soul be bound for eternal life."

William knew he would soon join Mary in the hereafter, but wanted to ensure that his store would carry on. The year after she died, after thirty-five years in business, William drew up the following legal contract with the assistance of his nephew, William Flegenheimer:

> William Thalhimer gives to Charles Thalhimer, Isaac Thalhimer, and Moses Thalhimer the entire stock of goods and merchandise consisting of dry goods, hosiery, furnishing goods and notions of every kind and description also all of the store fixtures, consisting of store shelving, counters, desks, tables & iron safe, also all of my books of account together with all

the debts outstanding and owing to me, in the said business situated, stored
located and being in the store room and cellar or basement in my house
at 601 Broad Street Richmond, Virginia, to have, hold, and enjoy all the
singular said goods, chattels, and personal estate. The business is now called
Thalhimer Brothers.

Thalhimer Brothers store at the corner of 5th and Broad Streets. (l to r) Gus Thalhimer, Jeff Kopple (Abraham and Henrietta Smith's grandson), Moses Thalhimer, unknown women, 1881.

The sign painter returned with a bucket of paint, ladder, and brush, and painted
"Thalhimer Bros." across the front of the store. After several incarnations, this name
would finally stick. Charles, Moses, and Isaac, the three Thalhimer brothers remaining in
Richmond, inherited their father's most prized possession: his store.

Six years later, Gus returned to Richmond where his brothers welcomed him home
and hired him as Thalhimer Brothers' bookkeeper. Gus jovially wrote to his brother Jake,

still living in San Francisco, "Fair week & lots of book keeping kept me busy. Ike was in New York…shipping lots of goods, and between receiving and selling we were fully occupied last week…Yesterday was the liveliest day this season, and Mose and I got no meal from breakfast till supper as we are so popular, you know, not being married." Back in Richmond, Amelia married a storekeeper down the street. Charles married and welcomed the first Thalhimer grandchild into the busy household above the store.

In 1878, Isaac married nineteen-year-old Amelia Blum. Amelia had been orphaned at the age of fifteen, left to raise her three younger sisters by herself. During summer buying trips to New York, Isaac had wooed Amelia with long love letters. "You have by your noble heart and soul won what no other mortal woman has succeeded in doing," he wrote. "Dear Amelia . . . you are all I care for in a woman."

When Isaac took his marital vows, he made another solemn promise to his new bride: he would care for her three younger sisters as if they were his own children. The youngest Blum sister Lina was deaf in one ear and blind in one eye, and Isaac took particularly good care of the sweet girl, promising her as fulfilling a life as her sisters.

⚜   ⚜   ⚜

In October, onlookers watched as President Hayes slowly paraded past Thalhimer Brothers in a carriage pulled by four majestic white horses. The President held his hat with one hand and waved with the other to the delight of the cheering masses, waving their handkerchiefs from street corners and windows.

An increasing number of wagons unloaded merchandise in front of the big stores, an optimistic indicator of good times to come. As bedsheets, stockings, yards of calico, cloaks, and rugs made their way into homes across Richmond, the Thalhimer name impressed upon its customers the hallmarks of quality, honesty and integrity. The Thalhimer Brothers guaranteed their shoppers fine merchandise, competitive prices, and personal attention.

Eventually, all five of the Thalhimer Brothers returned to work at The Store in some capacity, ensuring that at least one of them would carry on its legacy. William noticed that the two youngest boys, Isaac and Moses, showed particular promise as merchants.

William decided that after forty years in America, the time had come for his family to reside outside The Store. Bought on foreclosure, the Thalhimers' first freestanding home

William Thalhimer circa 1880. *Davis Gallery.*

stood at the corner of Fourth and Clay Streets among other German, Jewish, and English immigrant families on the edge of the neighborhood that would become known as Jackson Ward. The family home sprawled across two lots, although it provided fairly modest accommodations. It housed William, his adult children, and a growing assortment of spouses, children, and domestic help.

Only a few days after ringing up sales behind the register of his store in the spring of 1883, William Thalhimer fell ill with a horrible stomach ailment. While resting in bed, he passed away so quickly and calmly that the children and grandchildren at his bedside barely noticed their patriarch's spirit had flown.

Rabbi Abraham Harris conducted William's funeral at Beth Ahabah, where hundreds of Richmonders of diverse classes, conditions and creeds gathered in its pews. The pallbearers carrying William's casket included a city councilman, the first ranking Jewish officer from Richmond to fight for the Confederacy, a High Constable, and fellow dry goods merchants and clerks, Jewish and Christian alike. His whole literary society attended the funeral as a group. The respectable array of family and friends gathered to bury William beside his wife in Hebrew Cemetery, where he had once served as its Vice-President.

A letter to the editor by a man only identified as J.R.K. stated, "I am not a Hebrew, and am but little given to excessive praise of men, whether living or dead; but standing by the grave of William Thalhimer I could heartily wish that our Christian fellow-citizens would take counsel of the example of his life."[22]

William's newspaper obituary would have made his parents, Malke and Goëtz, the most proud. It said of William Thalhimer: "He leaves his children not only part of a competence honorably amassed, but what is better, the rich heritage of a spotless name."[23]

CHAPTER NINE

MR. IKE AND HIS BROTHERS
1884 - 1930

As sure as the pocket watch keeping time from his vest pocket, Isaac Thalhimer arrived at The Store as the first rays of sunlight warmed the cobblestone streets. With a brisk "good morning," he tipped his hat to neighboring merchants including his cousins at Abraham Hutzler & Sons and his Millhiser uncles. He checked the glass kiosk out front to ensure it displayed the newest, most attractive goods then unlocked the front door of Thalhimer Brothers at Fifth and Broad Streets.

Isaac chewed the end of his cigar as he climbed the creaky wooden stairs to his office on the mezzanine overlooking the selling floor. His stock boasted some of the finest dry goods in the city and, he liked to think, the whole of the south. He hung his hat and coat then sat down at his desk directly in the center of the balcony, like a king overlooking the expanse of his kingdom. Isaac inspected each ledger book to be sure the previous day's transactions had been recorded properly. A stickler for precision, he had to know The Store's exact financial status at all times.

The morning light spread like melted butter upon the rows of laces, linens, silks, cloaks, and spools of every colored thread. Thalhimer Brothers' recently expanded stock also included ladies' hats, carpets, crockery and house furnishings. Isaac's wife Amelia, who exhibited fine taste and an eye for quality merchandise, helped her husband attain a reputation as one of Richmond's best silk, woolen, and linen merchants. Amelia worked occasionally as a clerk at The Store, and hosted turkey dinners for employees at Thanksgiving and Christmas.

Isaac's secretary Ida Smith swept in, the bell dinging to announce her arrival. Miss Smith spent her days dutifully attending to the business correspondence of the day, informing customers of overdue accounts and handling invoices from the New York wholesale houses. Isaac could trust Miss Smith with just about anything and regarded her as highly as she did him. As a matter of fact, he considered her family.

Two more Thalhimer brothers arrived at The Store before the first customer of the day came to call. Moses selected which popular laces and trimmings to re-order and which ones to discontinue, and oversaw the ledger books for credit accounts. Charles, a lively, boisterous, and somewhat portly clerk, arranged merchandise on the shelves and prepared to ring up sales.

All three of Amelia's younger sisters worked as clerks at Thalhimer Brothers. Caroline Blum, endearingly called Lina by just about everyone, was a kind young woman with one glass eye and an ear horn to aid her hearing impairment. Lina took great pride in helping customers make their selections, gaining a loyal clientele.

A host of cousins and in-laws including Jeff Kopple, Myer Newman, and Charles Hutzler filled a variety of positions including store clerk, department manager, shelf-stocker, and errand boy, depending on what needed attention. Additional clerks like Messieurs Weller and Lamm worked in exchange for room and board at Isaac and Amelia's house.

As Isaac's pocketwatch ticked through the morning hours, customers streamed into The Store from the country's first streetcar system. This exciting new mode of transportation made it easy for Richmonders to travel back and forth from the outskirts of the city to the shopping district downtown. Visiting the stores on Broad and Grace Streets was no longer an all-day affair; women could conveniently drop by during lunch or shop in the evenings until as late as ten or eleven o'clock.

"From the furthest corners," boasted an advertisement in 1895, "you can hear the busy hum of the shoppers. We need no other advertising medium than for you to see the many gladdened souls that pass out of our store, each happy and pleased with their purchases." For the first time, The Store referred to itself as "Thalhimer's" and prided itself on being a "model one-price house." Its departments featured everything from fabrics and ribbons to parasols, German silver to baby carriages, fine china to oil stoves. A modern elevator carried customers to the basement where their children admired dolls, tin trains, pewter tea sets, hobbyhorses, ride-on wagons, and miniature printing presses in the toy department.

When the bell on the front door jingled, Isaac peered down from his perch in the

Thalhimers (right) and Miller & Rhoads (left) on Broad Street, circa 1890.

mezzanine, stroking his moustache. Occasionally he descended the staircase to greet loyal customers by name and introduce himself to newcomers. He proudly presented the newest piece goods he'd acquired: a richly woven brocade from New York, a supple piece of authentic Italian leather, or flowing silk from the Far East. He kept his golden thread counter at hand, always ready to show a customer the luxurious thread count of the goods he had so carefully selected.

With each sale, a salesperson put the customer's money and a certificate of transaction into a wire basket. Pulling the ropes of a pulley caused the basket to spring across the ceiling from the sales floor to the mezzanine. There, Moses inked his pen and entered each transaction into a large ledger book. He placed a receipt and the customer's change back in the basket, and back to the cashier it would fly.

The traveling basket delighted Isaac's children, and many years later his grandchildren, who would cradle mugs of hot Horlick's Malted Milk as they sat in the balcony and cheered the bouncing basket along. Sometimes Isaac would let them fetch the money from the basket and hand it to him. To the children, this was not just a balcony: it was Seventh Heaven.

Just after noon every day, Isaac placed the morning's proceeds into a black satchel and walked to the bank with one of his employees, Solomon Wells. They took care not to walk the same path each day as not to be robbed. Isaac never entrusted the black satchel to Solomon or anyone else. He clasped it tightly under his arm, protecting The Store's earnings with his own life.

Upon depositing the money, Isaac walked the short distance back home with the empty satchel. He sat down to lunch with his wife Amelia in the dining room then took a brief nap before one of the store's credit managers arrived. In the afternoons, the men spread out the ledger books on the dining room table to assess the state of Thalhimer Brothers' accounts.

William B. Thalhimer, age 6. *Jefferson Art Gallery, 1894.*

When time allowed, Isaac met friends at the Jefferson Club before supper. Over a round of poker or pinochle, he talked shop with other Jewish merchants including Leo Greentree of Greentrees men's clothing shop and W.H. Schwarzschild, one of Richmond's premiere watchmakers who founded a jewelry store bearing his name.

Isaac spent his evenings at home with his family, helping the children with their lessons and telling stories by the fireplace.

His children would beg, "Tell us a story, Father."

"A story?" His voice was gruff but his eyes twinkled. "Don't you know that I don't tell stories?"

But his tales captivated everyone down to the youngest child, little Ruth, only a toddler. Isaac told of how he threw stones at the Yankees in 1861, and grisly, detailed accounts of Civil War battles. He described how his mother and father, hardscrabble German immigrants, built their thriving business from nothing. As Isaac spoke, his eyebrows furrowed as his dark eyes met with those of his five daughters and two sons, William and Ira, whom he hoped would grow to be fine, capable merchants.

Isaac "Ira" Thalhimer, Jr. age 2, 1894.

Little Ira Thalhimer had been given the name Isaac, meaning "may God smile," after his father and his father's uncle back in Thairenbach. Isaac and Amelia hoped the name would bring a smile to their boy's lips when he reflected on the strength and dignity of his forebears.

One day in late April of 1895, just as the camellias were blooming, two-year-old Ira played on his rocking horse. As he laughed and rocked, his brown curls bounced up and down. Suddenly, Ira started rocking so hard that he almost fell. His mammy reached forward to steady him, but her cigarette grazed the horse's tail as she did. The toy burst into flames, and Ira's giggles turned into screams. By the time Amelia came outside and held her son in her arms, it was too late. Little Ira had burned to death.

Rabbi Calisch led a graveside service for Isaac "Ira" Thalhimer Jr. in his wee silk-lined coffin. Now William B. Thalhimer was Isaac and Amelia's only son. He would be The Store's only hope.

⚜   ⚜   ⚜

After celebrating his fiftieth birthday, Isaac decided his family deserved a more sophisticated residence. They had lived on the floors above the family store, in a modest dwelling on Grace Street, and in his father's lively home overflowing with relatives at the corner of Fourth and Clay Streets. Now Isaac wanted a stately home, a masterwork of art and architecture, a place that he and Amelia could call their own.

Aside from running the store, which had become quite successful, Isaac held significant interest in real estate. With an inkling that it was an up-and-coming area, he selected Monument Avenue as the address for his new home. From there he could easily walk to Thalhimer Brothers and Temple Beth Ahabah, the two locations he visited almost daily.

When Isaac announced his house-building plans to his wife Amelia, she cried – but not the tears of happiness he had expected.

"Oh, Isaac," she told her husband through passionate sobs. "I don't want to live out in the country!"

Amelia Blum Thalhimer, circa 1900.

Amelia only knew Monument Avenue as a dirt road lined by tobacco crops. Few people lived there, as the city of Richmond had not yet extended that far west. However, as other houses went up, she slowly acclimated to the idea of living on Monument Avenue. Nannies pushed buggies down the sidewalks where children played tiddlywinks and marbles. Periodically, crowds gathered in the median to watch as classically styled monuments honoring Civil War generals were hoisted upon their foundations. Before long, Monument Avenue blossomed into a grand, tree-lined boulevard with dozens of large, elegant homes. The dirt roads were paved over with cobblestones, making the noise almost impossibly loud when driving in Isaac's new automobile.

William B. Thalhimer in his father's Rambler. Circa 1912.

As the foundations for the home were laid, the family rented a home next door to observe the progress. They watched as expert craftsmen delicately carved wooden banisters and mantelpieces, stained glass artists installed oval-shaped windows to light the dramatic mahogany stairwell, and mosaic tiles were laid by hand on the front porch and in the bathrooms. The fireplace hearth of each room boasted its own personality with colorful stonework and an ornamental firescreen.

Upon the home's completion, Isaac, Amelia and their four youngest children, along with housekeeper Lillie Thornton and butler William Jones, moved into the newly built masterpiece. It was a wonder to behold its soaring entryway, with exquisite attention paid to even the smallest detail.

For the next ten years, 1824 Monument welcomed bustling activity from Friday night Sabbath dinners to stunning wedding receptions to formal affairs for Thalhimer Brothers' employees. Much to Amelia's delight, a noisy stream of visiting children and grandchildren tumbled through the front door, above which a stained glass window proudly declared the street number 1824.

⚜   ⚜   ⚜

William and Mary Thalhimer's children. Top row (l to r): Isaac, Amelia, Moses. Bottom row: Jacob, Gus, Charles. Front: Bettie, 1888.

Gus Thalhimer died at forty-eight years old. His eldest son William Gustavus, was hit and killed by a train. His other son, Morton Gustavus, would eventually find great success as a movie theater owner and realtor in Richmond.

Jacob Thalhimer remained in California for sixteen years. During that time he met and married a prominent Rabbi's daughter and they raised three children. Their family lived for a brief time in Richmond before settling in New York City. Their first son,

William Montefiore, would become a renowned physician whose serum, pathology, and blood banking research led to the development of dialysis.

Devoted sisters Bettie Thalhimer Solomon and Amelia Thalhimer Newman traveled extensively together, visiting Europe more than a dozen times. Amelia, a mother of three girls, died on a trip to Berlin. Bettie returned to Richmond with her sister's body for burial in Hebrew Cemetery. Bettie would marry twice and live to old age but would die childless in the Bronx.

Moses Thalhimer married and the couple's union produced only one child, the lovely and talented Irma Marie with her playful, bow-shaped smile. A gifted pianist from early childhood, Irma Marie married and moved to New York with her husband, a successful stockbroker. They would have two children, including a daughter they named Virginia in fond remembrance of Irma Marie's birthplace. Moses remained in Richmond, where he continued to manage Thalhimer Brothers with his brother Isaac.

With his protruding belly nearly popping his vest buttons, Charles Thalhimer proved to be both a mischief-maker and a dilettante. After he married, he dabbled in tobacco sales, ran a saloon, and sold wines and liquors on the wholesale market. Charles was convicted twice, once for owning and running a slot machine in his saloon and again for selling lottery tickets, for which he spent his day in jail.

Charles eventually sold his interest in Thalhimer Brothers to his brother Isaac and went into business with his friend Isaac Held, dubbing their short-lived store Held & Thalhimer. He abandoned that partnership to start a liquor business called Charles Thalhimer & Co. For the last fifteen years of his life, Charles returned to Thalhimer Brothers to work as a clerk. He died at the age of seventy-one after seven months of paralysis following a stroke. The lives of his five children, Samuel, Mary, Esther, Louis, and Rosa Lee, played out like Shakespearean tragedy.

Samuel raped a paraplegic girl and consequently was stabbed by her vengeful father, bleeding to death on the sidewalk outside Thalhimer Brothers. After Mary's husband died, her cousins cared for her until she died at age ninety, a childless widow. Esther, a clerk at Thalhimers, jumped from the roof of The Store and died instantly when she struck the pavement in the alley. Louis tied a bathrobe cord around his neck and hanged himself in a room at the Murphy Hotel. Rosa Lee married and had a mentally disabled son, Alfred Charles Blum, Jr., who bore no children.

CHAPTER TEN

In Memory of Alfred Charles Blum, Jr. 1998

On an overnight visit to New York City to do some genealogy research, Dad decides to look up his long lost cousin, Alfred Charles Blum, Jr., an elevator operator for the U.S. Postal Service. He calls Alfred's apartment a few times but it rings and rings, and there's no voicemail service to leave a message. On a whim, he hops a taxi to Alfred's neighborhood, so dismal and derelict that Dad tells the cab driver to wait outside and keep the meter running.

Growing more hesitant by the minute, Dad rides a rickety elevator upstairs. Upon finding apartment 24E, he knocks on the door. A woman answers, opening the door enough to see past the chain.

"Can I help you?" she says.

"I'm Bill Thalhimer," Dad replies. "Alfred Blum's cousin. Is he home?"

"No," the woman says, unhitching the chain and allowing Dad to enter. "I'm real sorry but Alfred is dead. He died last week and no one, no family or friends or nothing, has come to take his personal effects."

"I'm sorry to hear that," Dad says, taken aback. "I'm in New York doing some research and just wanted to meet my cousin."

"Like I said, I'm real sorry. I was just here cleaning up. He didn't have much," the lady says, her shoes scuffing across the floorboards of the sparse apartment. "Here's a bag. See what's on his desk and take what you want."

With trembling hands, Dad gathers Alfred's address book, a photograph, and several postcards into a plastic Rite Aid bag.

"I'm sorry for your loss," he says to the woman, who shrugs.

"I'm glad he had a cousin," she says, closing the door behind Dad.

"Thanks for your help," he says.

Confused and a bit shocked, Dad takes the elevator back down to the taxi waiting outside. On the taxi ride back to Manhattan, he dials a few numbers in Alfred's address book to inform his contacts of his death. The few people who answer don't seem to care. Then Dad calls me and recounts what just happened.

"I think that's the saddest thing I've ever heard," I tell him. "And I can't believe you were brave enough to go into that building alone."

"I figured I would try since I'm here. I sort of had it in my head that it would be like when we met Virginia Stern," he says. "It's amazing how a whole branch of the family tree can just snap off."

CHAPTER ELEVEN

TRADITION IS PRACTICE
1903 - 1922

Against the wishes of his parents, William moved in with his older sister Florence and her husband in Chicago after graduating from high school. He found a job at the renowned Carson Pirie Scott store, working his way up from being a stock boy in the basement to selling yard goods on the main floor. During his time in Chicago, he witnessed first-hand the dynamic expansion of Carson's and the theatrical flair of its competitor, Marshall Field & Company.

After two years working in Chicago, William felt he had earned the privilege of working at The Store with his father and Uncle Mose back home. He returned to Richmond where Thalhimer Brothers hired him as a buyer of toilet articles and all lines other than ready-to-wear and piece goods, which his father would continue to buy.

Early in his career, William had what he thought was a revolutionary idea.

"What if we separated the infants' and children's wear departments from those of women's ready-to-wear clothing?" he asked his father.

"You think women are willing to trek to a different department to shop for their children?" Isaac responded.

"Yes, I do." William said. "And I think when they get there, they'll spend even more, just as they would in a different shop."

"I don't know about that," his father said. "But you may give it a try."

Thalhimer Brothers adopted William's idea and, much to his delight, business picked

Annette Goldsmith Thalhimer, circa 1913.

up considerably. The concept even caught on in department stores across the country, children's wear quickly becoming one of the most profitable retail departments.

William also suggested adding a cosmetics counter, and with its success came a promotion to the position of Department Manager. Taking measured risks, he learned, could bring rich rewards. The young William B. Thalhimer quickly gained confidence but his self-assurance had a volatile intensity and moodiness about it. Once William made a decision, he wouldn't settle until he got his way.

Although he could be stubborn and difficult, William also possessed a tender side. When he met Annette Goldsmith, granddaughter of the founder of Lansburgh's department store in Washington, D.C., his happiness hinged upon her becoming his wife. Annette carried herself with poise and dignity, and her tasteful and elegant wardrobe was the envy of her friends. William Sr. was completely taken by her. After charming Annette with a series of passionate love letters and gentlemanly courtship, he asked for her hand in marriage. Quite romantically, he insisted that he would not accept "no" for an answer.

Annette had the unwavering strength of character to balance William's willfulness, and the couple married in 1913. Only a year later, William B. Thalhimer Jr. was born, named for his father and great-grandfather.

⚜   ⚜   ⚜

When William Sr. announced that he wanted Uncle Mose out of the business forever, forks fell around the dinner table. Everyone knew he meant business.

"Uncle Mose is a piddler. A trimmings buyer. A picayune," William Sr. roared to his father Isaac. "I'm not interested in working at The Store as long as he's there. Either Uncle Mose goes, or I do."

Moses had been devoted to his father's store since he was a boy. He grew up there, lining its shelves with merchandise and polishing men's shoes. For many years he served as a meticulous bookkeeper with excellent penmanship and a trimmings buyer with knowledge about the finest laces, buttons, and ribbons. Uncle Mose was respected and well loved by family and friends throughout the community.

Needless to say, it would be a difficult task for Isaac to ask his kindhearted brother to leave the business. But hearing his son's ultimatum and knowing that William Sr. provided the only hope as the next generation of leadership at The Store, Isaac had no choice.

When Isaac confronted Moses, the task proved much easier than expected. Moses willingly assented and surrendered his share of the business to Isaac and William Sr. without a struggle. As it turns out, Moses' wife Carrie was in fragile health and had been urging him to leave Richmond to live closer to their only child, Irma Marie, who lived in New York with her husband. Following a pleasant retirement party and solemn farewells to friends and family, Uncle Mose and Aunt Carrie packed their bags and moved to New York City, never again to live in Richmond.

Legitimate business partners now, Isaac announced to the Richmond newspapers, "It is the proudest moment of my life when I welcome my son into the business started by my father. The change means the opening of a new book and the turning of a new leaf in our commercial career."[24]

Thalhimers ad announcing William B. Thalhimer Sr.'s entry into the family business. *The Richmond Virginian, 1917.*

Also in 1917, tragedy befell 1824 Monument when Isaac's dear wife Amelia died at fifty-seven years old. Upon her passing, Isaac penned a poem in the family's Bible in her memory: "A precious one from us has gone, A voice we loved to listen is stilled, A place is vacant in our home, Which never can be filled."

Most of their children had moved away with the exceptions of Ruth and her sister Minna – now estranged from her philandering husband – and Minna's two daughters Aline and Jean. Dear old Aunt Lina continued to live in one of the upstairs bedrooms until Isaac found room and board for her elsewhere. Without his beloved wife, Isaac slept alone in the master bedroom on the second floor overlooking Monument Avenue, where the occasional automobile noisily chugged past. He kept his father's engraved pistol in the drawer of his bedside table, just in case.

To ease his heartache and keep himself occupied, Isaac traveled as often as possible with his children or grandchildren in tow. His voyages spanned from the American West to Paris, from Palestine to the West Indies, from New York to Cuba. Wherever he went, Richmond's Dean of Merchants sought irresistibly stylish, ready-made fashions and worldly goods for Thalhimer Brothers back home.

Now that Uncle Mose had left the business, William Sr. seized the opportunity to do things his way. He didn't want Thalhimer Brothers to be a mom-and-pop shop anymore. The Store's volume had grown in excess of four hundred thousand dollars, a princely sum. William Sr. saw unlimited, raw potential in the little store started by his grandfather in 1842. It was time to grow.

To start with, he hired Ed Broidy as secretary and comptroller. A capable and driven man, Broidy was active in organizations like the National Retail Dry Goods Association, attracting national attention to Thalhimers. He became William's business partner as well as a loyal friend.

Irving May, William Sr.'s first cousin on his mother's side, became a minority share-holder in the business and was hired as The Store's secretary. Mr. May's experience as an attorney brought added expertise to the business, his presence allowing William Sr. to concentrate exclusively on merchandising. Irving knew how to smile, shake hands, manage personnel, and work public relations to The Store's advantage. The "Maywill" cousins, Irving May and William Sr., made for a savvy pair of businessmen.

Another star employee, Miss Jennye Mitchell, attracted the national spotlight to Thalhimers when she became the first female buyer to embark on an overseas buying trip.

With her exquisite taste, Miss Mitchell shopped the Paris markets and brought distinctive and stylish French imports back to Richmond, including the designs of Chanel, Jeanne Lanvin, Robert Piguet, and Jean Paton.

Isaac and Uncle Mose, now living in New York, jointly made a real estate transaction that would only seem significant in later years. Having purchased the property with an eye for expanding their store further down the block, The Thalhimer brothers decided to sell it instead and move to a different block. Isaac and Moses sold their corner lot at the intersection of Fifth and Broad Streets to two retailers named Linton Miller and Webster Rhoads. Their store Miller & Rhoads, established in 1885, was on a rapid growth trajectory. It would soon consume an entire block in the heart of Richmond's business district and serve as Thalhimers' most formidable opponent for decades to come.

Miller & Rhoads' customers belonged to Richmond's "carriage trade," the upper class citizens who rode in well-appointed carriages and dressed accordingly. As Miller & Rhoads gained market share among Richmond's shopping elite, their spotlessly dressed children in tow, it only made William Sr. and Isaac scrappier and more competitive.

William Sr. and Annette welcomed another baby boy into the family in 1920, Charles Goldsmith Thalhimer. Not long after the birth of their second son, William Sr. effectively ran The Store while his father Isaac maintained the title and office of President.

Father and son agreed that to remain competitive with Miller & Rhoads they would need to make two major changes: incorporate The Store and secure a larger space with a more attractive storefront.

On February 2, 1922, they legally incorporated Thalhimer Brothers and privately floated common and preferred stock. The deal was this: Isaac received the majority of preferred stock and a handsome annual dividend. William received the entirety of common stock, which paid no dividends but gave him one hundred percent of the voting rights in running the business. Thus, William would have total control of Thalhimers after his father died. To run the business objectively, William Sr. would make sure his sisters and their husbands stayed out of store operations, although they would receive handsome preferred stock dividends. It was the shrewdest business decision William Sr. would make over the course of his career.

One Sunday, the whole Thalhimer family, including little William Jr., and scores of The Store's two hundred employees rolled big, red cartons down Broad Street. Perhaps expecting to see a parade, curious folks peered from their windows to see what the thundering ruckus was all about. Rumbling along the cobblestones, the cartons held the entirety of Thalhimers' inventory and fixtures, from boxes of buttons to stacks of pressed shirts, from the cash register to carefully wrapped mirrors. It was the biggest moving day in The Store's history as they traveled one block eastward to their destination: a magnificent, spacious five-story building on Broad Street between Sixth and Seventh. With the move, two hundred additional employees were hired, and sales surpassed one million dollars for the first time in Thalhimers' history. It surely would have made its founder, the first William Thalhimer, beam with pride.

The Store's headquarters would remain at Sixth and Broad for the next seventy years, but it was not the first time they'd been located there. William Thalhimer's store had stood on the same ground back in the 1860s. It's where Isaac's sister Bettie was born and his mother Mary had died of rheumatism, her family surrounding her bed. It was hallowed family ground, full of memories and significance.

"So, you see," Isaac said to a newspaper reporter during the 1922 move, "I'm just coming back to my old home."[25]

In the updated store, Isaac replaced the old pulley transaction basket with an innovative pneumatic pipe system. Each of The Store's departments had a pipe outlet in which a salesperson would place the customer's cash or credit number. With a whoosh, a vacuum suctioned the paper up to the office where a cashier made each transaction. It was a revolutionary development, making sales faster and more efficient.

Thalhimers fleet of horse-drawn wagons and coachmen had been replaced by motorcar delivery vehicles and uniformed drivers. Garages and oilcans replaced stables full of hay and feed bins.

After installing a modern lighting system at Thalhimers, Isaac wrote to the president of the lighting company, "In my fifty years of store experience, I have passed through the oil lamp, gas, arc light, incandescent and tungsten ages, making a change in our lighting system about every five years, but it was not until the present system was installed that I was fully able to appreciate the direct results it had on our business." Customers could literally see the merchandise in a new light.

When "Thrift Lane" opened in the basement, a small newspaper ad announced, "Thalhimers is opening a section in their basement for the sale of popular price ready-to-wear," and customers showed up in droves. On the very first day, the basement store sold three-quarters of its stock.

Looking at Santa down the center aisle of Thalhimers with its brand new lighting system, 1924.

"Give the lady what she wants," said famed merchant Marshall Fields, and that's what Thalhimers did. The ladies of Richmond no longer wanted to spend months hunched over a sewing machine making a single dress. They wanted to wear what New Yorkers were wearing and they wanted it *now*.

Isaac bought fashionable ready-made clothes from New York's wholesale houses and, with the rise of haute couture, Miss Mitchell continued scouring the French and Italian markets for the latest styles. Thalhimers' piece goods department shrunk smaller and smaller with each delivery.

Thalhimers models, 1924. *Virginia Historical Society.*

As Isaac's moustache faded to a salt-and-pepper gray, his grandchildren came to know him as a fiercely disciplined man with little patience, a harsh demeanor, and a baffling sense of humor.

On one of William Jr.'s visits to see Grandpa Isaac, his mother had scrubbed him clean, combed his hair with a perfect part on one side, and dressed him in a blue velveteen suit, a starched white blouse with a Buster Brown collar, and shiny white patent leather shoes. After taking a short drive across town in Annette's new car, the family arrived at Isaac's majestic house on Monument Avenue.

The housekeeper opened the door and welcomed them inside. Little William Jr. hid behind his mother's skirt, gripping it tightly with both hands.

Isaac got up from his favorite old chair in the front parlor to greet his guests. "Come here," he barked to his grandson.

His mother nudged him, but the little boy didn't move.

"Come here!" Isaac repeated, even louder this time.

Not knowing what to expect, the little boy inched his way over to his grandfather. The boy gasped as Isaac lifted his hand and set it atop his perfectly combed hair then tousled it roughly enough to make the boy squeal.

"No man ever made a success with hair combed like that," Isaac muttered gruffly.

Frightened, William Jr. ran back to his mother to bury his head in the folds of her skirt where he cried and cried.

That moment would remain forever etched in the little boy's memory. Decades later, he would take pride in disproving his grandfather's declaration. Perfectly combed hair or not, that little boy would become a much bigger success than Isaac ever could have imagined.

⚜   ⚜   ⚜

With the whole family gathered around the dining room at sundown, Isaac took his traditional seat at the head of the table. Since 1923, he had served as the President of Congregation Beth Ahabah, and strongly endorsed maintaining Jewish traditions in the home, including Friday night Shabbat dinners.

As he struck a match and lit the tall, white candles in their sterling silver candlesticks, Isaac recited the age-old Hebrew prayer, *"Baruch atta adonai elohenu melech ha-olam, asher kidshanu b'mitzvotav v'tzeevanu l'hadlik ner shel Shabbat."* He continued the translation in English, "Blessed are You, O Lord our God, King of the universe, who has sanctified us by Your commandments, and commanded us to kindle the lights of Shabbat."

After Isaac blessed the wine and bread with the appropriate prayers, the housekeeper entered from the kitchen. The tantalizing scent of the meal wafted across the dining room as perfectly pressed linen napkins went into laps all around the table. Quiet fell as everyone savored their dinner and adults sipped their wine. Knowing Grandpa Isaac would scold them if they didn't clean their plates, the children ate diligently. Isaac glanced slowly around the table at his brood, the Shabbat candlelight dancing in his deep brown eyes.

Suddenly, Grandpa Isaac stood and clapped his hands. The children jumped in their seats.

"Look under your plates," he commanded.

Each child carefully tipped up his plate to reveal a hundred dollar bill. Isaac watched with a self-satisfied grin as the children squealed with delight, waving the bills in the air. It was more money than most of them had ever seen.

Although Isaac loved treating his children and grandchildren to occasional surprises, he rarely surprised them by setting foot inside William Sr.'s family home on Richmond's North Side. Their relationship was kept strictly to business affairs, and their interactions occurred either at the store or in the parlor at 1824 Monument.

To visit with his grandsons, William Jr. and Charles, Isaac would pull up outside their house in his shiny black Packard automobile and honk the horn. The boys ran outside to sit with their cousins Jean and Aline in the backseat. The children laughed as they bounced on the leather seats, flying at the thrilling pace of thirty miles an hour up and down the hills past the coalmines.

One afternoon, Isaac pulled off the "dippy dip road" beside a persimmon tree and reached out the window to pluck four persimmons, one for each grandchild. He wiped the fruits with his monogrammed handkerchief then handed them to the curious youngsters. As they bit into the pungent persimmons, Isaac watched his grandchildren's little mouths pucker. Aline, the youngest, spat out the bitter fruit and started to cry. Isaac threw his head back with laughter as he pressed the pedal and steered back onto the road.

William Sr. and Annette's sons, Charles and William Jr., 1926.

⚜   ⚜   ⚜

On a cold February day in 1925, Isaac assumed something unusual was in the works. It was his seventieth birthday, so he expected some kind of surprise, but nothing along the lines of what he would receive.

When he arrived to work, early as usual, he turned the key to Thalhimer Brothers' front door and pushed it open to hear a resounding "Happy Birthday!" He gazed around the sales floor at hundreds of cheering and adoring faces, those of his friends, family, and employees. His children and grandchildren, gathered from across the country, ran forward to embrace him.

Stunned, Isaac walked up the stairs onto a platform erected in the center of the store and sat by a podium where Rabbi Edward N. Calisch, his close friend and spiritual advisor, offered a welcome address and the warmest of felicitations.

At Isaac's 75th birthday celebration, he is once again recognized by store employees. (Isaac just left of center with grandsons Charles and William Jr.) *Dementi Studios, 1930.*

Rabbi Calisch said Isaac's seventieth birthday was a time for "profound and serious happiness." He told of Isaac's long career filled with toil and tradition, his steadfast character, and his boundless generosity. Quite prophetically, he added that the Thalhimer grandsons William Jr. and Charles "will probably observe together the one-hundred and fiftieth anniversary of the store."

Isaac beckoned to his friend Douglas Southall Freeman, the esteemed editor of the Richmond papers, to deliver a speech to the gathered crowd. Dr. Freeman spoke on Isaac's behalf, knowing that his friend rarely spoke in public outside of the synagogue. He praised the work and dedication of the store's employees then took an opportunity to pay high, unexpected tribute to his dear friend Isaac.

Dr. Freeman then unveiled a bronze tablet that read, "In honor and affectionate appreciation of Isaac Thalhimer whose integrity, fine ideals, generous vision and noble character have stamped him as a citizen to be esteemed and as a man to be loved." The crowd clapped and cheered for Mr. Ike, the "Dean of Richmond Merchants."

That afternoon the whole Thalhimer clan gathered at 1824 Monument Avenue to continue celebrating Grandpa Isaac's birthday. Group photographs were organized and children read letters to their grandfather. Young Charles Thalhimer wrote in lopsided handwriting, "Grandpa, I have tried to follow your footsteps ever since I made that speech at the store and I think if I do so I will become as brilliant as you someday and maybe more brilliant...Signed, your devoted grandson, Charles."

Eleven-year-old William Jr. wrote, "My only desire is to follow your path...since I have been old enough, I have been very much interested in the firm and have noticed the wonderful achievements that you have performed, in business and private life. All of this inspires me, Grandpa, and makes a very high apex to my ambition."

The birthday celebration continued into the wee hours of the morning at the Woman's Club on Franklin Street, where nearly five hundred store employees and friends enjoyed refreshments, danced and sang, many of their songs written especially for the occasion. William Sr. gave a speech thanking everyone on behalf of his father. Isaac graciously accepted a silver loving cup from his employees as they joined in a raucous round of "Hail, Hail the Gang's All Here."

An editorial describing the celebration concluded, "Richmond is the richer for the character of Isaac Thalhimer. Great as has been his contribution to the material life of the community, his contribution to its spiritual life has been even greater…Upon the occasion of this happy anniversary, an entire city salutes Mr. Thalhimer. He has meant much to Richmond, and Richmond is not unappreciative."[26]

Several days after the birthday festivities, Isaac boarded the U.S.S. Megantic for a cruise to the West Indies with two daughters, Minna and Ruth, and two granddaughters, Aline and Jean. Looking out at the wide expanse of the ocean surely gave him pause as he counted the blessings bestowed upon him: a loving family, a stately home, a growing business, and – at the very top of the list – a diligent son, William Sr., who showed promise in minding the store.

Isaac with three of his daughers (l to r) Minna, Sadie May, and Ruth. Nice, France, 1929.

In 1929, Richmond's first skyscraper Central National Bank went up and the New York Stock Exchange plummeted. Despite the besieged economy, Thalhimer Brothers continued expanding. Investing nearly a million dollars to demolish the neighboring Odeon Theater, The Store increased its selling space to twelve thousand square feet and created an entrance on Sixth Street. That way, customers leaving Miller & Rhoads could easily cross the street and enter Thalhimers. At that entrance, inspired by a visit to Harrods of London, William Sr. installed a soda fountain with a case of sweets and baked goods. The scent of freshly baked honey buns and chocolate cakes wafted out the door onto Sixth Street.

At the opening ceremony of the new addition, little William Jr. and Charles unveiled an oil painting depicting their Grandpa Isaac's severe eyebrows, piercing brown eyes, and ever-present moustache. This painting remained conspicuously displayed above The Store's elevators where portraits of subsequent leaders would accompany it.

A flowery article in *Richmond Magazine* declared, "Consider it a moment: A structure not Colonial, but strictly modernistic in design; a store built from the designs of experts who had studied floor plans and window arrangements for the convenience and tastes of the multitude of Southerners

Isaac opens front door of new addition to store, 1929. *Dementi Studios.*

who will do business in this store; the latest devices in telephony, in delivery methods... Like the South, this establishment is unafraid of ideas, unafraid of progress."[29]

When autumn rolled around, the Great Depression was in full swing, but Thalhimers continued plugging along. Fueled by energy and idealism, William began to devote more time to the newly expanded Thalhimers store than his father did. Isaac worked at the store until September when his chest began to feel tight and constricted and he became more withdrawn. As the days grew colder, he spent most of his time resting in bed.

Isaac's weakened heart stopped forever on November 2, 1930, in his elegantly appointed bedroom as the autumn leaves drifted down to Monument Avenue. The following day, Thalhimers announced in a simple ad that The Store would be closed in memory of its beloved president.

An excerpt from Dr. Douglas S. Freeman's long, eloquent editorial upon his dear friend's passing read, "His employes he regarded as his children, whose joys and triumphs he shared...Always he was open to new ideas, quick to reject the impractical and to sense the sound, courageous in method, confident of the energy and intelligence of his organization, independent, determined, willing to trust the judgment of tried men, and not disposed to magnify an occasional mistake…The beautiful, the novel and the noble always awakened the enthusiasm that lurked behind his calm and serious face."[28]

Isaac's body lay in an open, satin-lined casket in the center of the parlor at 1824 Monument for visitors to say their last goodbyes. A long line of friends, employees, associates, and civic leaders extended out the front door and down the block. Following a service at his beloved Beth Ahabah, Isaac was laid to rest in a suit made expressly for him by The Store's finest tailor, Sam Brown. Rabbi Calisch watched sorrowfully as his friend's casket was lowered into the hallowed ground of Hebrew Cemetery.

Goodbye, Dean of Richmond Merchants. Goodbye, Mr. Ike.

Bustling Broad Street scene, Thalhimers at center, circa 1925.

CHAPTER TWELVE

IS ANYONE HOME?
2008

"So, where does this guy live?" I ask my friend Maribeth about her new boyfriend.

"1824 Monument Avenue," she says.

A shiver races down my spine, catapulting me out of my chair.

"I knew it!" I shout, clapping my hands, startling Maribeth. "I knew you were going to say that! I don't even know why, but I knew it."

"What? What did I say?" she frantically responds.

"That's Isaac and Amelia's house," I say to her, grasping her forearm. "My great-great grandparents."

"No way!" she says.

Quickly flipping through a file folder on my desk, I find a photograph with "1824 Monument" scrawled in pencil on the back. In the photo, the family gathers for a friend's wedding reception hosted in their home. Amelia sits next to Aunt Lina on a velveteen sofa with William Sr. and Isaac standing behind them. It's the only photograph I've ever seen depicting William Sr. and Isaac together.

"See?" I tell her as we gaze together at the photograph. "Isaac built it when Monument Avenue was practically new. There were, like, tobacco crops in the median. I've been waiting for years to see that house. I've left messages for the landlord but he's never returned my calls."

"Well, if you want to see it that bad, then let's go," says Maribeth, pulling her cell phone from her pocket to dial her boyfriend's number.

⚜   ⚜   ⚜

My finger poised to snap photographs and my heart pounding, Maribeth's boyfriend turns the key to the front door of 1824 Monument Avenue. I'm suddenly struck by a sinking fear that I will be disappointed. What if Isaac and Amelia's ghosts aren't home? What if it's just a bunch of messy apartments full of college kids? Maybe this is a mistake.

Above the front door, colorful stained glass displays the number 1824. It looks authentic, unaltered by the march of time, and gives me the confidence to step over the threshold.

Right away I can see that the house has been divided into apartments by dry wall partitions, but a few exquisite details remain: the bronze chandelier above our heads, the hand-tiled floor, a swooping carved banister, the decorative carvings of the fireplace beside the front door. A porcelain teapot rests on the mantel.

The stairs creak as I slowly climb them, snapping pictures with each step. Maribeth laughs at me when we get to the landing and I knock on a door.

"What are you going to say if someone answers?" she asks. I shrug.

A young woman opens the door.

"Can I help you?" she asks us.

"Hi. This is going to sound weird," I explain, "but this is my great-great-grandparents' house and I've never been in here before. Their names were Isaac and Amelia Thalhimer. I've just always wanted to see this place. I think they may have even died in here, in your apartment. Sorry, I'm Elizabeth. This is Maribeth and her boyfriend, who actually lives in the basement. Could we, maybe, come in and take a look around?"

Maribeth quickly adds, as a sort of endorsement for my request, "she's writing a book."

Instead of politely turning us away, which would have been a perfectly reasonable response, the young woman smiles and says, "Sure, come on in."

We step into her living room, which Grandpa once told me was Isaac and Amelia's bedroom. I look out the grand bay window and imagine Amelia parting layers of lace curtains to wait for Isaac's Rambler to come rumbling up on the street below.

"It's been a great apartment for me," says the young woman, "but the kitchen is really small."

"Oh, I love the kitchen. It's small, but has everything you need," I respond absently from my trancelike state as I look for evidence of Issac and Amelia's ghosts. Don't they know I'm here?

We cross back through the living room and walk into the bedroom, which I suspect was a dressing room. It boasts yet another beautifully carved firescreen and mantel. A woman's face is carved into the metal of the firescreen. Is it Amelia's?

"This is so comfortable," I say. "Plenty of space."

I'm trying hard to have a normal conversation about normal things, but in my head it's all haywire. What about that fixture? Is that an original oil lamp? Did Isaac read books here by gaslight in the evenings? What did he read? Is this where he lay when his heart stopped? Was this firescreen, perhaps a likeness of his beloved Amelia, the last thing he saw before his eyes closed forever?

"I like living here," the girl says as I move some candles without asking and photograph the firescreen. "It's convenient to everything downtown."

"Do you mind if I look in the bathroom?" I say, pushing open the bathroom door.

"Um, sure," she laughs.

The stainless steel fixtures, porcelain sink, claw-foot tub, and tiled floor look original. I swoon with the notion that Isaac and Amelia's hands might have grasped these very faucets.

"Can I use the sink?" I ask her as I hold and turn the knob with my right hand, feeling its steely coolness as the water flows into the ceramic basin and swirls down the drain. What would Isaac say if he knew I was here in his house using his sink?

I turn the knob back.

Not wanting to appear crazier than I already do, I say, "Well, thanks for letting us poke around your place."

On our way to the door, she says, "No problem. I can't wait to read your book!"

"I'll be sure you get a copy. Thanks again for letting us barge right in," I say as we return to the hallway.

"Okay. Bye!" she says, shutting the door.

Maribeth says sarcastically, "Well, that wasn't weird."

"Whatever," I reply. "This is awesome."

Going downstairs, I gently slide my hand down the wooden banister where Isaac and Amelia's hands once touched. I know they did. I can practically feel the warm energy of their presence.

Nearing the front door, Grandpa's voice echoes in my head saying, "My only memory of Amelia is of her lying on a little couch in a room at the end of the hall past the dining room." He was only three years old when she died, so in his recollection she must have been near death. I'm not sure why, but I want to see that spot.

I knock on the door of the room at the end of the hall. Silence. I knock again. No one answers.

Likewise, no one is home in the apartment by the front door. I wanted so badly to see the living room where Isaac kept a talkative parrot in a birdcage. As the parrot cawed, Isaac would synchronize his gold pocket watch with the mantel clock every day at noon. When the parrot died, Issac's grandchildren buried it in a shoebox in the backyard.

We go outside and down another set of stairs for a quick tour of the basement apartment where Maribeth's boyfriend lives.

"So, have you ever seen any ghosts down here?" I ask him.

"Uh, not lately," he jokes as we walk through the apartment.

"I'm serious," I say. "What's behind that door? Is that a closet?"

He says, "I don't go in there. Honestly, I don't really know what's in there."

I open the door to a dimly lit, dank space and move slowly through the shadows. My right foot hits something hard. A trunk full of old photographs and books? Isaac's shoe?

"Oh my gosh. What's this?" I shout.

"That's the water heater," says Maribeth.

I can't help but laugh. There are no ghosts here except the ones in my head. Without a word, we climb back up the stairwell into the bright daylight of reality.

We sit and chat for a few minutes on the front steps of the house where Grandpa once learned how to jump on a pogo stick and his cousins, Aline and Jean, sang *Tea for Two* as they jumped rope. Isaac used to chide the children for sliding down the thin iron banisters flanking the stairs.

Sliding my hand down one of the rails, I catch a glimpse of my watch and realize it's practically dinnertime. Ryan will be home soon.

"Well, thanks for showing me around. I'll never forget it. Let me know if you see any ghosts," I say.

"Hey, no problem," says Maribeth's boyfriend. "You'll be the first to know."

A breeze shuffles the leaves of the tree beside us, its branches swaying delicately in unison. Before getting into the car, I look up to the second floor balcony, just in case Isaac and Amelia are waving goodbye. The French doors are open but no one is there.

In the parlor at 1824 Monument Avenue. Standing (l to r): William Sr., Isaac. Sitting: Ruth, Amelia, and Amelia's sister, Lina Blum, circa 1910.

William Sr. speaking on WRVA radio. Douglas Southall Freeman seated behind him, 1936.

CHAPTER THIRTEEN

ADVERSITY BUILDS CHARACTER
1930 - 1934

William Sr.'s side of every conversation consisted of curt, abrupt sentences if he spoke at all. He had no patience for frivolous small talk, refusing to attend a party if there were women present; their gossip made him impatient and irritable. If he planned to attend a party, he asked his gentleman friends to arrive early to talk business and enjoy a drink then he'd depart when the women arrived. He didn't care what anyone said about him as long as he, in his own conscience, knew he was a good man doing the right thing.

Arthur Ashe Sr., father of the legendary tennis player, worked as William Sr. and Annette's chauffeur. Mr. Ashe once drove his employer down the road to see a man about buying a piece of land. When they arrived, the man ranted and cussed about selling his property to a Jew. William Sr. remained still and silent throughout the one-sided conversation. At the end of the man's tirade, William Sr. calmly but firmly made an offer and the man accepted.

When he got back into the car, Mr. Ashe asked, "Mr. Thalhimer, why did you take such insults from an inferior?"

"Arthur," he said, "I came out here to purchase that piece of land. I got the piece of land. It belongs to me now, not to him. That man can go on cursing me as long as he likes. I have the land."[29]

William Sr. admired ambitious achievers who favored action over talk: his cousin and real estate and movie theater entrepreneur, Morton G. Thalhimer Sr.; king of the Richmond newspaper empire, John Stewart Bryan; Pulitzer Prize-winning author and newspaper editor, Douglas Southall Freeman. Accomplished gentlemen such as these were the company he kept.

William Sr. proved to be an aggressive merchant with a vision ahead of his time. He sought to grow his business like fellow merchants John Wanamaker and Marshall Field, and showed great potential to do so. That is, until tragedy struck.

William Sr. was only thirty-seven years old on a trip to Briar Cliff Manor, New York, with his wife and boys when he clutched at his chest. His first heart attack nearly killed him.

During the days that followed, he sat in a patio chair facing a fan blowing hot air over a block of ice, his eyes closed as beads of sweat dripped down his face. Blindsided by the unexpected, his head reeled with the prospect of how his hard-earned business would go on without him. Who would succeed him if he didn't survive the next heart attack?

Thirteen-year-old William Jr. sat cross-legged in the living room, listening intently to KDKA Pittsburgh on a crystal set radio he had made from a cigar box. Tuning out his surroundings, the boy focused hard on the radio set. He wanted desperately to get Lindburgh and The Spirit of St. Louis over to Paris, but his father wanted something else. In light of his faltering health, he needed a contingency plan and a successor. Seeing in his son a fierce determination, a fire that could be stoked, William Sr. decided he would groom his namesake to be the finest merchant The Store had ever seen.

⚜   ⚜   ⚜

The way William Sr. saw it, his sisters were nothing but a drain on store profits. They came sweeping into Richmond and shopped like mad, taking every benefit of their hefty family discount and annual payouts from their father's preferred stock. Finally, William Sr. put his foot down. He limited the family discount to only his immediate family members and retired all preferred stock. These decisions made his sisters and their spouses red with anger, but William Sr. saw no alternative. He was willing to risk his relationships with his sisters to maintain the integrity of the family business.

To further increase volume and profits, William Sr. joined forces with the National Retail Dry Goods Association and Cavendish Trading Corporation, a retail buying association that included reputable stores like D.H. Holmes of New Orleans, Goldsmiths

William Sr. and his sisters. (l to r): Sadie, Florence, Ruth, Helen, Minna. Circa 1936.

of Memphis, and Ivy's of Charlotte. Membership in distinguished groups like these gave Thalhimers advantages like joint buying with other stores, stocking international merchandise, and bulk purchase discounts. As a result, The Store passed along the savings to their customers. William Sr. also enjoyed fostering relationships with other merchants on the national retail scene.

Cavendish boasted dozens of buying offices around the world. Although the stock market had crashed along with the American economy, William Sr. decided to take his family on a three-month tour of Europe to visit the Cavendish offices, do some buying, and enjoy a long family vacation. He might not live long enough to see another opportunity like this to travel with his wife and sons. Time had become far more precious than money.

Dozens of friends and cousins gathered to shout "Bon voyage!" and "Happy trails!" as the train pulled away from Broad Street Station, carrying the William B. Thalhimer Sr. family towards the ship in New York's harbor that would ferry them across the Atlantic.

Upon arriving in Europe, William Sr. rented a car in Antwerp. From there, he took his family from the windmills of Holland to Europe's largest synagogue in Budapest, from the fjords of Norway to the harbors of Finland, and from the mineral waters of Baden Baden to the Eiffel Tower. Along the way, William Sr. treated Annette to exquisite dinners and antique-buying sprees while William Jr. and Charles went out on their own, enjoying their first tastes of beer and independence. For boys of only sixteen and ten years old, the trip was the greatest, most liberating experience imaginable.

The Thalhimers visited jewelry houses, art galleries, furriers, and manufacturers of fine linens and porcelains. At the international Cavendish offices, William Sr. and Annette selected exotic merchandise to be sold in The Store's Connoisseur Shop and advertised in attention-grabbing window displays. William Sr. referred to these visionary purchases as "getting people what they want before they even know they want it."

Annette carried herself with utmost elegance and dignity; her petite hands in their long, ivory gloves with pearl buttons were as graceful and captivating as a dancer's. Her

Annette dressed for a costume party, circa 1925. *Foster Studio.*

impeccable sense of style influenced every outfit to grace her willowy figure, from the simplest silk blouse and headscarf to the most ornate sequined evening gown, diamond drop earrings, and mink stole. Arguably, Annette served as one of the most persuasive advertisements for her husband's store.

The Thalhimers visited department stores in nearly every major city across Europe, from Le Bon Marché in Paris to KaDeWe in Berlin. Meeting with the heads of these stores, William Sr. not only learned about business trends but became aware of something far more disturbing. He began to sense a growing instability and fear within the European Jewish community, noting the presence of brown-shirted Nazi party members in Germany. Something evil lurked beneath the surface of this pleasant vacation.

The boys, however, remained blissfully ignorant of any political unrest. Charles continued to tag along behind his big brother. William Jr. scratched entries into his daily journal, taking note of interesting goods, fixtures, building details, and business practices, sounding more like a businessman than a teenager.

In one entry he jotted down, "In afternoon went to Karstadt department store. New type of elevators. Cheap goods. (One idea to have ventilators on the showcases.) Next to Werthimers. This is the most beautiful store and largest in all the world. All stores have sky lines. We saw a couch on wheels with mattress on it. Very comfortable. Good item." He also took note of such delights as driving the rental car, playing shuffleboard with pretty girls, and drinking lager with Charles, but, above all, William Jr. took great pleasure in learning the retail business in the shadow of his father.

⚜   ⚜   ⚜

When they got back home, William Jr. found that it was an easy walk from John Marshall High School to Thalhimers' delivery department on Seventh Street. Much to his parents' chagrin, William Jr. snuck out of school whenever he could to run off to The Store. There, he would help Joe Parsley wrap packages in the packing department then hop into a delivery wagon with Hezekiah Jackson. William Jr. smiled as Mr. Jackson pressed a quarter into his palm. He was finally getting paid to work at The Store.

Outside of school, his father insisted that he socialize with peers outside of the Jewish community, so William

Richmond Times-Dispatch article. April 29, 1934.

Jr. left Beth Ahabah's youth group for Boy Scout Troop Two over on the North Side. There, the other boys roughed him up for being the troop's only Jew. One time, a fellow scout tied an oyster to a string and made William Jr. swallow it before pulling it back out, gagging him as the other scouts laughed. In Boy Scouts, he learned what it meant to be an outcast but he also learned how to cope. He eventually developed friendships with some of the boys and found a confidante and mentor in the troop's leader.

During his senior year at John Marshall high school, William Jr. decided he wanted to attend Washington & Lee University. He wasn't an A-student and lacked aptitude for subjects like Latin, which he failed four times, but William Jr. possessed intense ambition and natural leadership ability. He had an uncanny knack for arithmetic and statistics and wanted to further his understanding of finance, management, and economics.

But before William Jr. so much as started to fill out his college application, an unexpected meeting altered his plans.

One early evening after school let out, Dr. Douglas Southall Freeman invited William Jr. to meet with him in his editorial office at the newspaper. The young man obliged right away and headed downtown on a city bus.

"Good afternoon, Dr. Freeman," William Jr. said as he shook hands with his father's friend in the doorway of the office.

"Son," Dr. Freeman said, "Please sit down. I have something important to discuss with you."

William Jr. sat in a chair facing Dr. Freeman's desk and watched as the old man carefully removed his small, round eyeglasses and placed them on the desk between them.

"You know your father and I are very good friends," Dr. Freeman said.

"Yes sir, I do."

"I need to tell you something important that your father wants me to convey to you. He knows you love the business. He also knows you are planning to attend Washington & Lee. He wants you to seriously consider a different path. He asked me to convey to you his sincere wish that you forego college and get started at The Store."

William Jr. sat for a moment, considering the gravity of his father's request delivered by this most unusual of messengers. It would be unwise for him to say "no" to someone as upstanding and prominent as Dr. Freeman.

"I will think about it, sir," said the young man. "Is that all?"

"Yes, that's all," Dr. Freeman said.

William Jr. took the bus home. When he opened the front door, he found his father waiting for him.

"I talked to Dr. Freeman," William Jr. said.

"And?" his father asked expectantly.

"And I've thought about it," the young man said, weighing his words carefully. "I'll do what he says under one condition: that I will be permitted to learn the business away from home. On my own. Just like you did."

"What do you mean?"

"I want to go to New York and get a job."

It certainly was a valid request. After all, William Sr. had spent the first two years of his career at Carson Pirie Scott in Chicago against his parents' wishes. He too had wanted to learn the retail business away from home, away from the inherent pressures of seeing his surname on every sales ticket. The father had no grounds for refusing his son's request.

"All right," William Sr. said. "It will be so."

And that was that.

After graduating from John Marshall high school, William Jr. took the train from Richmond's familiar Broad Street station to the towering skyscrapers and teeming sidewalks of New York City. There, he settled as much as he could into the one-room apartment Thalhimers' owned on Madison Avenue behind the B. Altmans store. The apartment seemed busier than a bus station, with buyers coming and going daily. He found the constant activity distracting and annoying.

William Jr. decided to ask his Aunt Ruth and Uncle Leo if he could move in with them on the Upper East Side near Central Park. Having no children of their own, they obliged their nephew's request with open arms. William Jr. basked in the undivided attention of his aunt and uncle, and quickly felt at home in their lavish apartment.

As he searched for a job, William Jr. dressed in his best suit, pressed shirt, and freshly shined shoes for each interview.

"How can I help you, Mr. Thawl-meyer?" the interviewer would say. Or "Have a seat, Mr. Tall-heemer."

The young man from Richmond had sought this lack of recognition but hadn't expected doors to slam so abruptly in his face. He went to Macy's. No luck. He went to B.

Altmans. Not hiring. He went to Saks. No entry-level opportunities. He went to Bloomingdales. Nothing. The routine became tiresome.

Finally, with the last bit of confidence he could muster, William Jr. showed up for an interview at Stern Brothers on Forty-Second Street.

"Young man," said the interviewer. "I'd like to offer you a job in the marking and receiving room. Fifteen dollars a week."

William Jr. could barely contain himself.

"Thank you, sir. I'll take it," he said, his right hand outstretched. The interviewer shook William Jr.'s hand then handed him a blue smock and a key.

"The lockers are that way," he said, pointing down a hallway. "You can start today, if you'd like."

William Jr. walked directly to the cabinet corresponding to the number on his key and placed his jacket inside. He put on the blue smock and went straight to work, learning from his new associates how to mark items for sale. He could have burst with enthusiasm. From a job like this, there was nowhere to go but up.

During his first few days at Stern Brothers, William Jr. met the hosiery buyer, Mr. Alvin Hirschman. Every day, Mr. Hirschman would come over and talk to all the young men in marking and receiving, giving them instructions on how to properly mark each brand and style of hosiery.

"Good morning, Mr. Hirschman," William Jr. would say, taking a moment to shake the man's hand.

"Good morning, son."

One day, William Jr. felt particularly emboldened. When he got up the nerve, he asked, "Mr. Hirschman, don't you need a stock boy?"

"Well, come to think of it," Mr. Hirschman said, "I do need someone to stock the bargain booths on the main floor. The job is yours."

"Thank you, sir," William Jr. said. "Is this a promotion?"

"I'll give you eighteen dollars a week."

Turning in his blue smock, William Jr. felt like he'd been promoted to General Manager. He held his head high as he walked in the door of his aunt and uncle's apartment that evening, placed his hat on the hat rack, and headed straight to the telephone in the foyer.

He picked up the phone and asked the operator to ring up his parents' house in Richmond.

"Hello?" William Sr. answered.

"I got a promotion!" the teenager exclaimed breathlessly to his father. "I talked to Mr. Hirschman and I'm working the bargain booths. I got a raise to eighteen dollars a week."

"You're going to spend your whole damn raise on the telephone," William Sr. replied irritably. "Writing a letter would say the same thing."

The line went dead.

Bang. William Jr. felt like he'd been shot. He hung up the phone and cried.

✢   ✢   ✢

The Depression brought business to a near-standstill at Thalhimers. William Sr. invited the manager of every department to meet with him at a folding table in the driveway of his home in Ginter Park. Sitting face-to-face with each employee, he asked bluntly, "What can we cut out?"

With each meeting, he cut and cut and cut. He cut services, expenses, nonessential things, and some essential things The Store would simply have to learn to live without. He eliminated jobs by the dozen. He kept a tight inventory of office supplies. In order for an employee to get a new pencil, he had to turn in the stub of the old one.

By the end of the year, Thalhimers barely eked out a profit. Both William Sr. and his store had weakened pulses, but both were still alive.

Two years later, the situation became even bleaker. The banks stopped lending. Thalhimers' account books began to show red. The Store didn't have sufficient funds to pay its employees or purchase new merchandise. William Sr. came home each day more agitated and tense than the last. Annette feared the business would flatline along with her husband's heart.

In an uncharacteristic moment of weakness, William Sr. phoned his friend Frank Rabinowitz up in New York to ask for help. Rabinowitz owned a successful millinery company called Ogust, Rabinowitz and Ogust that stocked Thalhimers, Saks Fifth Avenue, and an array of other department stores with millinery merchandise. Despite the recession, the haberdashery business continued to thrive. Plus, the Rabinowitz family and Annette's mother's family, the Lansburghs, had been friendly with each other for years.

"How much do you need?" Rabinowitz asked.

William Sr. took a deep breath and responded, "I need one-hundred and seventeen thousand dollars cash."

Silence.

Then Rabinowitz said, "I'll give it to you. Pay me back when you can."

No contracts were signed, no interest or fees discussed, and nothing was established other than a gentlemen's agreement that the debt would be repaid. In those days, having a gentleman's word was as good as money.

Rabinowitz' agreement presented a new challenge. How would William Sr. safely transport one hundred thousand dollars cash from New York to Richmond during such desperate times? Certainly not through the postal service or by hiring a messenger, and he couldn't travel on his own, fearing another heart episode.

Then William Sr. had an idea.

"Son," he said to William Jr. "I need you to visit a gentleman by the name of Mr. Frank Rabinowitz at sixty-five West Thirty-ninth Street. He will give you several stacks of cash. Place the money in unmarked brown paper sacks and bring it down here to me. Immediately."

William Jr. asked no questions and headed directly to Mr. Rabinowitz' office.

With sweaty palms, the teenager carefully took the stacks of bills from Mr. Rabinowitz and placed them in paper bags, just like his father had said. He asked his friend Sam Stern, a Thalhimers' buyer shopping the New York markets, to travel with him on the train from New York to Richmond.

The two young men went directly to Pennsylvania Station and boarded a Pullman car on a train headed back to Richmond, both of them scared pale at the prospect of the bags of cash being lost or stolen. After he shut the door to the cabin and the wheels started rolling, Sam said to his friend, "Bill, go to the bathroom and do what you need to do. Then get up on your berth, put the money under your pillow, and stay there. Don't you dare move your head until we hit Broad Street Station."

William Jr. did just as Sam instructed. He dutifully went to the bathroom, washed up, got into the top berth, put the bags of money under his pillow, then laid his head down. As the train chugged rhythmically down the tracks through the dark of night, he closed his eyes and fell asleep.

William Jr. awoke the next morning to the sound of the train's brakes screeching into the station. With tousled hair, he shot up from the depths of sleep, groggy and terrified, and thrust his hand under the pillow. What would his father say if he lost the money? His heart raced.

By the grace of God, the two brown paper bags were still there. Tucking the bags tightly under their arms, the boys disembarked the train as the early morning sunlight beamed through the tall windows of Broad Street Station and ran straight to the taxi line where they hopped into the first cab.

"To Thalhimers, please," Sam told the driver.

As the taxi pulled up to The Store, John Harper, the night watchman still on duty, took out his jingling key ring and opened the Broad Street entrance. The three men marched straight through The Store to the safe. Their fingers fumbled to unlock the door; no one could remember the right combination. They panicked.

Mr. Harper frantically phoned Mr. Allen, a store manager, who arrived with the correct combination and placed the bags of money in the safe before shutting the heavy metal door.

William B. Thalhimer Jr. could breathe much easier now. The future of the family business had literally rested in his hands, and he had delivered.

Thalhimers' fleet of delivery trucks and drivers, 1935.

Thalhimers rebounded from debt and repaid the load to Mr. Rabinowitz within the next two years. Years later, when hats went out of fashion and the haberdashery business dried up, Rabinowitz embarked on a career in real estate. When the real estate market went on the skids, he found himself in debt and phoned his friend, William B. Thalhimer Sr.

"William," he said. "Remember the money I lent you back in '32? Well, the tables have turned. Now I need *your* help." William Sr. did not hesitate to provide Rabinowitz with the same loan in reverse.

"That was a very satisfying feeling," William Jr. said many years later. "My father and I talked about Rabinowitz often. Things like that keep you alive: the unsung heroes."

⚜   ⚜   ⚜

William Jr. ended up leaving his job at Stern Brothers to return to Richmond for his doctor to remove a cyst from his back in the summer of 1934.

That summer, William Sr. had planned to take Annette on another trip to Europe. Ed Broidy, Thalhimers' Treasurer and one of William Sr.'s closest, most trusted associates, had suddenly announced he was leaving the business. William Sr. couldn't bear the stress of losing such a vital business partner.

"I can't take this trip," he told William Jr., still home recuperating from his medical procedure. "Here are two tickets for the S.S. Excalibur to Naples. I'm shipping the Chevrolet. Find a friend and drive around Europe for three months. Keep your expenses to an absolute minimum and learn as much as you can."

Ecstatic, William Jr. invited his cousin and friend Will Flatow Jr., a grandson of Jacob Thalhimer, who readily accepted the offer. Giddy with independence, the young men traveled overseas where they hopped into the Chevrolet and road-tripped across Italy, Switzerland, France, Belgium, Holland and England. They spent their weekdays in museums, art galleries, department stores, and castles. On weekends, they climbed mountains, swam in natural springs, played golf, danced with beautiful girls, bet on horse races, and went sailing. They kept meticulous records of everything they spent, right down to their daily newspapers.

William Jr. faithfully wrote letters home describing his adventures. He assured his father that he was making the best of each opportunity to learn about history, culture,

Page from William Jr.'s scrapbook of his European trip with cousin, Will Flatow Jr., 1934.

art, and, especially, business. He and his cousin Will visited Associated Merchandising Corporation offices across Europe. They watched lace being made in Valenciennes and the glassblowers at work in Venice.

Across Europe, William Jr. made contacts with manufacturers and department store executives, noting to his father, "I'm doing my best to make real acquaintances which I know are going to be a big help to our store in the future. Rather, I should say, a big help to me." At that point, at the tender age of nineteen years old, he knew he would be taking over the family business.

Occasionally he wrote with suggestions his father could implement at The Store.

"What do you think of running a promotion," William Jr. wrote from London, "if not this winter maybe next, of real fine imported Scotch fleece Kynock single and double breasted coats that you could retail from forty-five to fifty-five dollars? It's not only a good prestige act and building up of fine merchandise, but we can still make a good thirty-five to forty-five percent mark-up, depending on its retail value. I believe we can make a good deal."

From Paris, William Jr. wrote, "Today I paid a visit to Charles Roditti, also Printemps and Galeries Lafayette. These stores are very disappointing as they can't touch the values of ours. Prices are extremely high. Have had some swell escargot snails."

He continued in a more serious vein, "Dad, I've thought a lot along the lines of my first step down at the store, and I am convinced that your plan of selling first is the most sensible as I realize the importance of my knowing merchandise. I am really excited about coming home again and going down to the store which I've looked forward to all my life!"

At the suggestion of Mr. Kena, an American Consulate and a friend of Will's father, the boys were specifically instructed not to visit Germany on their trip. "There's too much instability there," said Mr. Kena. "The political climate is too dangerous." Needless to say, it proved a wise decision for two young Jewish Americans traveling Europe in 1934.

In Venice, the boys saw a group of uniformed officials saluting a distinctive man they recognized immediately as Adolph Hitler, the Chancellor of Germany. They had heard of Hitler's hatred of Jews. Mr. Kena had forewarned them.

After Chancellor Hitler and his entourage entered a building and the door shut behind them, the boys waited around for the crowd to dissipate. Then, making sure no one was watching, they unzipped their trousers and urinated on the front stoop.

⚜   ⚜   ⚜

Upon his return from Europe, William Sr. handed his son the keys to the family car along with two hundred dollars.

"Welcome home," he said. "You will spend the next six weeks driving through Virginia and North Carolina. Meet our vendors and see how things are made. Introduce yourself to people. The only way to succeed in life is to learn how to do these things for yourself."

As usual, young William did as his father said. He knew his father had a plan.

In Suffolk, Virginia, William Jr. saw a fascinating experimental television set with a rotary disk. He asked questions and made notes, calling his father to suggest that Thalhimers get a demonstration of this revolutionary contraption. William Sr. had no complaints about this phone call and arranged for one of Richmond's first television sets to be displayed at The Store.

William Jr. visited Fieldcrest Mills and saw towels being made by machines. He watched as seams were sewn up the backs of women's stockings at the May Hosiery Company in Concord. At the Cannon Mills, he heartily shook the hand of Mr. Charlie Cannon, and at Cone Mills he introduced himself to Mr. Benjamin Cone.

Returning home after six weeks on the road, William Jr. drove straight to Thalhimers where he took the elevator to his father's office. Placing the car keys on his desk, William Jr. told his father, "I'm still not coming to The Store until a job opens up. I refuse to take a job away from anybody."

"Fine," William Sr. said, taking the keys.

Not too many days later, Thalhimers' Art Needlework Buyer quit. William Jr. interviewed and was offered the position by his cousin Irving May. Without hesitation, he accepted.

"Boy, I want to tell you how glad I am that you are about to enter into the House of Thalhimer," Irving wrote William Jr. about his decision. "You know, without my telling you again, of my deep love for you, and insofar as within me lies, I want to help in every way I can so you can be to us what we know and expect you will be – a real merchant; a good fellow; and a pride and joy to all your dear ones." William Jr. vowed to live up to his cousin's expectations.

Starting with zero knowledge of Art Needlework, William Jr. asked other buyers for assistance in selecting attractive trimmings, buttons, and ribbons for his department. He learned which yarns and threads were appropriate for the various textile arts. He learned the difference between crochet hooks and knitting needles. He talked to female customers about which piece goods were best suited for children's dresses and which were intended for draperies.

Mr. Wallenstein, a salesman from B. Blumenthal's button house, arrived periodically with hundreds of buttons glued to big pieces of cardboard. If it wasn't raining, Mr. Wallenstein would lay the cards out on the roof of The Store for William Jr. to make his button selections.

When Armistice Day came around and William Jr. had forgotten to stock his department with American flags, his father chided him, "Son, you'd better figure out fast how to find some flags!" William Jr. then went down to the shop of a local flag maker and purchased several dozen flags, which he marked with prices and displayed on the Art Needlework sales counter back at The Store. After arranging the flags, he wandered off, assuming it was someone else's job to sell them.

"William," his father's voice boomed from the sales counter. "You get on this floor and you stand here and sell every single flag in stock." Dutifully, he did as his father said. William Jr. would never forget this important lesson and would someday make it an employee motto: Everyone Sells at Thalhimers.

Having shown mastery as a buyer, William Jr. soon got promoted to Divisional Merchandise Manager of the Home Department, full of ranges, refrigerators, washing machines, radios, lamps, draperies, and rugs. He stocked a popular new gadget called a record player and bought Thalhimers' first selection of records. He also managed the Toy Department for six weeks a year during the Christmas season, stocking the finest toy in each category, including stuffed animals, dolls, trains, and wind-up toys. The art of the game was to end up with nothing left in January, an enticing goal he quickly learned to achieve.

Most importantly, William Jr. observed his father's commitment to the values of honesty, integrity, quality, and service. He learned the importance of interacting with customers on the selling floor, creating an environment in which each employee and shopper felt important and respected.

On his twenty-first birthday, William Jr. received a promotion to the position of Secretary and Treasurer of Thalhimers' Board of Directors. Standing alongside his father, the rest of the Board of Directors clapped vigorously when the official announcement was made. William B. Thalhimer Jr. didn't know what college was like, but it couldn't have been better than this.

The busy corner of Sixth and Broad by Thalhimers' clock, 1936.

CHAPTER FOURTEEN

THE UNSUNG HEROES
1935 – 1941

"I refuse to close The Store on Saturdays or Jewish holidays just because my father did," William Sr. told his sons. "We're going to be a competitive business. We're going to run this business like it ought to be run, not as a personal affair or a religious affair. Mark my words: We are going to grow."

William Sr. clearly struggled with balancing his Jewish identity and his business persona. He recognized undercurrents of anti-Semitism in his own community and became increasingly aware of its impact in Europe. He saw the carriage trade patronizing Miller & Rhoads across the street, and knew some of their customers still considered Thalhimers a "Jew Store." He wanted as much as possible to disassociate himself with the stigma of being Jewish.

On the other hand, William Sr. felt strong ties to the Jewish people and wanted to help his co-religionists in need. He was not alone; his views reflected those of many other American Jews of his generation. William embraced his faith as a form of ethical responsibility while rejecting it as organized religion.

"I don't have to go to Temple to be a good man or a righteous man. Reading the same damn thing over and over and over again. It doesn't mean anything," he grumbled to his sons. "I see a lot of these guys go down there and read all that stuff then go out and get drunk and lose their money playing cards. They don't do anything for humanity. You call that being religious?" The boys certainly couldn't argue with their father's observations.

The Thalhimer family did not attend Friday night services or light Shabbat candles, but William Sr. faithfully took William Jr. and Charles to religious school every week at Temple Beth Ahabah. William Sr. and Annette instilled in their boys the importance of Jewish values and philanthropic involvement in the Jewish community.

"Giving back," William Sr. maintained, "is of utmost importance." If the Jews didn't take care of their own people, no one else would. Of that he was certain.

Although he had a social circle of close Jewish friends, William Sr. wanted to ensure that his boys fostered friendships outside the Jewish community. He prescribed to the motto that Jews had followed for centuries, "Be more silent than water and lower than the blades of grass." He knew about the brown-shirted Nazis he'd seen on his trip to Germany in 1930. He had read about the frightening rise of Adolph Hitler.

Violence in Germany escalated steadily after the Nuremburg Laws were enforced in 1935, stripping German Jews of most of their rights. Desperate refugees sought shelter anywhere in the world that would take them. Only three years after the laws passed, German Jews vied annually for the available twenty-six thousand American visas. Due to governmental "paper walls" and other unfortunate circumstances, only five thousand visas would ultimately be issued each year.

The typically genteel anti-Semitism and anti-immigrant attitude of the United States revealed its ugliness more overtly in an intra-government memo written by Assistant Secretary of State Breckenridge Long. His memo, which made it as far as the desk of his friend President Franklin D. Roosevelt, stated, "We can delay and effectively stop for a temporary period of indefinite length the number of immigrants into the United States. We could do this by simply advising our consuls to put every obstacle in the way...which would postpone and postpone and postpone the granting of the visas." Although Long would eventually be demoted and widely criticized for this extremist stance, his actions limited the number of German Jews able to seek refuge in America.

Back in Richmond, William Sr. set out to aid German Jewish refugees escaping the Nazis. He helped set up the Richmond Jewish Community Council, which would become known as the Richmond Jewish Federation, and built upon the foundations of the Hebrew Benevolent Society, later to become Jewish Family Services. Both organizations gave much-needed assistance to refugees as well as providing for the poor and sick of Richmond, in the Jewish community and beyond.

Minna Thalhimer Livingstone, one of two sisters with whom William Sr. maintained a relationship, had been involved with the Joint Distribution Committee for years. Initially, she may have been the one to encourage her brother's involvement in national refugee relations.

William Sr. was invited to serve on the Board of the American Jewish Committee in 1929, and often traveled to New York City for AJC meetings, especially if he could combine them with merchandise buying trips. Other merchants on the AJC board included Fred Lazarus Jr. of Lazarus department and famed philanthropist William Rosenwald of Sears, Roebuck & Co. They saw William Sr. as a well-grounded leader with a no-nonsense, workable approach to resettling refugees. He had the ability to produce plans and follow through, making complex situations understandable and workable.

Mr. Rosenwald conveyed first-hand news about Nazi atrocities in letters written to him by German relatives. He shared these letters with fellow AJC members and others within the Jewish community, warning them that the Nazi regime was growing more virulent and dangerous by the day.

Through his AJC participation and subsequent involvement with the American Joint Distribution Committee and National Coordinating Committee, William Sr. became aware of a man by the name of Dr. Curt Bondy in Gross-Breesen, Germany. After Hitler stripped him of his profession as a renowned psychologist and university professor, Bondy ran a training farm affording German Jewish teenagers the opportunity to learn agriculture and life skills.

At Dr. Bondy's Gross-Breesen training institute, students learned to manage a dairy, raise chickens, and sow fields. Young women learned to cook and sew, and students of both genders received instruction in foreign languages, Jewish studies and philosophy. Famed philosopher Martin Buber even visited the farm, teaching them, "Love thy neighbour, for he is like thee."[30]

Through a combination of discipline and education, Dr. Bondy taught the importance of self-respect, strength of character, spirituality and endurance. His goal was to prepare his students to resettle overseas as a group, establishing a new Gross-Breesen community somewhere like Brazil or Argentina, or anywhere they would be safe from the Nazis.

Upon hearing about Dr. Bondy's project, William Sr. had an idyllic vision. He would purchase a farm in Virginia and resettle the young German Jews from Gross-Breesen, giv-

On a wagon at Hyde Farmlands. (l to r) Dr. Jacob Billikopf, Frederic Borchardt, William Sr., Ingrid Warburg, 1938. *Beth Ahabah Museum and Archives.*

ing them refuge in America and allowing them to continue their studies. But William Sr. quickly learned that this vision was far more complicated than it seemed.

Through painstaking communications in the form of slow-moving overseas letters and cables, Dr. Bondy, William Sr., and several others worked together to develop what they called the Virginia Plan. William Sr. and his cousin Morton G. Thalhimer Sr. had located the perfect spot: a sprawling, fifteen-hundred-acre tobacco and cotton plantation called Hyde Farmlands in rural Burkeville, Virginia. The Virginia Plan became more than just words when William Sr. purchased Hyde Farmlands.

After a complex series of deliberations and negotiations among the U.S. State Department, Labor Department, and Consulate General of Berlin, Hyde Farmlands ultimately incorporated. Leroy Cohen, general counsel at Thalhimers and a confidante of William Sr., had the necessary legal expertise and served as chief negotiator in these dealings.

Student driving a horse wagon on the farm, 1939. Refugees eating lunch at Hyde Farmlands, William Sr. and Morton G. Thalhimer Sr. in background, 1939. *Beth Ahabah Museum and Archives.*

Simultaneously, the Thalhimer cousins and their sons signed hundreds of affidavits in an attempt to bring refugees to America. According to unofficial estimates, as many as seventy or eighty refugees fled Nazi Germany using these affidavits. In all, twenty-one of the original twenty-five Gross Breeseners who were selected for the Virginia Plan made it to Hyde Farmlands. The remaining four students became trapped in Holland after the Nazi invasion and died in a concentration camp.

The fortunate residents of Hyde Farmlands lived and worked as farmers in a self-sustaining microcosm, hidden away from the urban masses of nearby Richmond. On Fridays, William Sr. urged the students to speak English so they could better assimilate into American society. They read the newspaper every morning, especially enjoying the comic strips. On special occasions, they gathered around an upright piano, brought to them by William Sr. and Annette, and sang songs in English as well as German. Somehow they found the courage and energy to sing despite the brutality that had so recently murdered many of their relatives back in Germany.

William Sr. visited the farm as often as he could, gathering the students to talk on the back porch. He gave them his word that should the Hyde Farmlands project fail, he would take personal responsibility for each of them, serving as their mentor and protector.

In springtime of 1941, before the United States entered the war, Hyde Farmlands disbanded. Mort Thalhimer Sr. helped his cousin William Sr. sell the farm. Ending this refugee project was a difficult decision ultimately reached due to William Sr.'s worsening heart condition, the realization that no more refugees were coming, and growing financial strain. Most Hyde Farmlanders enlisted in the American army, some even returning to Germany to fight.

William Sr. held true to his word, helping the refugees however he could. The dog tags of Isidor Kirschrot, one of the refugees, listed William B. Thalhimer Sr. as "next of kin."

About a third of the Hyde Farmlanders went on to pursue careers in agriculture. Several became teachers. One of them, Ernst Cramer, moved back to Berlin and became Chief Executive of prominent publishing house Axel Springer. All of them developed successful careers, started families, and led productive, dynamic, grateful lives. Seven refugees became Thalhimers employees, although they received a lukewarm reception at The Store.

Carola Thalheimer had found out about William Sr. through a friend at Gross-Breesen, and couldn't help but find hope in their shared last name. "Dear Cousin," she wrote to William Sr. on August 2, 1938, "I am very happy and also very proud that we could find out you quite by chance…Our name Thalheimer has here always a good sound. And in the States, you and your name is well-known in such a large country, special now through the honorable and admirable work. So we all hope that our one child, also a boy, the youngest 'Thalheimer' now in the entire family, may be always proud with his name and shall give also his best in the future. You know the situation here a little bit, and may be, perhaps, we have the fortune one day to start to the States too."

This note was a polite request to save their lives, which William Sr. did. Carola, her son Jack and her brother-in-law were brought over on affidavits signed by William Sr. Carola eventually found work at Thalhimers, and Jack often joined William Sr. to dig in his garden. They always considered themselves cousins, although both parties knew the truth.

Hiring refugees like Carola proved to be a public relations nightmare at Thalhimers. The Depression had hit hard, and the last thing American workers wanted was German Jewish immigrants taking jobs away from them. William Sr. skirted the issue until the backlash grew too fierce. He addressed the rumor, declaring that no Thalhimers employee would lose his or her job to an immigrant. Even *The Richmond News Leader* came to Thalhimers' defense in an editorial that stated, "All Richmond will be humiliated to think that a store which has exemplified good citizenship in every respect should be the object of a preposterous rumor."[31]

For the rest of his life, William Sr. would not discuss Hyde Farmlands unless specifically asked about it. He emphasized moving forward and not dwelling on the past. William Sr. certainly didn't consider himself a hero, and no doubt wondered how many other lives he could have saved if given the opportunity.

William B. Thalhimer Sr. at work, 1938.

Hyde Farmlands main house. *Courtesy Evan Silverstein, 2010.*

CHAPTER FIFTEEN

VISITING HYDE FARMLANDS
2004

Hans George Hirsch, ninety-one years old and one of the original Hyde Farmlanders, sits in the passenger seat as Dad steers the Suburban away from the Virginia Holocaust Museum towards Burkeville, Virginia. Mom and I share the back seats along with three descendents of a deceased Hyde Farmlander.

We listen to Hans George's stories about his experiences as a refugee as we watch the landscape turn from suburbia to farmland. After about an hour, when it looks like we're smack in the middle of nowhere, Dad says, "I think we're getting close." I wonder how they ever found this remote farm, especially back in the 1930s when cars drove so much more slowly.

As we pull into the driveway of Hyde Farmlands, my heartbeat quickens. Soon a dilapidated oasis of a plantation appears amidst acres of woodland and grassy fields. The massive main house looks proud from a distance, but once we get inside, it's clear that the once immaculate home has changed over the last seventy years. Piles and piles of clutter extend from the eighteenth century wooden floorboards to the cracked plaster ceilings. Stuffed bears and dolls, thousands of baskets, hand tools, mediocre landscape paintings, and metal folding chairs crowd its rooms. We traipse around the house, astounded by the owner's junk collection and the dangerously exposed electrical wires, then settle outside on the patio for lunch. The farmland itself is beautifully serene, with birds chirping and cows grazing in the fields near the chicken houses.

Five of the original Hyde Farmlanders have returned for this reunion along with dozens of spouses, widows, children and grandchildren. One gentleman from North Carolina has just discovered that his deceased father was a Hyde Farmlander. Raised Baptist, this man never even knew his father was Jewish. Representing the Thalhimer family are my Mom and Dad, our cousin Morton G. Thalhimer Jr., my great uncle Charles G. Thalhimer Sr., his new wife Sibyl, and me.

Tall grasses and weeds brush against our legs as several of us walk through the field towards the chicken houses, away from the farmhouse. I swat away mosquitoes and pick a tick off of my arm before it latches on. I immediately regret having worn my favorite jeans, now dotted with thorns and burrs I'll have to individually tweeze from them later. I brought along a microphone and DAT recorder, borrowed from a friend.

"So this is what you did every day?" I say into the microphone to Ernst Cramer, who walks a few steps behind me. A spry and robust ninety-one years old, Mr. Cramer has flown in from Berlin for what will be the second-to-last reunion of Hyde Farmlanders. He has no qualms about trekking through an overgrown field on a muggy day, although he breathes heavily as we walk.

"It was different back then," Mr. Cramer says into the microphone in his thick German accent. "The fields were neatly kept. The house was immaculate."

Crossing over a small ditch, I ask him, "Do you need help? Let me take your arm."

"No," he says breathlessly. "I'm fine."

Of course he doesn't need my help; I should have known that. He is a survivor. I make a mental note not to forget.

As we approach a series of small, crumbling wooden structures, he says, "We built these chicken houses."

"Let's see – one, two, three, four, five, six, seven, eight chicken houses," I count as I open the door to one of them and peer inside. "But no more chickens. Now it looks like… what's that? There are *Encyclopedia Brittanicas* in here."

"Well, we had very educated chickens," Mr. Cramer says, and we share a good chuckle.

"We also built that house up there," he says, pointing to a two-story structure behind the main farmhouse. "We mixed the cement and made the cinder blocks ourselves. We had a hand-operated cinder block machine. I made those blocks."

"With those two hands?" I ask stupidly. I wish I could ask better questions in the presence of a man like Mr. Cramer, who lost his entire family to a concentration camp. I feel inferior beside him, like I've never had to work hard enough for what I have.

"We did everything on the farm. My main duty was to drive the truck. I brought in feed, which we bought in Richmond once a week. We got there, we went to a store downtown where they sold wholesale feed, and I had to buy all the stuff the girls couldn't get in Burkeville and Crewe. Like stuff for soap and so on."

"What else did you grow here?"

"Mostly potatoes for home use and for the tenant farmers. And feed for the mules and other things."

"So you ran a self-sufficient farm?"

"That's that William Thalhimer wanted. He was an idealist," he says.

"That's what I've heard."

"Your great-grandmother, I only saw her once. I was deeply embarrassed because she had a little dog along, a female dog, and we had a male dog. I had to try to get the dogs apart, but they had other things to do. Mrs. Thalhimer didn't mind. I minded."

Again, we share a laugh.

"Was my great-grandfather here when you arrived?"

"No," Mr. Cramer says, as if I should have known. "I think he came out in September 1939. When he came, my friend asked him for a raise. He was making four dollars a month. Mr. Thalhimer said, 'What for, for instance?' 'Well,' my friend said, 'For instance, to buy a Coke.' Mr. Thalhimer led him by the arm, over to the well, and said, 'Pull up the water and drink. This is much better for you and much cheaper than a Coke. No raise for you.'"

At noon, we all gather to enjoy a picnic on the patio, eating sliced oranges and cookies in the sun as we chat and make new friends. Every time one of the Hyde Farmlanders tells a story about William Sr., I naively expect my great-grandfather to seem valiant and heroic. But in their stories, he was the same unyielding businessman who kicked his uncle out of the family business and snubbed his sisters. He was not a saint, but he did a saintly thing.

"There is no doubt that your great-grandfather's action was our escape route out of Germany. He saved our lives," says Hyde Farmlander George Landecker.

Looking around the picnic, it occurs to me that Gramps and others like him not only saved a handful of refugees, they saved children and grandchildren and great-grandchildren. Generations upon generations of families that will flourish until perhaps, one magical day, they add up to six million people.

CHAPTER SIXTEEN

HAPPY DAYS
1938 - 1946

Although the Cavendish buying offices kept Thalhimers stocked with sophisticated, worldly merchandise, William Jr. encouraged his father to pursue involvement with a larger, more respected trading office. Eventually, father and son applied for membership in the highly regarded Associated Merchandising Corporation; Thalhimers was ready to roll with the big boys.

Membership in the AMC would allow Thalhimers access to some of the most prestigious fashion buyers and desirable goods in the world. It would introduce them to the best practices in management and operations exercised by their retail peers. They would receive national market recognition and press coverage. One final advantage brought a rare smile to William Sr.'s lips when he so much as considered it: membership in the AMC would give Thalhimers a critical edge over Miller & Rhoads. The pressure was on.

William Sr. attended a meeting of AMC store principals in Hot Springs, Virginia, where his grandmother had once come to partake of the healing waters. He told the retail magnates about Thalhimers' progressive return policies, brotherhood of employees, customer satisfaction guarantee, and recent expansions. In conclusion, he said to his distinguished audience, "We are proud of our store, which lies in the heart of a beautiful city. I wish to extend to each of you an invitation to come to Richmond as our guest, so that you may see and become aware of that which is our own."

The AMC elected to send its review committee, comprised of retail giants from across the nation, to Richmond to judge whether or not Thalhimers would make a good addition to the team. One requirement for membership was five million dollars in annual sales. The Store had just surpassed that mark and showed promise for exceeding it during the coming year. Another requirement was aggressive growth potential. Thalhimers had recently bought out the seventy-six year old Cohen Company, retaining its stock, fixtures, and employees. The Store was poised for nothing but growth.

When the AMC team arrived, hundreds of smiling Thalhimers' employees stood to greet their distinguished guests. Fixtures and display cases shined. Each shirt had been steamed and pressed, and each metal nametag polished.

William Sr. outstretched his hand to greet each representative, personally welcoming them to Thalhimers. He shook hands with retailing heavyweights Lou Ayers from L.S. Ayers in Indianapolis, Fred Rike of Rike-Kumler in Dayton, Ohio, and Oscar Weber of J.L. Hudson in Detroit.

In the weeks that followed, Thalhimers' executives and Board of Directors eagerly awaited a response letter from the AMC. A secretary finally delivered a letter with an AMC seal to William Sr.'s desk. He called his son into the office, where they read its contents.

That night, father and son poured two celebratory glasses of bourbon.

"Happy days," they toasted, clinking their glasses.

In April 1939, William Sr. sent his namesake to attend Thalhimers' first AMC meeting in California. It would be a good business experience for him, while allowing William Sr. to stay home and focus on Hyde Farmlands and minding The Store.

Upon his arrival in California, William Jr. was welcomed to the AMC by top executives from Bloomingdales, Dayton's, Hudson's, Carson Pirie Scott, David Jones of Australia, and Harrods of London. At twenty-five years old, he felt like a member of an exclusive club, mostly because he was.

One evening after a meeting at the Emporium department store, his colleagues discovered that William Jr. was the only single man in the AMC. One of them set him up with a date for a social function the following evening, but the girl fell ill and sent along her best girlfriend from college instead. That girl's name was Barbara Jacobs. She should have been in classes at the University of California at Berkeley, but she had come home to recover from an emergency appendectomy.

Barbara's charm, quick laughter, ruby red lips, and easygoing elegance charmed William Jr., who fell in love on their very first date.

"I've found the girl I want to marry," William Jr. told his parents when he returned to Richmond.

His father said, "Go back to California and make sure you're sure."

William Jr. telegrammed his girl then hopped a train back across the country to take Barbara Jacobs on a trip to Lake Tahoe. From there, he cabled his father and said simply, "I'm sure."

In early autumn, Barbara chose not to return to college and traveled across the country to meet her future in-laws. William Sr. and Annette held a magnificent reception for Barbara in their home on Old Locke Lane, introducing her to the meaning of Southern hospitality. Only nineteen years old and knowing no one at the party aside from her fiancé, Barbara

Barbara Jacobs Thalhimer's wedding portrait. San Francisco CA, 1939.

carried herself with absolute confidence and her sunny, Californian manner put everyone at ease.

William B. Thalhimer, Jr. and Barbara Jacobs married in an intimate candlelit ceremony several days after Christmas in the bride's aunt and uncle's living room in San Francisco. After spending a two-week honeymoon in Hawaii, the happy couple returned to Richmond to settle into their first home. Within the year, they welcomed their first child, a baby girl named Barbara after her mother.

⚜   ⚜   ⚜

Following another massive expansion, Thalhimers' annual sales shot up to six and a half million dollars. The phone nearly rang off the hook with AMC executives from around the country calling to congratulate William Jr., who now served as Vice President but clearly held the management reins.

Family portrait. (l to r): Barbara, little Barbara, William Jr., Annette, William Sr., Charles, 1942.

One morning, William Jr. received a call from Dick Rich, head of Rich's of Atlanta. They had developed enough of a friendship that Rich already had a nickname for William Jr.

"Willy," Rich said, "I'd like to congratulate you on your success with the AMC. But Rich's needs to be a part of this thing too. Will you sponsor us?"

William Jr. said, "of course," and enjoyed the implied power of such an affirmation. At Thalhimers' request, Rich's was accepted into the AMC. The Store would later sponsor Burdines of Miami as well. Still a single-store operation in Richmond, Thalhimers was finally rolling with the big boys.

In 1942, Thalhimers celebrated its one hundred year anniversary with the "Centurama" extravaganza. A special song, "My Mem'ry of the South," was written for the occasion and sold as a recording. Eighteen nostalgic display windows celebrated Thalhimers' and Richmond's shared history. More than two hundred leading fashion editors, manufacturers and businessmen came down from New York for the occasion. When the windows were unveiled, nearly five thousand people gathered to admire them.

As part of Centurama, Thalhimers embarked on its first national advertising program, placing ads in popular magazines like *Vogue, Harper's Bazaar, Mademoiselle,* and *House Beautiful*. Special items created expressly for the event included Centurama clothing, jewelry, slipcovers, and handkerchiefs.

Old Thalhimers delivery wagon displayed outside The Store for Centurama. *Dementi Studios, 1942.*

At the height of the festivities, fifteen hundred employees gathered around a stage erected on the first floor of The Store. In the shadow of a worldwide war, the remarks of Douglas S. Freeman and William Sr. emphasized tradition, community, and patriotism.

"Over the hundred years that Thalhimers has played its part in the life of Virginia, many things have happened" said William Sr. "But this I believe with all my heart. That if we keep our courage, if we are willing to make sacrifices for our country, if we live the ideals of our democracy, then we can face the future with clear-eyed confidence…

Thalhimers shall do its part, is doing its part, earnestly cooperating and working for our country. LIFE...WORK...MUST GO ON!"

The late Mr. Ike's secretary Ida Smith stood next to William Jr., holding two-year-old daughter Barbara in his arms, and together they pulled a velveteen curtain from the wall. The audience burst into applause when the drawn curtain revealed William Thalhimer Sr.'s portrait, freshly hung next to those of his father Isaac and his grandfather William, marking one hundred years and three generations of Thalhimers in Richmond.

❧   ❧   ❧

William Jr. and baby Barbara unveil William Sr.'s portrait as Ida Smith looks on. *Dementi Studios, 1942.*

During the Second World War, William Jr. left The Store and spent three and a half years serving as a Second Lieutenant, then a First Lieutenant, then finally as a Captain in the United States Marine Corps at a base in North Carolina. He would be honorably discharged in 1946 following a court-martial case over alleged transactions between the post exchange under his supervision and Thalhimers department store. William Jr. would never again talk about the case except to say that it was unfortunate, and he was proud of his service as a Marine Captain. After his military service, he returned to Thalhimers.

The Store engaged in home front efforts supporting the war, changing the title of its employee newsletter from *TBI Talks* to *TBI Fights*. They held canteens on the weekends for the soldiers from Camp Lee to socialize and dance with their girlfriends in the empty parking lot outside The Store. Thalhimers established a government contract providing uniforms for the Pinks and the Second Lieutenants graduating from the Quartermaster Corps at Fort Lee. Officers came to The Store to get measurements for their uniforms taken by the tailor, Sam Brown. Display windows along Grace Street educated customers and passersby about war efforts. One window showed a sample of what troops ate at sea, including a remarkable new invention called "instant coffee." Another exhibit in the empty parking lot displayed actual Air Force planes.

Thalhimers joined other private companies in advertising War Bonds to help finance war efforts and keep inflation at bay. William Jr. even discussed Thalhimer's war bond drive with Secretary of the Treasury Henry Morgenthau, who had sold the very first War Bond to President Franklin D. Roosevelt.

The Store's sales more than tripled during the war years. A stock boy barely had time to unpack a box before the merchandise was on its way out the door in a shopping bag with a sales ticket. Americans were spending money like never before, and Thalhimers thrived along with department stores across the country.

Despite keeping his sisters out of the business, William Sr. made strides in granting employment opportunities to women. Ever since Amelia Earhart, noted aviatrix, author, and designer, had come to Thalhimers in 1934 to promote her line of ladies' activewear, he'd been interested in her progressive remarks about women in the workplace.

"Women have to do so many things that men have done, just to prove that they can," said Miss Earhart at Thalhimers. "Women should earn their own salt and men should do their part of the housework. They should help bring up the children, too!"

However revolutionary it seemed, women like Miss Earhart were edging their way into traditionally male dominated professions.

Acknowledging that women were an important part of his business on both sides of the cash register, William Sr. developed the Business Girls Advisory Council and oversaw the founding of the popular Teen Council, a group of local high school girls serving as an informal focus group for merchandising. Many women established their first independent credit accounts at Thalhimers, allowing them to take out loans and establish financial independence. William Sr. began hiring sharp, savvy women not just as salesgirls and buyers, but in higher management positions as well. During a time when female executives were a rarity, he promoted Miss Elizabeth Bauder to run sales promotions at Thalhimers.

Cosmetics counter salesladies, 1940s. *Virginia Historical Society.*

CHAPTER SEVENTEEN

TEA WITH BETTY BAUDER
2004

"My dear, can I get you some tea?" Ms. Bauder says to me in that lilting Vuh-gin-yuh accent that's disappearing along with her generation. I take a seat at her dining room table as she returns to the kitchen to remove a whistling teakettle from the stove.

"Yes, ma'am," I reply, a bit bashfully.

I recall one day, when I was maybe thirteen or fourteen, when Dad took me to work with him. He asked, "What do you want to do today?" and without hesitation I replied, "I want to work in advertising with Ms. Bauder."

He walked me past the old Thalhimers delivery wagon in the hallway to the advertising department, where Ms. Bauder set me up at my very own easel with a blank cardstock canvas, a thin paintbrush, and a glass jar of black ink. I watched in awe of the artists seated in a row in front of me, their brushes flicking effortlessly across the cardstock as they illustrated the delicate slant of a woman's eyebrow, the simple pleats of an A-line skirt, the commanding point of a Ferragamo shoe. I tried my best to channel their artistry and skill as I picked up the brush and inked an image of an impossibly slender woman wearing a sleek dress and an enormous brimmed hat. This painting still hangs in my office, reminding me how very much I wanted to show up for work every day to create such things.

If I'd become an artist in the advertising department, I would have walked down the hall to Dad's office at noon and asked him to join me for lunch in the Richmond Room. We would have eaten buttery popovers and Chinese chicken salad or a cup of creamy clam chowder and a deviled crab before returning to work. On the occasional afternoon, we would have taken the elevator downstairs to split a freshly baked chocolate éclair from the bakery. I imagine these things when I gaze at my painting of the waiflike woman in the wide-brimmed hat. It marks the beginning and end of my career at Thalhimers.

Returning from the kitchen holding two teacups, Ms. Bauder starts, "My father brought us up to think that things were changing and women were coming up in the world." I pick up my pen and begin jotting notes.

She sets my teacup in front of me and asks, "cream and sugar?"

"Yes, please."

With the regal poise of a queen, she tips a tiny pitcher into my cup and offers me a bowl of sugar cubes.

"Father wanted us to be self-sufficient. I got my first job in high school as a model at Miller & Rhoads. When I got out of college I went to New York to be interviewed at Lord & Taylor. It was the only department store, to my knowledge, with a woman executive. They offered me thirty-five dollars a week. Can you imagine? I would have had to live in a loft with four roommates!"

"I really can't imagine," I laugh politely.

"When I got back to Richmond, Thalhimers had a female Director of Sales Promotion and two women as Divisional Merchandise Managers. There wasn't any other business in the state of Virginia with that many high-placed women. I talked to my father and said, 'I've been in both stores, and I'm going to work for Thalhimers. These gals have already broken the ceiling.'

"And when I arrived, your great-grandfather was ab-so-lutely wonderful to me," Ms. Bauder says enthusiastically, shaking her head back and forth with each syllable of "ab-so-lutely."

"Really?" I ask, baffled by her glowing words about someone who always sounded intimidating and gruff.

"We used to call him 'Mister Senior.' He was the cat's meow. If you caught his eye and hopped-to when he needed something done, he really let you run with it. A very original man full of lively ideas. A modern man. A man of tremendous creativity, and very self-assured."

I interrupt with a sugarcoated nod to my real question. "Forgive me for saying this, but I've heard William Sr. was…tough. And maybe a little unpleasant."

"Yes. But tough as he was, it was worth it when he scolded you because ninety-nine percent of the time he was right. He was one of the smartest men I've ever known."

As she speaks, I begin to understand just how smart Ms. Bauder is. Smart enough to match her boss in toughness then couch it in feminine graciousness, southern charm, and irresistible style. Clever enough to play his difficult personality to her advantage.

"When things came about in terms of public interest, he jumped on them. He had sparks flying all over the place. He'd go off on these journeys, drag his wife halfway around the world, and come back with extraordinary things and want them displayed in The Store. He didn't miss a trick. Tunics from Greece, precious stones from South America. We had to figure out how to display them and sell them.

"One year he went to Africa. When he came back I got a phone message to come to the building across the street. Mister Senior was unpacking what he brought home: Zulu shields and an elephant's foot. Well, he was excited about all of these things. In that long, ninety-foot Grace street window – the longest continuous display window in the United States – our very clever display people made that elephant's foot into a coffee table. The Zulu shields hung like paintings on the walls."

Taking a sip of tea every so often, Queen Bauder goes on and on about how she intends to write a book about the extravagant window displays featuring live baby animals and elaborate fashion shows where guests sipped champagne and ate lunch along the runway. I infer that this ambitious book will never exist outside of her intentions, but hope I'm wrong. It would be a rollicking read.

Ms. Bauder offers me a scone and I oblige. She continues, "You know, your great-grandfather created Thalhimers' Fine Foods department – the first on the east coast below New York. Foods from around the world.

"We even had a food consultant. I don't know of any other store in the AMC at the time that had one…must have been an idea he brought back from Europe. We became known for our catering, boxed lunches, and those black-and-white checkered bakery boxes. Mr. Senior wanted to offer the best candies, the best hams – Smithfield, of course, lobsters flown in from Cape Cod. The fine foods market was simply a magnet for attracting customers. It didn't make much money, but kept people in the store. Customers went gaga for the honey buns, Sally Lunn rolls, lemon chess pies, and the legendary six-layer chocolate cake with a cherry on top."

I can practically taste the chocolate buttercream icing between layers of moist cake just thinking about it. My sisters and I always fought over who would get the shiny, caramelized cherry on top. I usually won.

"Mister Senior let me sample everything before he placed an order. 'Come down here,' he said to me on the phone one day. 'I want you to taste this ice cream.'" Betty laughs at her imitation of his serious tone. "And when I tasted it, I said, 'it's delicious!' He looked at me with this piercing look and said 'hmph,' but I knew he liked it too. He just needed someone to validate him.

"We were the first in the country to display original photography, and I was very lucky he let me do some of the things I did, being so young, and The Store having such a limited budget. One year he went to Japan and brought back these magnificent, authentic kimonos in exquisite fabrics into the French Room. We tried to sell them, but I didn't pay much attention to them. He said, 'we're not selling these kimonos and they should be selling. Do something.' I responded, 'Well, they'd make wonderful evening coats.' Mister Senior didn't say anything, which was his typical response, but the wheels were turning. In the end, we displayed the kimonos as evening coats, and they sold like hotcakes."

"What other kinds of promotions did you do?" I ask.

"One year, pink was the rage all over Paris. When I came back from there, Mister Senior said, 'Let's do this whole store in pink in late January.' Well, we had pink everything. Pink azaleas in the windows, pink birdcages with live pink birds. I had the most fantastic job.

"We brought celebrities and dignitaries to The Store. Oleg Cassini. Estée Lauder. Maurice Rentnor. Gloria Swanson. Oscar de la Renta. Julia Child. Sammy Snead. Mary Martin. Milton Berle. Even Salvador Dalí.

"In the 1960s, we held two-weeklong festivals called Bravo Brittania and Bravissima Italia. Big, overblown productions. Neiman Marcus started the idea. When we did Brittania, we got an amazing reception. We recreated the Sixth Street entrance as Trafalgar Square. We had a town crier and a real double-decker bus. We visited Richmond, England, for inspiration, and the mayor greeted us there. We were able to display the royal mace in Richmond, which was priceless. We had an English art collection that ended up being circulated through stores across America. British food in the restaurants, British hairstylists in the salon, Shakespearean performances and Punch and Judy shows in the auditorium. A few years later, for Bravissima Italia, we had glassblowers from Venice,

Florentine leather crafters, and authentic gelato. Your grandfather received a medal from the Italian government – the Cavaliere Ufficiale – for the whole thing."

I don't even have to ask questions at this point. It's like she's interviewing herself.

"We had a great sense of theater, above and beyond Miller & Rhoads," Mrs. Bauder says, looking out the window with a reflective smile as she lifts her teacup. "Oh, we had pizzazz."

William Sr. and Fine Foods buyer John Highfill discuss products with a buyer. Circa 1955. *Valentine Richmond History Center.*

Betty Bauder, VP of Sales Promotion, examines a Christmas display, 1970s. *Photo Courtesy: Betty Bauder.*

Shoppers at Thalhimers' Grace Street entrance, circa 1950. *Valentine Richmond History Center.*

CHAPTER EIGHTEEN

HONESTY, INTEGRITY, QUALITY
1946-1959

At only thirty-two years old, William Jr. was promoted to the office of Vice President of Thalhimers. In a letter to William Sr., Morton G. Thalhimer Sr. wrote, "William Jr. has the intuitive ability that I think Uncle Ike had, and above all else, is forthright and direct and honorable. I have often told you that I think he is doing a good job, but now I want to tell you I think he is doing a superb job."

Empowered by his newly gained status as Vice President, William Jr. asked Thalhimers' Board of Directors, "Do you want to remain a single store operation or grow into a multi-branch chain? Because if we want to grow, we're going to need O.P.M.: Other People's Money."

The board unanimously opted for growth, and Thalhimers floated preferred stock with Wheat First Securities and Kidder Peabody partnering as lead brokerage houses. Once Thalhimers began to build more equity, they borrowed more money, strictly keeping the debt to equity ratio at no more than thirty percent. Under William Jr.'s lead, Thalhimers made its initial public offering of common stock. Stock sales quickly brought in two million dollars of O.P.M. At the same time, Thalhimers borrowed an additional two million from the banks at an attractive rate. All of a sudden, The Store had brought in four million dollars without so much as selling a shirt.

William Jr.'s financial savvy quickly became evident. With millions of dollars of Other People's Money, Thalhimers grew in every direction. A walking bridge was con-

Cousins Irving May and William Sr. chatting on a walk after an AMC meeting in Westchester, New York, 1946.

structed across Seventh Street, connecting The Store to its warehouse. Thalhimers gobbled up the neighboring YMCA and Seventh Street Christian Church. It built up three floors on one side and, including a new loading dock, eight floors on another. It bought out Kauffmans, a beloved local competitor, absorbing its merchandise, fixtures, and employees. The Store now encompassed an entire block's frontage between Sixth and Seventh on Broad Street, setting the stage for real battle against its gallant competitor, Miller & Rhoads.

For three years, The Store operated under its first non-Thalhimer President, William Sr.'s first cousin Irving May. William Sr. continued on as chairman, making all major decisions and guiding his cousin Irving as if he were his own brother. Eventually, William Sr. hoped William Jr. would assume the presidency.

William Jr. continued to climb the corporate ladder, keeping his relationship with his father close but businesslike. As William Sr. raised his high expectations even higher, his eldest son continued to meet them. They maintained a passive-aggressive relationship that revolved around authority, respect, love and fear.

After William Jr. fired someone without his father's approval, he found a note scrawled across the yellow legal pad on his desk. It said, "Any more decisions like this and your days are numbered. W.B.T."

In a more formal letter, William Sr. expressed confidence and pride in his son. He wrote, "For obvious reasons of emotional restraints or influence of emotion whether voluntary or involuntary, I wish to acknowledge in this manner how proud I am. First, as a father, of your personal development and family accomplishments. Secondly, to be lucky enough to feel you have inherited many of my gifts which are more or less inborn, and in addition to the orderliness and the mastering of many details of financing, again claiming what I think I have and have evidenced, salesmanship, drive and leadership." He signed it, "Your Chairman of the Board of Directors and Your Father."

William Sr. had a far less complicated relationship with his younger son Charles. In 1947, Charles entered the family business after graduating from Washington & Lee, the school his older brother had wanted to attend. After graduation, Charles worked for the Newport News Shipbuilding and Dry Dock Company then served in the Merchant Marines, where he was eventually commissioned as an ensign in the Navy. During his military service, Charles served on a transport ship carrying troops to France and England and bringing the wounded back to America.

At Thalhimers, Charles began his career as Operations Assistant under the direction of Mr. Glavé. There, he helped establish leases and devise construction contracts until a

Charles and William Jr. sing "Happy Birthday" to Thalhimers' basement on its 29th Anniversary as buyer Benny Perlin laughs. *Wray Selden, 1958.*

vacancy came about for a sales position in the Men's Hatwear department. Within three years, he had been promoted to buyer of that department, followed by another promotion to Divisional Merchandise Manager of Children's Wear, Juniors, Piece Goods, and Art Needlework.

A dapper young man, Charles was chatty and personable. He enjoyed the game of buying and selling, but was most at ease sport fishing with his father or telling comical stories over cocktails with friends. He and his new bride Rhoda enjoyed visiting museums and galleries, developing a shared appreciation for fine art. He entered his family's business with a distinct challenge cut out for him: establishing a career alongside that of his domineering brother, who was already Vice President of The Store.

⚜   ⚜   ⚜

In 1948, Thalhimers began staying open for evening shopping, and on the first night they could barely handle the mobs. Shoppers jam-packed the elevators and escalators, shoving each other, causing women to get their skirts caught in the escalator's moving stairs. Women crowded the cash registers, pulling their metal Thalhimers Charga-Plates from their leather pouches and waving them in the air, insisting, "I'm next! I'm next!" Off-duty firemen monitored the crowds, shouting, "Hold on, ma'am. Please don't push. Wait for the next elevator."

Overcrowding posed a challenge William Jr. had only dreamed Thalhimers would face. While showing unprecedented growth potential, it also revealed a need for more inspired management. William Jr. said to his father, "I'm worried. I think The Store is in danger of spinning out of our control."

He had worked under William Sr.'s leadership long enough to see his weaknesses: a vice-like grip on controlling every decision, an inability to delegate, and a relative lack of financial savvy. The Store, he thought, required more agile leadership. William Jr. could never address these flaws to his father's face, but he felt they were serious enough that they could prevent Thalhimers from achieving its full potential. Something had to be done.

While his father was away on a buying trip, William Jr. sought information on various business analysts and requested proposals. The first day his father was back in the office, William Jr. made an appointment to see him.

Sitting in the green leather chair facing his father's desk, he said, "We can't handle the amount of business we're doing with the current management structure. We need to either get our act together or close up shop. I'd like to recommend that we hire a third party to complete an objective business study and make recommendations. Give me three months, and I'll get it done."

"I didn't ask you for a study," his father said, banging a fist on the desk as he stood up. "I'll make up my own mind about the future of this business."

William Jr. said nothing as his father stormed out of the office.

A month or so later, William Sr. called William Jr. back into his office and said, "Son, would you mind repeating to me what you told me that first day after I got back from my trip?"

After William Jr. repeated his suggestion, William Sr. thought for a moment then said impulsively, "Get a hold of Irving and whoever else is on the Board and let's call a meeting. Right now."

That very afternoon the Board met, William Jr.'s proposal was approved and they unanimously voted in favor of launching a search for a business analyst. Ultimately they selected Cresap, McCormick and Paget, whom they felt would provide an entirely fresh and unbiased point of view on how to improve operations, shore up management, and grow the business.

At the conclusion of the analysts' three-month study, the Board members took seats in the green leather chairs for a presentation of the thick documents awaiting them around the executive boardroom table. In the lengthy, detailed report, Cresap, McCormick and Paget made some bold recommendations.

First, they suggested that thirty-three-year-old William B. Thalhimer Jr. be promoted to the position of President, the top executive spot. William Jr. heartily disagreed with this recommendation. He wanted to prove himself before receiving such a significant title. The Board voted not to change his title to President, but to give William Jr. the responsibilities of President. His title would remain Executive VP, General Manager and Treasurer for the next three years. If he proved successful, he would succeed his father as President. If he failed, the Board would hire someone else and save William Jr. the public embarrassment of not having lived up to his title at the business bearing his last name.

Second, the report suggested that seventy to eighty employees immediately be fired. Management needed to clean house, allowing the business to build a sharper, more focused team. The board put William Jr. to the task as a preliminary test to determine if he could handle the responsibilities of General Manager.

William Jr. didn't have much experience with letting employees go. He had done it once before and been roundly chastised by his father, so he was nervous when he called Mo Breitstein, the first name on the list, into his office.

After fighting in the war, Mo had come to Thalhimers to serve as an Office Manager. William Jr. had been friends with Mo for years. He was a loyal employee who had never caused a problem.

"Mo, I can't help it," William Jr. said with a quivering voice, "but I've got to fire you."

"OK, Billy," Mo said.

Then the two men hugged and cried together.

William Jr. composed himself then promised, "Mo, I'll do everything I can to help you relocate." He would in fact find Mo another job, and their friendship continued through the years.

One particular layoff didn't go as planned.

William Jr. had called The Store's architect, Fritz Koch, into his office.

"I'm sorry, Fritz," said William Jr., "But we no longer need the services of an internal

A backyard business meeting at Old Locke Lane. Mo Breitstein pours William Jr. a glass of water as Sam Stern looks on, 1939.

architect. I'm afraid we're going to have to let you go."

"Bill, I don't agree. I want to think about it," replied Mr. Koch in a German accent.

Taken aback by his response, William Jr. said, "Fritz, you don't think about it. It's a decision the Board has made and I'm telling you that we don't need an architect. In simple language, you're fired."

Mr. Koch cocked his head, paused for a moment, and said, "I'll think about it. I will see you in the morning."

The next day, Mr. Koch returned to William Jr.'s office and sat in the green leather chair facing his desk. "Bill, I think we're going to build one hell of a business, and you're going to need architectural help. If you hire someone from the outside, you'll never get what you need for my price."

Pursing his lips and pausing to think for a moment, William Jr. responded, "I admire your audacity, and I think you might be right. You can keep your job, Fritz. I'll let the Board know of this change."

It ended up being a positive move, as The Store soon entered a period of enormous growth, keeping Mr. Koch busy until his retirement from Thalhimers three decades later.

As he made his way down the layoff list, William Jr. toughened up a little more with each firing. Finally he had laid off ten, then twenty, then fifty people. The Board of Directors noted that William Jr. had passed an important test on his way to earning the title and position of President.

The analysts' report also suggested careful expansion outside of the single Thalhimers store, so William Jr. began looking for opportunities beyond the city of Richmond and the state of Virginia.

Thalhimers' first major acquisition was the Sosnik specialty store in Winston-Salem, North Carolina. In exchange for Thalhimers' stock, Mr. Morris Sosnik agreed to sell his longtime family business, an elegant and well respected store with more than three hundred employees. Charles stayed up all night helping Mr. Sosnik do inventory and prepare The Store for re-opening under the name Sosnik-Thalhimers. Charles also played a critical role in securing the lease and handling operational details.

Several years later, William Jr. made a visit to Danville, Virginia, to scout locations for a Thalhimers branch. He arrived around dusk after a full day's work, strolling down Main Street after dinner. He cupped his hands to peer into the windows of the handsome four-story L. Herman's store just as the Captain of the Danville Police Department turned the corner, walking his beat.

"Can I help you?" the policeman asked the suspicious stranger.

"Yes, sir," William Jr. responded politely, "I like your city and am thinking about buying this place. Who can I talk to?"

"Well, Mr. Herman owns it," said the baffled policeman.

The following spring, William Jr. shook hands with the highly respected Mr. Herman as his store became Thalhimers' next acquisition.

These branch stores allowed William Jr. to run the business from afar, testing whether or not he and his management staff were up to the challenge of expansion. Traveling back and forth by car between Virginia and North Carolina took too much precious time, so Thalhimers purchased a private airplane to make travel easier for its executives.

Ever since riding his bike to Byrd Field in 1927 to see Lindbergh land "The Spirit of St. Louis," William Jr. had wanted to fly an airplane. His wish was granted when the pilot allowed him to share the controls and help land Thalhimers' plane. William Jr. loved the soaring rush of traveling at astonishing speed, seeing the majestic view from thousands of feet above the ground, and being in control of something so incredibly powerful.

William Jr. surrounded by congratulatory flowers on the occasion of his promotion to president of The Store, December, 1950.

*   *   *

After spending three years auditioning for the role, the Board of Directors finally cast William B. Thalhimer Jr. as President and General Manager of Thalhimers. On his wife Barbara's birthday in the winter of 1950, William Jr. and his family gathered to celebrate at a lavish dinner party at William and Annette's house.

"To the future of Thalhimers," William Sr. toasted to his son in glasses engraved with *William B. Thalhimer Jr., President.* "Happy days."

For dessert, they enjoyed a cake intricately styled by Thalhimers' bakery to replicate the downtown store. William Jr. thought it tasted particularly delicious.

Several days later, Thalhimers' new President got a call from Ray Hickok, President of Hickok Manufacturing, which produced a very popular line of belts. Mr. Hickok said, "Bill, I'm starting a national group called the Young Presidents' Organization for corporate presidents under the age of forty. We've heard your news, and I'd like for you to be one of our first members."

William Jr. accepted. At thirty-six years old, he was one of the youngest corporate presidents in the nation.

⚜   ⚜   ⚜

One summer, William Jr. and Barbara visited their friends the Reynoldses in Jamaica where Richard S. Reynolds' company, Reynolds Metals, mined bauxite for its aluminum products. The two executives kicked back on the beach to enjoy a few beers, which Reynolds bragged were brewed and bottled by Lord Beaverbrook of England.

"Anodized aluminum," Mr. Reynolds said to his friend. "It's the next thing."

"No kidding?" said William Jr. "We should coat the store in it." He snickered, showing the gap between his front teeth.

"Now that's an idea." Mr. Reynolds said, with utter seriousness. "We've already created aluminum siding for homes. Billy, I'll tell you what we're going to do. We're going to cover your store in aluminum. Reynolds will engineer the whole thing…present you a diagram to show you how it'll look, install it, turnkey, whatever it costs us to put up there. You cover the materials, and that's it."

"Are you joking?" William Jr. said.

"I'm dead serious. Aluminum retains heat in winter. Keeps things cool in summer. It's self-cleaning. You'll never pay a dollar's worth of maintenance on it. It'll be the first commercial building in the country to wear a jacket of aluminum."

They'd both had enough beers that it seemed like a good idea.

"All right, let's do it," said William Jr., and the two men stood up and shook hands on the beach.

Reynolds' engineers worked to design and install enormous grooved aluminum plates covering the exterior of the downtown Thalhimers store, extending an entire block

A crowd assembles to watch the unveiling of Thalhimers' new aluminum front, October 1955.

from the clock on Sixth Street all the way to the loading dock on Seventh Street. When the construction was complete, thousands gathered on Broad Street to watch as workers on the roof raised the world's largest continuous piece of cloth, which was made by Virginia's Dan River Mills, revealing the most modern looking façade Richmond had ever seen. A spectacular celebration followed, crowning an "Aluminum Queen," distributing aluminum mint julep cups to store executives and local dignitaries, and announcing that the fabric of the curtain would be made into children's clothing and donated to orphanages.

The modern-looking Thalhimers store boasted so many departments, a shopper could spend all day there. Beside the Fine Food and Sweet Shop at the entrance, the Metropolitan Main Floor featured the Men's Store, the Silver Store, the Smoke Shop, costume accessories, cosmetics, books, and stationary. Ads for the Homemaker Floor, with its linens, china, appliances, draperies and rugs, boasted, "This is the floor that shows many a homemaker how to save time, save steps, save energy, and conserve precious time so that she may have more leisure to enjoy her home and her family." Everything a shopper bought could be delivered to their home by way of a Thalhimers delivery truck, and oftentimes the drivers knew their customers by name.

Popular fashion designer Maurice Rentner (far right) shows off an evening dress he designed. Buyers accompany Jennye Mitchell (seated center), Sam Stern (standing center) and William Jr. (seated right), 1955.

And oh, the Fashion Floor. Miss Mitchell's "French Room" brought haute couture to the ladies of Richmond. Other specialized services on the Fashion Floor included the Bridal Counsel, Lingerie Fitting, Fur Salon, Maternity Shop and Lovely Lady Shop, for women of a "certain size." The Young Virginians Floor featured cradle-to-college boutiques, including the ever-popular toy department with its train tables and Madame Alexander doll collection. The Budget Floor offered smart fashions at thrifty prices, as well as the Sewing and Needlework Center for women still inclined to make their own clothes.

Other special services at Thalhimers included The Humidor, a temperature-controlled vault with individual lockers for frequent Smoke Shop customers, an interior decoration and home planning service, a travel agency, a beauty salon, an optician, a portrait studio, and the Thalia personal shopping service.

If an exhausted shopper needed a break, she could visit the Ladies' Lounge to freshen up with a shower. Thalhimers was the only department store in the country to offer showers, an especially popular feature for rural shoppers coming to the "big city" for the whole day.

If a shopper developed an appetite, he or she could enjoy a Chinese chicken salad at the swank Richmond Room, afternoon tea at the T-Cart, a root beer float at The Soda Fountain, shrimp salad from the Fine Foods department, or an éclair from the Sweet Shop. Men dined at the Men's Soup Bar on the mezzanine, where many a business transaction occurred over navy bean soup and a "three-way" sandwich. Women weren't allowed. When the women's lib movement finally forced its way into the Men's Soup Bar, sales dropped. Women took up all of the tables and gabbed for hours over chicken salad croissants and iced tea.

⚜   ⚜   ⚜

One morning, William Jr. received another phone call from Dick Rich of Rich's of Atlanta. "Willy," he said, "Meet me in New York. I have an idea."

Not wanting to miss a ripe opportunity, William Jr. jetted off to meet with Mr. Rich in his New York apartment.

"Look, Willy," Rich said, "I want to form a group of retailers, something like Federated that the Lazarus boys put together. I want Rich's, Thalhimers, Hutzlers, and Woodward & Lothrop. What do you say?" He handed over a proposal outlining the benefits of such a partnership.

William took a look at it, pursed his lips, and said, "We'll think about it."

A few days later, Rich called William Jr. back in Richmond. This time he shouted, "Willy, we can't do this thing!"

"Why's that, Dick?"

"You own a controlling interest in Thalhimers. You'd own so much damn stock in our group that you'd be my boss!"

The proposal was taken off the table immediately. Thalhimers would not become part of a national conglomerate. Not yet, anyway.

As department stores around the country began selling out to larger holding companies, William Jr. called Dick Rich to see if a rumor he'd heard was true.

"Are you selling to Federated?" William Jr. asked.

"Over my dead body," Mr. Rich told his friend.

Not long after that phone call, Mr. Rich had a stroke and died shortly thereafter. The subsequent President of Rich's, Mr. Harold Brockey, decided to merge Rich's with Federated. So the merger did, in fact, happen over Dick Rich's dead body.

Not long after these merger discussions, William Sr. asked his son to stay home from work. Walking side by side with his son around the rolling acres surrounding his home at Old Locke Lane, William Sr. said, "Son, I'm concerned about your health. You and I are very similar. You're burning the candle at both ends, and I'm afraid about what may happen. Maybe The Store ought to belong to a group. That way if anything happened to you, our equity would be protected."

"That's a great idea," William Jr. told his father. "But not now. I'll know when the time is right."

Shoppers enjoy pre-summer bargains on Thalhimers' main floor, 1950s.

CHAPTER NINETEEN

THE WESTMORELAND STORY
2003

As usual, Grandpa and I take seats in our respective wicker chairs on the sun porch of his house for another interview. The sun beams in through the glass walls, illuminating Grandpa's silhouette so much that I squint to look at him.

"Let me adjust the blinds," he says. He stands up, opens the closet door, and presses a button to activate automatic awnings that descend to just the right spot to block the sunlight.

"Thanks, Grandpa."

After pulling a notebook and pen from my canvas Thalhimers bag, I lift the lid of the blue and white ginger jar to scoop out a handful of sesame sticks.

"Once I became President, I was quick to realize we had to grow," Grandpa tells me, picking up from our last interview. "And all the merchandising smarts in the world do you no good without money and growth. We needed to keep building the strength to borrow and the ability to create equity."

Oh no, I think to myself as I pick up the pen and notebook. He's going to launch into that story about the land on Westmoreland. I must have heard it a hundred times. But this time I decide to really pay attention. I want to understand why this story is so important to him. Placing the sesame sticks on a napkin, I recline into Gram's needlepoint pillows to focus hard on his words.

"So we found this land. It was the old Deep Run Hunt Club on Westmoreland. It was about thirty-five acres. We bought it, figuring we would build a modern-type, one-floor distribution center there with plenty of room to grow."

I'm familiar with this area since Ryan and I live only a few blocks away. It's now choked with car dealerships, fast food restaurants, and an off-track betting operation.

"What was it like in those days?"

"Staples Mill was a dirt road. There were no stoplights. No water lines. No electricity. No bus line. Nothing. They called it Siberia.

"On a Saturday afternoon, the phone rang in my office. No one was at the switchboard. A lady said, 'Mr. Thalhimer, I own land next to the parcel of land your company just bought. Will you take mine, too?' And I asked her, 'How many acres do you have?' She said, 'I have 55 acres.' So we bought her land for very little, and we had some eighty-odd acres total.

"We only paid a half million dollars for the two parcels of land, then we sold Richmond Motor Car Company seven acres at the corner of Westmoreland and Broad for half a million dollars.

"My way of calculating is, and this has nothing to do with Latin, it's just simple arithmetic, if we paid half a million for eighty-eight acres and we sold seven acres for half a million, we owned the balance of the property for nothing. We sold off the other parcels of land to Blue Cross Blue Shield, Life of Virginia, and Mr. Valle of Valle Steakhouse in Wellesley, Massachusetts. We sold him the property for half a million dollars, which he thought was a great deal. He didn't know it was just gravy to us. Then we went ahead and built a Distribution Center, which later turned out to be a wonderful location for a pilot study for our third branch store in Richmond: the Westmoreland store.

"We gave a man named Mr. Bowles a few acres provided he would install sewers, drains and roads on the property named Thalbro, named for Thalhimer Brothers, and Maywill, named for Irving May and William Thalhimer. So we put no money in the infrastructure.

"Long story short is, we brought several million dollars into the business. We ended up with a two hundred thousand square foot distribution center and a seventeen thousand square foot branch store with no rent. That store ended up being a very profitable unit, even though it was in an industrial area.

"It was one of the best forward pieces of financing we ever did in the business. We didn't realize it at the time, but as I look back on it, it somewhat saved us because we had to keep our debt-to-equity at a respectable level. These transactions increased our borrowing capability and gave us the funds to expand."

As the sun sinks below the awning, illuminating Grandpa's silhouette once again, I finally get it. The Westmoreland story is about making something out of nothing. It's about creatively taking advantage of unexpected opportunities. It's the reason Thalhimers had the money to go on without joining Federated or Allied early on, like so many of its competitors. It's about small decisions adding up to big success. It's the story of how Grandpa's mind worked.

William B. Thalhimer Jr. looks towards the future outside Thalhimers, 1955.

William Sr. and William Jr. on the family's fishing boat, the Annette II, Cape Cod, 1961.

CHAPTER TWENTY

POWER SHIFT
1960 - 1969

When William Sr. suffered another heart attack, his doctor told him, "You need to get away and relax somewhere. Slow down. You're suffering from too much stress and your heart can't handle it." William Sr. and Annette took the doctor's advice seriously and began spending their winters in Fort Lauderdale and summers on Cape Cod.

In their rental home on the Cape, William Sr. slept with a coffeepot on the bedside table. Moments after he awoke, he'd turn on the coffeepot, fill it with a big mug of water and chug the near-boiling water to start his day. He watched the birds linger on the bird-feeder outside the window and feed their young in a nest on the sill. He read books about everything from business history to meteorology. He spent hours sport fishing on his fishing boat, the Annette II.

At the annual lobster dinner and clambake celebrating his birthday, William Sr. would occasionally find a tiny soft-bodied crab inside an oyster, place it in his mouth, and let it crawl down his tongue. His eyes widening, he would crunch down and swallowed the crab whole. "They're a delicacy," he said. His six grandchildren shouted, "Ooh, yuck!" and "Mommy, Gramps ate a baby crab! Can I eat one?"

In the late afternoons, Annette watched out the window as her husband sat in his lawn chair and watched the boats sail past. He was a different man away from the pressure and drama of The Store.

While Annette focused on her children and grandchildren and keeping her husband in good health, she pursued personal interests as well. She traveled across New England

William Sr. and his cousin Morton Sr., Cape Cod, 1967.

in search of Early American antiques, ornate oriental rugs, and colorful Sandwich Glass, a popular glassworks of the mid-1800s. An avid flower gardener, Annette raised a variety of orchids, caring for them like children. She also became quite a golfer, having won Richmond's citywide golf championship one year. Most of all, Annette enjoyed seeing her husband so unusually content.

William Sr. became more reflective and sentimental, taking the time to read a brown leather-bound volume embossed with "The Thalhimer Family" on its spine, a gift to him and Annette from their sons. Although the majority of the scrapbook's pages would remain blank, the boys put together a brief family history and genealogy then glued a few newspaper articles about Thalhimers inside.

Sensing the importance of connecting with his family's roots, William gathered memorabilia that had been passed down to him: his grandfather William's German passport, Kiddush cup, letter received from a cousin in 1844, and engraved pistol; a letter written by his grandmother Mary before leaving for America; his father Isaac's golden thread counter, family Bible, and cufflinks; and an old photograph of the store at Fifth and Broad. Without much explanation, William Sr. passed these mementos down to his eldest son, William Jr.

⚜   ⚜   ⚜

Back in Richmond, William Jr. had ambitious plans for Thalhimers to surpass Miller & Rhoads in volume and sales. The Store had always been runner-up to the powerhouse next door, finally catching up during the war years. After the war, both stores' earnings leveled off and they maintained competitive sales.

Told to keep his friends close and his enemies closer, William Jr. befriended the gentlemen across the street. He approached Webster Rhoads, Jr. of Miller & Rhoads and invited him to partner with Thalhimers on several business and community endeavors, including building downtown parking garages.

"The nucleus of our cooperation," he told Mr. Rhoads, "is that two rivals will be working together to strengthen Richmond's downtown. In turn, it will strengthen the growth of our two department stores. We are competitors in some respects, but we can cooperate to improve the city."

Mr. Rhoads agreed, and the rival businessmen shook hands to form Sixth Street Enterprises, in which the two stores held equal stock. Sixth Street Enterprises built two parking garages downtown and launched a paper engraving business that allowed the stores to print stationary, fulfill customer orders, and print their own ads for the newspapers. Sears, Roebuck & Co. joined in on the venture as well.

At the end of each fiscal year, William Jr. and "Web," as he became known, engaged in a friendly competition, betting their favorite whiskey on whoever had the best sales and profits. William Jr. was bourbon, Web was scotch.

"Dear Billy," wrote Web. "It is going to be a close race – it may be possible that you will win one half and I will win the other...Of course, this depends upon what our bet was, and it will probably take several bargaining sessions and several lawyers to help us negotiate an agreement."

"Dear Web," William Jr. responded the next day. "I would like to move that we do not have lawyers mediate in our burdensome problems, but once again, because of my esteem in you and confidence in your judgment, integrity and ability to be

Miller & Rhoads executives laugh at Thalhimers' annual report. (l to r) William Byrd, Jr., Edwin Hyde, Alfred Thompson, Webster Rhoads, Jr., 1953.

Thalhimers execs indicate Miller & Rhoads' numbers get a "thumbs down." (l to r) Charles Sr., Newman Hamblet, William Jr., Dan Schiller, Herb Leeds, Walter Fisher, 1961.

fair, accompanying this letter is a bottle of scotch – a full bottle of scotch – and I will leave it to your judgment to take what you feel is fair…The reason I am sending this in advance of receiving your Statement is that I don't want to miss my timing, which I am sure you realize is extremely important in our kind of business."

For the next few years, bottles of Walker's Deluxe continued to arrive at the office of William B. Thalhimer Jr. Every time he opened one of these packages, he chuckled, revealing the charming gap between his front teeth. Thalhimers had finally outdone Miller & Rhoads, and everyone knew it.

CHAPTER TWENTY-ONE

MORE THAN BRAVE
2003

Grandpa opens the door and I give him a kiss on the cheek, knowing exactly what he's going to say. He taps his watch and grumbles, "You're five minutes late."

"I know, Grandpa," I tell him, "I'm sorry. I was at a JFS meeting that ran a little late." It seems like I'm always late, whipping around town at a frantic pace. Grad school classes. Client meetings. Volunteering. Whatever my excuse, no matter how legitimate, I silently curse at myself for my lack of punctuality with Grandpa.

"Hmpf," he grunts. "It's disrespectful." His disapproval stings every time.

I try to dress in business attire for our meetings, but life gets in the way. Sometimes I show up in workout clothes and he'll ask, "You wouldn't wear that to a business meeting, would you? Just making sure."

After we take our customary seats on the sunporch, Gram comes beaming in like sunshine.

"Please don't stand up," she says as I stand up and give her a kiss on the cheek.

After a bit of polite conversation, Gram leaves the room to do some knitting while watching a ballgame on TV. Although she's long since given up her avid volunteer work, she still knits squares to make into blankets for terminally ill children.

"Grandpa," I say. "Today I want to talk about the sit-in protests in 1960."

"It was a Saturday," he begins. "I had gone home for lunch. I hadn't even sat down to the table when the phone rang and a voice said, 'Mr. Billy, we don't know what's going on down here, but the whole soda fountain by the Sixth Street entrance is totally taken over by black students. They're just sitting there doing their homework or reading books, but they're not ordering.' I said, 'Hold on. I'll get down there as quick as I can.' I went down there and I couldn't believe my eyes. We had no notice of anything. It happened exactly like that. What we did was, we immediately closed the soda fountain.

"Then, on February twenty-second, this is 1960, same thing happened all over again. But this time they came into the store and went up to the Richmond Room and the fountain and occupied all the tables and so forth. We closed the store completely. I never will forget seeing Oliver Hill standing there with his arms folded like this, observing."

Grandpa crosses his arms over his chest, leans forward in his chair, and peers down his nose at me. Oliver Hill, the legendary Civil Rights attorney and crusader, towered over my grandfather in height. Grandpa must have known that Mr. Hill's stare meant business.

Although the situation seems as distant as any historic conflict that happened before I was born, I can feel its intensity in the narrow space between Grandpa and me. I can't imagine a time when racial differences dictated restaurant seating. Segregated water fountains and dressing rooms sound as primitive and foreign as Jews not being allowed to have last names or women being denied the right to vote.

"What happened next?" I ask.

"The police came and politely asked the students to leave, but they wouldn't. So they arrested them on charges of trespassing and the wagons came and took them away. We didn't know what to do," Grandpa says, still leaning forward in his chair, his voice as agitated as if these events happened yesterday.

"Miller & Rhoads had a similar thing happen to them right after us," he continues. "Then the two of us were boycotted. I recall very definitely going to Web Rhoads Jr. We went to see Tennant Bryan. I don't know why we thought Tennant could do something. He was the head of the Richmond newspapers. I think he was as baffled as anyone else. We just didn't know what to do.

"Web and I began to meet in a neutral place, mostly on the fourth floor of the parking garage, which we owned jointly, in the back seat of an automobile. We discussed what we were doing to see if we could coordinate and do it together. After all, most of our business was done with the white community and we didn't want to do anything to run against the grain."

Thalhimers exec Newman Hamblet listens as VUU student and sit-in leader Frank Pinkston explains his actions, February 22, 1960. *Valentine Richmond History Center.*

Right then, Gram jauntily strolls into the sunroom and asks, "Can I get you a glass of wine?"

"No thanks, Gram," I say with a smile. "We're talking about the sit-in protests."

She raises her eyebrows and slides both hands into her pockets. As always, Gram's head shakes back and forth involuntarily, as if she's saying "no, no, no." She rarely sits down during my interviews with Grandpa, but this time she takes a seat in the empty chair across the coffee table from us.

"We were picketed for months," Grandpa continues, more flustered than before. "Shown in national magazines. Ruth Tinsley – a very prominent member of the black community – being dragged by policemen with dogs outside our store."

Mrs. Tinsley served as a senior advisor to the NAACP's Youth Group, and her husband had once been president of the NAACP's local chapter. Two policemen had asked Mrs. Tinsley to move away from Thalhimers' entrance during the boycott, and she refused, saying she was waiting for a friend to pick her up. They removed her by dragging her across the street, accompanied by a German Shepherd guard dog.

Civil rights picketer outside Thalhimers, 1960.

Soon after that day, Mrs. Tinsley said at an NAACP fundraising rally, "We are going to bring one store at a time to its knees." A *Richmond News Leader* editorial spitefully commented, "To their knees, eh? Not for a while, Mrs. Tinsley; not for a while." Two weeks later, Mrs. Tinsley wrote, "Any time Thalhimers and the other stores are willing to treat all buying guests the same, we will be glad to return; we forget atrocities quickly...Hate is for those who are weak."[32]

Grandpa fiddles with the gold chain hanging from his pocket.

"Were you scared?" I ask him.

"You're damn right, I was scared," he barks. "I was literally scared to death. There is no way that I could today, because it's been so long, transmit the fear that was here...almost a nervous breakdown that I personally...we had to have police living in our home."

Gram interjects, sensing Grandpa's tension. "We were more afraid for our children. We had threats and phone calls. Policemen lived in our breakfast room for months. We had threatening letters about hurting the children. Personally, it was hard to do anything about the situation. Grandpa's doctor sent him to Florida to relax."

Grandpa breathes deeply and removes his glasses, closing his eyes and massaging the bridge of his nose with a thumb and forefinger.

"I thought that was the end of the line for our business at that particular point in time," he laments, shaking his head. "Almost put me to the end of the line. I'll never forget the train ride down to Florida. I got on the train, and who was sitting across from me at the dining room table but Tennant Bryan and his sister, his wife, and a couple of guys from the press. I just spoke to them very politely. Later on, Tennant said he wouldn't bother me. He knew what I was worried about. Apparently it showed. Couldn't help but show. I was silently sitting there, crying all by myself."

"It must have been hard," I say, at a loss for more appropriate words. "I just can't imagine. Did the protests ever escalate and become, you know, violent?"

"Not to my knowledge," Grandpa says. "That very unfortunate photo that received so much press made it look more rowdy and ugly than it was. Some of the picketers knew me. When I came into The Store past the picket lines, they'd say, 'Hi, Mr. Thalhimer.'"

Mrs. Ruth Nelson Tinsley being dragged away from Thalhimers' Sixth Street corner by police, 1960. *Library of Congress photo by Scott Henderson.*

"That's funny," I say, imagining the paradoxical scene. "I didn't realize it was like that."

"It wasn't funny at all," Grandpa balks. "I thought it was the end for us. I could see us losing everything we had."

"I didn't mean funny, Grandpa. I meant surprising. Unusual." It's too late to explain myself. Grandpa looks agitated. He'll probably stand up and ask me to leave, but I want to know more.

"Elizabeth," Gram says, attempting to lighten things up, "Can I fix you a Coke?"

"No thanks, Gram. I'm good."

"I know you're good. Being bad is more fun, you know."

We both laugh, but Grandpa is still in 1960. He grunts "hmpf" and picks up where he left off. Gram leaves the room to return to her knitting.

"During that period, you see, we were trying to figure out how to integrate without ruining our whole patronage. Our reputation and business were at stake. In 1960, which includes the boycott, we dropped three point nine percent in sales. That's the only year in the history of the company that we went down on our sales *and* earnings.

"Incidentally, our downtown store was a more important factor in 1960 than it was as time went on. The basement operation was an enormous part of our volume. Of course, the middle-income black community made it possible for the basement at one time to do eight million alone. It was big business. We took a giant drop in sales that year and we never really, really built that back."

"How did you decide to integrate The Store?" I ask, carefully choosing my words as not to disquiet him further.

"Judgment and instinct told me that integration was the right thing. People are people under God. We didn't *decide* to be Jewish. No one *decides* to be black or white," Grandpa says. To my surprise, he adds, "We were more than brave."

I had always considered the protesters to be brave, admiring their strength and courage in standing up, or sitting down, as the case may have been, against overt oppression. I never really thought about it the other way around.

"Thalhimers had lots of black employees," I note. "Did they protest too?"

"I don't recall that the pickets had any impact on our black employees because we never really separated them. In our minds, they were employees. Black and white were just as important as one or the other. We had already integrated our employee cafeteria years before. That we could control; it was not for the public.

"We would gladly have done all of it. We wanted to do it years before we ever thought anything like this would happen. We didn't think it was fair that we had to have separate fitting rooms. We didn't think it was right to have separate bathrooms. We didn't think that it was right that we could sell blacks dresses, suits, and everything else but we couldn't let them use the restrooms."

I nod in agreement with his egalitarian perspective, but his use of polarizing words like "we" and "them" grates on my inner sense of political correctness.

"During the year," he continues, "Web and I became acquainted with the leaders of the black community. We wanted to correct everything. We agreed that we would issue an invitation to leaders of the black community to have dinner with us. This was symbolic of our changing policy.

"So I invited several heads of the black community to have dinner with me in the Richmond Room and Webster invited some to have dinner with him in the Tea Room, both on the same evening right after Thanksgiving in November. That was the beginning of quietly integrating our restaurants. After that, we integrated everything. From then on, we had one employment office, blacks and whites together. We cut out the black and white toilets so it was just a men's room and a ladies' room. We cut out separate fitting rooms; everybody used the same fitting rooms."

By January of 1961, less than a year later, Thalhimers' facilities were open to all.

"That was pretty good progress, and that was the beginning of the end of segregation. Of course, in the meantime, the whole country was experiencing similar things in different places."

Rifling through file folders in my Thalhimers tote bag, I find a newspaper clipping.

"This Western Union telegram dated May 29, 1963, I want to know more about it. From your personal perspective, I mean. May I read it to you?"

"Sure," Grandpa says with a grunt, staring at the floor and pressing his fingers into a triangle shape in front of his lips. It feels like we're in a press interview. Sometimes I wish he would sit beside me, put his arm around my shoulders and tell me what really happened, what he and Web Rhoads Jr. really said while sitting in the back of the car in that garage. But he never does.

I read aloud, "At five o'clock on Tuesday, June 4, I am meeting with a group of business leaders to discuss some aspects of the difficulties experienced by minority groups in many of our cities in securing employment and equal access to facilities and services generally available to the public. These subjects merit serious and immediate attention and I would be pleased to have you attend the meeting to be held in the East Room of the White House. Please advise whether you will be able to attend. John F. Kennedy."[33]

"It was a Saturday, several years later," Grandpa says. "I was in my office after I'd come back from Florida when the phone rang. Nobody was on the switchboard, so I answered it myself. The voice on the other end said, 'Mr. Thalhimer' – and she pronounced it with a TH- sound – 'just a minute, the President wants to speak to you.' And I said, 'The president of what?' I thought my friends were pulling my leg or something. I really didn't know. I was never more flabbergasted, shocked, and surprised. It was President Kennedy. He said that he'd been following me with a great deal of interest with what was going on down here and in other parts of the country, and would I be good enough to come up there and share some of what we were doing."

"What did you say to him?"

President John F. Kennedy (speaking), Robert F. Kennedy (standing), and Lyndon B. Johnson (seated), lead a meeting of retailers at the White House. (William Jr. sits immediately to the right of Robert Kennedy.) *Courtesy TIME Magazine, 1964.*

"I said all right, and I went to Washington. I took Alex Parker with me because I just didn't know if I would need a lawyer. I don't know why I took a lawyer except that I had a lot of confidence in him. He never did come into the meetings. In the East Room of the White House, a meeting was called with President Kennedy, Vice President Johnson – future President Johnson – and Bobby Kennedy, who was the Attorney General. They met with the heads of retail establishments across the country: Sears-Roebuck; Montgomery Ward; there were no Walmarts in those days; there were no Price Clubs; J.C. Penney; Federated; Allied; Associated; all the different groups; maybe about sixty, seventy people there. We had a full, free discussion of the entire thing.

"I believe that was when we gained more respect from people in the community. I had always tried to do the right thing, but you respond to the whims of your community. I always believed in equality of rights."

"Do you remember what was said in that room? Specific things?"

"I really don't. I remember what I just told you."

I don't push him for details, although I later wish that I had. Richmond may have escaped violence and riots because of what Grandpa did. By being the first major retailer in Richmond to integrate his entire store, he risked his business and his reputation to do what was right. He not only integrated, but he made a point of including blacks in the store's hiring and promotion practices and even hired several of the protesters who sought jobs.

In 1964, Grandpa went so far as to hire Thalhimers' first black management trainee, Mr. Abbot J. Lambert. A year later, Mr. Lambert was promoted to the position of Senior Vice President and General Merchandise Manager. A true people-person with drive, humor and innate talent, Mr. Lambert proved that skin color had no bearing on one's ability to be an exemplary executive.

On February 21,1965, Grandpa received the annual Humanitarian Award from Reverend H. D. Knight of Sixth Street Baptist Church, who had led a picket line outside Thalhimers only five years prior. The congregation selected Grandpa as the recipient of their Fourth Annual Brotherhood and Citizenship Award, presented to him during a church service.

"In discussing the matter of presenting this award to Mr. Thalhimer, it was my feeling that it should be presented to the company," preached the Reverend Mr. Knight. "Mr. Newton Hamblet, a vice president, made this statement. 'No, Mr. Knight. I don't think that the honor should go to the company. It is my candid opinion that the credit should go to Mr. Thalhimer. He was not pushed by his board to do what has been done. He made his decisions on his own. We simply implemented his wishes.' Such a man we come to honor today!"[34]

William Jr. smiled at his wife Barbara and their three children as the congregation rocked with cheers and thunderous applause. William Jr. accepted a commemorative plaque then clasped an arm around Mr. Knight in an emotional embrace.

"The most thrilling thing I ever received was that award from Reverend Knight," Grandpa said. "Come on. Let's go downstairs and I'll show it to you." He struggles a bit to hoist himself from the chair, so I help him stand.

"You're good to your old Grandpa," he says to me, leaning on my shoulder.

"There's no where else I'd rather be right now," I tell him, and I mean it.

(above) William Jr. accepts brotherhood and citizenship award (below) from Rev. H. D. Knight, 1965.

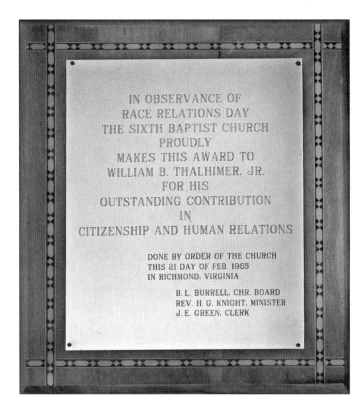

IN OBSERVANCE OF
RACE RELATIONS DAY
THE SIXTH BAPTIST CHURCH
PROUDLY
MAKES THIS AWARD TO
WILLIAM B. THALHIMER, JR.
FOR HIS
OUTSTANDING CONTRIBUTION
IN
CITIZENSHIP AND HUMAN RELATIONS

DONE BY ORDER OF THE CHURCH
THIS 21 DAY OF FEB. 1965
IN RICHMOND, VIRGINIA

B. L. BURRELL, CHR. BOARD
REV. H. G. KNIGHT, MINISTER
J. E. GREEN, CLERK

CHAPTER TWENTY-TWO

TWO ELIZABETHS
2004

On the blustery afternoon of February 22, 2004, with Ryan's arm around my shoulders and our pug Rocky sniffing around at our feet, we join the crowd of about forty people standing on the Broad Street sidewalk outside the downtown Thalhimers building. Some of them hold signs commemorating the event much like they during the original protests forty-four years prior, only these signs say things like "Civil Rights Day of Remembrance" and "Equality Rules." Passing cars honk – in solidarity with the signs, I assume and hope.

On February 22, 1960, inspired by the sit-in protests in Greensboro three weeks earlier, two-hundred Virginia Union University students marched from their school's campus into downtown Richmond. Thirty-four of them entered Thalhimers and took seats in the swanky Richmond Room restaurant and the first floor soda fountain, where they sat to read books and talk quietly. Some of them tried unsuccessfully to order coffee or Cokes.

Shivering from the wind whipping down Broad Street, I zip my coat all the way up to my chin as the sit-in protesters tell their stories. Listening to Elizabeth Johnson Rice, a large, dignified woman wearing a full-length fur coat over a royal blue silk dress, I feel an unusual connection to her. We have the same name: we are both Elizabeths. I'll bet she likes to shop and eat out with friends and get the best seats at the movies, just like I do. Hearing her words, I try hard to imagine a time when those things would have separated us.

With her own multiracial family in the audience, Mrs. Rice recalls, "My mother and father said to us, 'Now we know things are happening around the country, and we don't want you all to get hurt and get involved in this.' And so we told them, 'Of course, Mom and Dad. We're not going to do anything. If we do anything, we might go down to Thalhimers.' Once we went down to Thalhimers and got to the store...the next thing I heard was 'We're going in.' So we decided to sit at the counter. All of us filled seats around the counter, as many as were available. People were just amazed at what was going on. We were called names, and from what I can remember, some things were dropped in our laps. I thought, 'I said I wasn't going to get involved and here I am.'

"Then all of a sudden I saw these police wagons pull up and the German Shepard dogs on chains were coming out. And I said, 'Oh my goodness. This is what I've seen on television.' I really got a little scared there, but all of us were still very nonviolent. Very quiet. Next thing we knew, they said, 'You all are gonna be arrested if you don't leave.' And everybody looked at everybody else, and...we realized we'd come that far so we really weren't gonna leave. They were gonna have to do what they were gonna do. So we got into the wagons. And I thought, 'Oh my gosh. Here we go. Here we now are going to jail!' I'd never had a spanking – all my life. Here I am a college student...we were there for maybe an hour or two.

"As we were coming out, there were people lined up. People were yelling and screaming and giving high fives and clapping. It was like a parade! We all were taken by cars to the Eggleston Hotel. When I got out of the car, I looked across the room and there was my mother and father. My father, instead of looking really angry, he had his hands behind his back looking like he was burstin' his buttons. He was so proud that we had done something."

Later in 1960, Mrs. Rice appeared on the *Today Show* to represent the Virginia Union student body as she discussed the sit-in protests with hosts Florence Henderson and Dave Garroway on national television.

As Mrs. Rice speaks, Grandpa's words echo in my head: "more than brave." Would I have had the strength and resolve that she had to stand up against oppression – in college, nonetheless? Even if I did, I certainly wouldn't have done it on television.

I whisper to Ryan, "I'm going to talk to that lady afterwards, ok?" and he nods. Rocky sits patiently with his ears folded back, watching the cars pass on Broad Street.

Towards the end of the ceremony, plaques are presented to the original sit-in protesters. Then all of us link arms and sway gently back and forth in a circle as we sing two verses of "We Shall Overcome," our breath creating tiny vapor clouds in the winter air. Because of the actions taken by people like Grandpa and Mrs. Rice, we're all able to link arms and sing together forty-four years later. Although there are many unsung heroes, we are singing now. We are singing for them. I breathe deeply between verses so I won't get choked up.

After the song ends and the crowd disperses, I sweep Rocky into my arms and walk over to the podium where Mrs. Rice gathers her things and greets friends and family. Ryan and I stand nearby until she has a spare moment.

"Mrs. Rice," I say. "I enjoyed hearing your story. You were so brave to do what you did in college."

"I was a lot skinnier back then, too," she laughs heartily. "Please call me Liz."

I reach out my hand. "My name's Elizabeth, too. Elizabeth Thalhimer Smartt."

"Thalhimer?" she says, still shaking my hand. "You mean like the store?"

"Yes, ma'am. You probably saw my grandfather at some point during the protests. He was General Manager at the time. His memories of that day are pretty different from yours."

Without a word, she lets go of my hand and reaches inside the podium. I look at Ryan and transfer Rocky to him, which is like handing someone a water balloon. Mrs. Rice pulls out two plaques engraved with the names William B. Thalhimer Jr. and Charles G. Thalhimer Sr.

"Then one of these is for your grandfather and one for your great uncle, I suspect. We honestly didn't think anyone from your family would be here."

"Well, I read about this event in the paper. You know, it's weird. 1960 was a hard year for my family, but I know it was way harder for you. I just wanted to come here and tell someone that."

"Good gracious," she said. "I'm so glad you did. I hope you'll convey to your family how much we appreciate what they did."

"I will," I assure her, taking a pen and paper from my purse. "Do you mind if I contact you sometime? I want to know more about you and your experiences."

"I look forward to it," she says, leaning on the podium to write her email address on the scrap of paper.

"Likewise," I tell her. "I'll be in touch, Liz."

"Please do, Elizabeth," she says. "You give my best to your family."

❧   ❧   ❧

That afternoon, I deliver the plaque to Grandpa. He grunts when he reads it, then I take a picture of him balancing the plaque awkwardly on his lap. He still seems overcome with fear, like he might pick up the phone and call his lawyer at any moment. I try to convey to him Mrs. Rice's appreciation and how she wanted him and Charles to have these plaques, but Grandpa just says, "I'm not feeling so good today. Can you come back another time?"

"Of course, Grandpa," I tell him. "I'll be back on Friday."

He kisses me on the cheek, and before I leave, I place the plaque on the table by the front door.

In the months and years that follow, Liz Rice and I become friends, writing each other emails and occasionally getting together when she comes to Richmond. One day she treats me to lunch with her husband, grown son and adorable granddaughter in the dining room at Virginia Union University. I accept, although it seems backwards. I had intended to treat her to lunch. I smile at the irony of her gesture.

"Cheers," Mrs. Rice says as we clink glasses of iced tea.

"Happy days!" I say to her. "That's what my family always says."

A happy day, indeed, that we can sit together – just a couple of Elizabeths – and enjoy our lunch.

Elizabeth Johnson Rice and me on the 50th Anniversary of the Thalhimers' sit-in, February 22, 2010.

CHAPTER TWENTY-THREE

GIVING BACK AND MOVING FORWARD
1958 – 1978

Inspired by a wildlife exhibit Thalhimers sponsored in 1944, William Sr. had an idea. He wanted to create a wildlife park right in the middle of Richmond where low-income, urban families could step off a city bus and see everything from bison to foxes to black bears in their native habitat. He wanted all children, regardless of their social status or background, to be able to experience the wonder and beauty of nature.

Accompanied by a letter explaining his intentions, William Sr. sent ten thousand dollars to Mr. Horace Edwards, Richmond's City Manager, to get the project started. At the time, the city managed Maymont, the Gilded Age estate of James and Sally Dooley along with its one hundred acre grounds near the James River. It was the perfect spot for William Sr.'s animal park. Established in 1958 as the Thalhimer-Virginia Wildlife Park, the name would later be changed to Maymont in order to better solicit state funding. In the middle of the park, on the edge of a peaceful wooded area, a plaque dedicated to William Sr. was unveiled by his grandchildren.

Although Hyde Farmlands and Maymont were arguably his biggest contributions outside of The Store, William Sr. contributed to other endeavors as well. Along with several other businessmen, he helped convince President Franklin D. Roosevelt to legalize the deduction of charitable gifts from income tax returns. He also played an active role in establishing Richmond's Byrd Airport, raised funds as Chairman of the Jewish Welfare Fund Campaign, and served as President of the Richmond Area Community Chest, later

William Sr. and his grandchildren. (l to r) Ellen, Harry, Charles Jr. Bobby, and Bill III admire the Thalhimer-Virginia Wildlife Exhibit plaque at Maymont, November 1958.

the local chapter of the United Way.

Following in their father's footsteps, Charles and William Jr. became involved with charitable causes of their choosing. Charles and Rhoda gave significant time and money to Maymont, the Virginia Museum of Fine Arts, Virginia Commonwealth University, and the Jewish Community Federation. William Jr. and Barbara supported the Crippled Children's Hospital, the Jewish Community Center, the Virginia Historical Society, and the Science Museum of Virginia. Both brothers and their wives started family foundations that would ultimately donate millions of dollars to these organizations and many more across the city, serving as role models for the next generation of Thalhimers.

The Thalhimers continued to support Beth Ahabah, their family's house of worship for generations, although they attended few services and raised their families to celebrate secular versions of Christmas instead of Hanukkah. At the prodding of his beloved Aunt Minna, William Jr. joined the Board of Beth Ahabah and eventually became its President. He helped establish the Sunday school there, later to be called the Barbara and William B. Thalhimer, Jr. Religious School.

One of the high points of William Jr.'s philanthropic life came when he was tapped by the executive branch of the White House to serve Radio Free Europe as the Chairman of Virginia, heading fundraising efforts across the state. He accepted the volunteer position, viewing it as an interesting challenge different from anything he'd ever done before.

Radio Free Europe sought to provide up-to-date, objective broadcasts across Communist countries Poland, Hungary, Czechoslovakia, Romania, and Bulgaria. It finally allowed public access to propaganda-free news from the Western world as well as within the Communist bloc.

In September 1963, William Jr. traveled with thirty-five other business and civic leaders to Munich and both West and East Berlin, crossing through the Berlin Wall. Upon their arrival in East Berlin, an official took away their passports and money and watched the visitors intently as they boarded a bus. They drove past areas where people had fallen to their deaths from the wall or been shot while trying to escape. William Jr.'s legs shook for the entire trip until his feet once again stood firmly on American soil.

✤   ✤   ✤

Over the years, William Jr. fostered relationships with retailers across the country including Cubby Baer of Stix, Baer & Fuller in St. Louis, Joe and all the Hudsons at J.L. Hudson, the Daytons, the boys at Emporium in California, the team at Strawbridge's in Philadelphia, Burdines in Miami, J.H. Holmes in New Orleans, Rosenwald of Sears Roebuck, Avery of the Montgomery Ward group. He'd known Stanley Marcus of Neiman-Marcus for years, even hosting him as a houseguest, and enjoyed his entertaining camaraderie.

Inspired by these merchants and the growth of their department stores, William Jr. and his trusted management team reverted back to the recommendations of Cresap, McCormick and Paget. Thalhimers had followed their business plan meticulously for more than ten years and was ready to take the next step: expansion.

Following the AMC meeting at Thalhimers, (l to r): Bob McBrier (Woodward & Lothrop), William Jr., Dick Rich (Rich's), Ralph Lazarus (Federated), 1967.

William Jr. had no prescribed format in mind for a new store's size or layout. He opened Thalhimers' Career Shop boutique on Richmond's Main Street, Thalhimers' Young Virginians' boutique at River Road Shopping Center, a college store on the campus of Wake Forest University in Winston-Salem, and the smallest branch store above a dance studio in Durham, North Carolina. He made expansion decisions purely based on instinct, what the company could afford, and working out a good deal.

"The most important thing is to make a decision," he said. "It might not always be right, but at least you're moving forward."

Within a single week in 1960, three large Thalhimers stores opened in Richmond at Westmoreland, River Road, and on Hull Street. Additional Thalhimers stores sprung up across Virginia and North Carolina every year until the chain boasted twenty-two locations by the end of the sixties.

William Jr. continued taking managed financial and operational risks, which oftentimes paid off. However, a few risks did not prove worthwhile, including Thalhimers' tire stores, insurance sales, and, most notably, a fast-food chicken venture called Golden Skillet. When Thalhimers obtained worldwide rights to Golden Skillet, they envisioned it becoming the next Kentucky Fried Chicken. Thalhimers managed Golden Skillet franchises within their stores and elsewhere, as close by as Petersburg, Virginia, and as far away as Hawaii.

After a year, William Jr. realized that Golden Skillet's profits weren't worth the effort and focus the chain required of him and his management staff. It detracted from his ability to expand the family's retail business. He dropped Golden Skillet like a hot piece of fried chicken and decided to stick to what he knew best: minding the store.

As William Jr. maintained his leadership position as CEO, Charles rose through the ranks from Vice-President and Director of Sales to Senior Vice-President of Branch Store Development and finally to President and Vice-Chairman of the Board. He continued to oversee operational functions, work closely with architects designing new stores, and maintain relationships with merchandise vendors, clothing designers, and visiting dignitaries and celebrities. More importantly, Charles created a positive public image as the face of the business at store openings, ribbon cuttings, and other community events.

People loved Charles. He had a sharp sense of humor and a more easy-going, relatable personality than his brother.

"Take all that family division of responsibility for what it's worth," said a retail competitor in *Womens' Wear Daily*, "but Billy runs the show…and he deserves to. Charles is a great salesman, but Billy is a financial and managerial whiz, as well as being a hell of a merchant. He runs rings around some of us. I'm not sure it's something you can learn either…a lot of it is intuitive. He has the ability to surround himself with good, sharp minds – minds that can grow – and he listens to what they say. But once he's made up his mind, that's it. You don't argue with him, because he simply doesn't answer back."[35]

The Thalhimer brothers worked side by side for decades, much like the Thalhimer Brothers of the prior century. According to former Retail Analyst Kenneth Gassman, "In terms of Billy & Charles, my sense is that there was a split. It was not antagonistic. One did this, the other did that. It takes that kind of a couple to run a business. It takes a visionary and a mechanic. Businesses err when someone tries to fill both of these roles."

Barbara and William Jr. were now the proud parents of three children, Barbara, Billy III and little Bobby. Not far behind them, Charles and Rhoda welcomed babies Charles Jr., Ellen and Harry. At least one of these children, the brothers hoped, would represent the next generation of Thalhimers' leadership at The Store.

⚜   ⚜   ⚜

Thalhimers' annual Christmas Toy Parade delighted Richmonders with more than a dozen marching bands, scores of floats, forty giant balloons, and, to kick off the holiday season, Santa Claus in his sleigh. Thousands of revelers gathered beneath the clock to watch Santa ascend into one of The Store's second floor windows where the Thalhimer children awaited his arrival. Giant candles lined Broad Street, and elaborate animated display windows rivaled those of the legendary Macy's.

Christmastime brought thousands of shoppers downtown to Richmond's Grace and Broad Streets. Smaller stores like Berry-Burke, Montaldo's, LaVogue, and Cokesbury Books garnered crowds, but most people came to experience the festive magic of the flagship stores, Thalhimers and Miller & Rhoads. Mothers dressed their children in their winter finery to sit on the lap of "the real Santa" (as he was known due to his real, snowy white beard) at Miller & Rhoads then dine on Missouri club sandwiches while listening to Eddie Weaver play Christmas carols on the organ in the Tea Room. Hundreds of families gathered in Thalhimers' Richmond Room for Breakfast with Santa followed by a visit to the magical Santa Land in the auditorium.

Upstairs on Thalhimers' sixth floor, the atmosphere was completely different. Nobody went up there unless they had to, especially during the holidays when the tension

Christmastime crowd watches Santa climb into a window at downtown Thalhimers in Richmond, following the Toy Parade, 1960s.

was palpable. The success of a retailer's year hinged upon holiday sales.

Emerging from the sixth floor elevator, a long hallway led to a frosted glass door that read EXECUTIVE OFFICES. Beyond that door was a boardroom with green leather chairs and a brown leather sofa and armchair. Behind the boardroom was what appeared to be a residential bathroom, with a black and white mosaic tiled floor, monogrammed towels outside the shower, and a cup with a toothbrush and toothpaste by the sink. The bathroom also featured a massage table where William Jr. would get deep tissue massages from his masseur once a week.

As he got older, William Sr. occasionally reported to work in his wheelchair. He moved into a small, simple office next to the boardroom.

Next to the boardroom was Charles' well-appointed office with comfortable furniture, framed family photographs, and a Blue Marlin displayed prominently on the wall. His secretary Mary Kidd's desk stood nearby.

Betty Wells, William Jr.'s trusted secretary and confidante, sat at her desk just outside the entrance to her boss' office. In her raspy, smoky voice, Ms. Wells could rattle off the store's earnings, the family's net worth, and any other critical information needed by either of the Thalhimer brothers at a moment's notice. She had a key to The Store's vault and knew every bit of its contents.

The Chief Financial Officer and Controller sat in offices adjacent to William Jr.'s. That way, he could walk next door to get financial information as quickly and efficiently as possible. Although he didn't have a temper like his father's, William Jr. liked to get what he needed without delay. He had no patience for lateness, rudeness, or lack of manners.

William Jr. subscribed to the "reverse pyramid" philosophy that his customers were most important – at the peak of the pyramid – employees came next, and executives were at the very bottom. For this reason, he refused to invest in improving the executive offices unless absolutely necessary. The walls featured what looked like wood paneling but was actually wood-grain patterned wallpaper. He replaced the modest carpet and draperies only once when they began to dry rot. The most extravagant features of his simple office were two picture windows overlooking Grace Street.

No one ever showed up without an appointment, but William Jr. maintained an open door policy. Other than a handsome Dirk Van Erp hammered copper desk set, William Jr.'s oversized desk remained immaculate at all times. "Clutter on a desk is clutter in the mind," he upheld. The only consistent items on his desk were his ever-present notebook, pen, and what he called his bible; a book full of daily statistics on debt to equity figures and various other indicators he watched like a hawk. Behind the desk stood a piece of furniture specifically designed for him with pigeonholes for organizing all paperwork by category. On the opposite wall hung a childhood portrait of William Sr. with a plaque his father had inscribed with the words, "Son, I just want to be near you."

Every night when William Jr. went home, he joined his wife in the sunroom for one or two highballs of Walkers Deluxe on the rocks. She enjoyed joining her husband for "happy hour" and helping him unwind from the day. When the children came downstairs from doing their homework, the butler, Dayton Allen, would come in and announce, "Dinner is served." Margaret Jeter cooked in the kitchen and Anna Jackson, who lived in the housekeeper's quarters, helped raise the children and did the family's laundry. Mr. Houghton, the primary groundskeeper, and Oliver Hargrove, the gardener, took care of the yard, including the rose garden, three large flowerbeds, plus the pool and tennis court.

Dinner was served nightly in the dining room with silver and china. Barbara had a little bell under the table to ring if her husband needed a refill of ice water or one of the children wanted seconds. William Jr. usually ate dinner in business attire, but very rarely did he talk business at the table. Conversation mostly revolved around the children's activities, and Barbara never lacked for something clever or pleasant to say. After dinner, Mr. Allen returned to clear the table.

At six o'clock every morning, William Jr. did his Canadians – self-resistance exercises involving running in place, sit-ups, and arm circles. Anna served breakfast in the breakfast room, where the children joined their father at the table. He would teach them the basics of finance by counting the bubbles in his coffee. One bubble was a quarter, four were a dollar.

William Jr. had a small, tight-knit group of friends to whom he was fiercely loyal. He and Barbara took exotic vacations with their dear friends Nathalie and Phil Klaus, visiting places from Tanzania to Bora Bora, from China to Antarctica. William Jr. hedged weekly football bets with Jack Myers and Dick Schwarzschild in their "I'll Bet a Dollar on Anything" club, complete with custom t-shirts.

On Sunday mornings he took his three children to Byrd Park to feed the ducks, Broad Street Station to watch the trains coming and going, and Maymont to feed the animals. Weekends were filled with family tennis matches and swimming in the cold backyard pool, and each summer featured a trip to California to visit Barbara's family.

When each of the children turned sixteen, William Jr. took them on a trip of their choosing: Mexico with Barbara, Europe with Billy, Africa with Bobby. "These times made up for the fact that Dad worked seven days a week," said Bobby years later.

With his family gathered around the elegant Thanksgiving table every year, William Jr. would clink his glass and stand to make a toast. First, he would remember his parents and his wife's family, and everyone who had passed on. Then came a most special moment for every member of the Thalhimer family. Each child, grandchild, and spouse held a crystal wine glass in the air as William Jr. took pride in reciting their individual, crowning achievements for the year. It felt good to hear his approval, and made them want to achieve something even more significant the following year.

At the end of the toast, William Jr. choked up when he turned to his wife Barbara and credited her for all of his success and happiness in business and at home.

"Without you," he said, "none of us would be where we are today."

Then everyone clinked glasses, declaring "Happy Days."

⚜   ⚜   ⚜

Thalhimers' basement store featured rows of bargain tables selling everything from candy to ladies' dresses to silver-plated servingware, as well as an additional lunch counter called The Patio. When the basement became overly crowded with bargain hunters, William Jr. said to his father on the escalator, "You know what my biggest worry is? We're doing too much business in the basement in relation to the total business. I'm afraid we'll get a reputation for being a budget store rather than a fashion-forward store."

William Sr. replied simply, "Then you'd better figure out how to get more business up here."

Compelled by the challenge, William Jr. decided to place less emphasis on sale goods and more on cutting-edge trends, tapping into Miller & Rhoads' more affluent market. Thalhimers started a Fine Jewelry department, outfitted to compete with local favorite Schwarzschild Jewelers, and offered a full selection of silver, glassware, and china.

Inspired by Neiman Marcus, Wanamakers, and Macy's, Thalhimers' supported charitable causes in dramatic fashion. Elaborate lunchtime fashion shows benefiting the Sheltering Arms rehabilitation hospital entertained sold-out audiences. The Store held a multitude of events and exhibits in conjunction with organizations from the Richmond Symphony to the Crippled Children's Hospital to the Virginia Historical Society.

Community-wide events welcomed customers participation in everything from an annual tennis tournament to learn-to-swim programs to juried art exhibitions with buses ferrying customers back and forth from the Virginia Museum of Fine Arts. A billboard at Richmond's baseball field featured a big Thalhimers ad, and fans celebrated Thalhimer Night at summertime ballgames. Employees enjoyed activities including softball teams, bowling leagues and Camp Thalia summer retreats.

Having comfortably surpassed Miller & Rhoads in volume and sales, Thalhimers enjoyed its status as Richmond's hub for fashion as well as the latest innovations. The National Cash Register Company took a particular interest in retail uses for modern technology and developed a relationship with William Jr. After eight years of research, Thalhimers installed electronic scanners at all cash registers and later adopted the revolutionary NCR315 computer, which converted two hundred thousand customers to automated billing. It was the largest computer system ever installed in Richmond: it required five thousand square feet of space. NCR footed most of the bill for these new systems, allowing Thalhimers to enjoy cutting edge technology without significant expense.

"Today, Thalhimers is among the nation's leading retail stores which have taken this progressive step forward in the development of modern business methods for the future," William Jr. announced to the press.

Above all, Thalhimers' stellar customer service continued to exceed expectations. One evening, a woman called William Jr. at home and told him she needed to buy a dress for her husband's funeral the next day. He opened up the downtown store just for her, even calling in a seamstress to make last-minute alterations. He opened the store again on Christmas Eve for a customer who had purchased the wrong sized shoes as a gift and needed to exchange them without the recipient's knowledge of the error.

"The customer is always number one," William Jr. maintained.

At the close of the sixties, William Jr. couldn't have been more pleased with The Store's progress. He knew it made his father very proud, and that approval meant everything to him.

Behind the better service you get at Thalhimer's Department Stores is 125 years' experience.

And an NCR computer system.

With one store in Richmond, Va., it was easy for Great Grandfather Thalhimer to know what his customers wanted. It's even easier for Bill Thalhimer, Jr. with 23 stores. Every single sale rung up on NCR control registers is taped for his NCR computer. The computer tells Bill Thalhimer what his customers are buying, passing up, paying for and charging. Without sifting through mountainous reports, he gets information he needs to stock what customers want, keep charge accounts straight, and run a store that serves its customers well. Useful information is NCR's business. Always has been.

THE NATIONAL CASH REGISTER CO., DAYTON 45409

NCR ad shown in national magazines including *Newsday* and *Business Week,* William Jr., in front of his great-grandfather's portrait, 1968.

William Sr. had a stroke in the mid-1960s and became paralyzed from the waist down. Ever the merchant and businessman, he continued reporting to his sixth floor office in his wheelchair. One day he rolled into William Jr.'s office and a scowl came over his son's face.

"I don't want you to think I'm disrespectful," William Jr. said to his father, "but please don't ever come back to my office in a wheelchair. I don't want to remember you that way."

From that point on, William Sr. would sit behind his desk and summon William Jr. into his office to talk. That way his son couldn't see the wheelchair.

At the insistence of William Jr., Charles, and the Board of Directors, William Sr. remained Chairman of the Board at Thalhimers until the day he died. His friends, family and associates gathered for his funeral at Beth Ahabah, one of the only times he had ever been to temple. Police horses, kept in stalls formerly owned by Thalhimers, led the funeral procession to Hebrew Cemetery.

Thalhimers closed all stores for two days in memory of William Sr.

More notably, a half-page ad stated, "We deeply mourn the passing of William B. Thalhimer, Senior, whose creative leadership and contributions to the business and cultural communities of Richmond and Virginia will long be appreciated and remembered." But it was not a Thalhimers advertisement; it was sponsored by Miller & Rhoads.

View of Thalhimers on Broad Street, 1960s.

Stained glass window at Congregation Beth Ahabah dedicated to William and Mary Thalhimer by their children. *Photo by Wayne Dementi, 2010.*

CHAPTER TWENTY-FOUR

HEBREW CEMETERY
2007

Dad drops me off a block from Temple Beth Ahabah on Rosh Hashanah, the Jewish New Year. After I shut the car door, he rolls down the window and says, "Save me an aisle seat in a back pew on the left," before driving off to park the car.

Inside the synagogue, I walk around to say hello to a few of Gram and Grandpa's friends then find our seats. I'm comforted by the familiar wooden pews with red velveteen cushions, the soaring domed ceiling, the golden candelabras on the bimah, and the arc holding its ancient Torahs.

To my right is the solemn stained glass window, depicting the walled courtyards of King Solomon's temple surrounded by the Judean hills, dedicated to William and Mary Thalhimer by their six children. Behind me hangs a Yahrzeit memorial plaque bearing Isaac Thalhimer's date of death, its tiny light bulb glowing with hundreds of others.

One hundred and four years ago, the pristine, impressive synagogue opened its doors to worshippers, and Isaac was there. For many years, he stood on the bimah as President of the congregation. I imagine Isaac's moustache turned up at the corners as his spirit quietly smiles upon me. I think he's glad I'm here.

It used to be tradition for the whole Thalhimer family to attend high holiday services en masse; we took up a whole pew. Grandpa would wink at my sisters and me from the bimah, signaling that we would go to Baskin Robbins for Chocolate Peanut Butter ice cream after services even though we were supposed to be fasting for Yom Kippur. Katherine and I would hide notes in our prayer books and pass them down to Stanton, our oldest cousin. It was a game to make him laugh during the sermon and we usually won.

Over the years, our family has taken up less and less seats. Last year, there were four of us in attendance. Today it's just Dad and me.

At the end of the service, Dad kisses me on the cheek and asks, "Thirty-one flavors?"

"I don't know," I tell him. "I was kind of thinking we should go to the cemetery."

Dad smiles and says, "Now you're talkin'."

When he was elected Hebrew Cemetery chairman, Dad was so excited that he had black baseball caps embroidered with HEBREW CEMETERY for all of the staff and board members at the Temple. I was lucky enough to get an extra one. Where is it acceptable to wear a baseball cap that says HEBREW CEMETERY? Certainly not to a baseball game, and certainly not to the cemetery. I've never worn it anywhere, but enjoy seeing it sitting on the shelf of the coat closet. I like to think of taglines to embroider on the back like "We're dying to have you," or "For the final inning."

Hebrew Cemetery resides in a seedy, dilapidated part of the city. Pockets of it have been revitalized, but it's mostly a crumbling, poverty-stricken neighborhood. Somehow this makes it even more poignant to visit the Jews on the hillside. They're surrounded by whining ambulances, passing trains, the constant hum of the interstate, and occasional gunshots.

Approaching the cemetery, we notice a lock on the gate and realize that it's closed for the Jewish holiday.

"It's not *really* closed," Dad says, walking along the fence to a point where he can hop over.

"See?" he says, smiling mischievously, and reaching out a hand so I can climb after him.

Dad takes my hand as my high heels teeter precariously across the gravel on the cliff overlooking the train tracks. He guides me through a construction zone in the older part of the cemetery. The hillside suffered a devastating landslide during Tropical Storm Gaston three summers ago and the temple finally raised enough funds to begin repairs. A few gravesites slipped down the hill during the storm. Dad couldn't find any descendents of the already-deceased victims, but he assures me that they will all be cared for.

"See those?" he asks, pointing to a bunch of tombstones lying on their sides. "We had to pile them up so the construction equipment could get through. But they will all be returned to their places," he says, seemingly to quell his own discomfort. "They will all be returned to their places."

Sauntering around the headstones, looking at names and epitaphs, Dad asks questions like we're playing a trivia game. "What do you think the Millhisers did?" Four of their gravesites are marked by handsome stone cash registers, and the other four are decorated with tobacco leaves.

"Let me guess. Half of them were retailers and the other half worked in tobacco?"

"You got it," he says. "Who was Mary Millhiser?"

"William Thalhimer's wife. Isaac Thalhimer's mother."

"Right. Where was William Thalhimer born?"

"Thairenbach. That's easy," I reply. "Do you think we'll ever go there?"

"Nah," Dad says. "Why would we want to go when William is right here?"

Instead of honoring the dead with flowers, it's Jewish tradition to leave a stone on a gravesite to commemorate your visit. I like to think it's because stones are more lasting than flowers, but I'm not sure that's the real reason.

On Rosh Hashanah of the Jewish year 5768, Dad and I lean down together and leave stones on the graves of William and Mary, Isaac and Amelia, William Sr. and Annette. I bend down to leave a stone on the grave of little Ira Thalhimer, Isaac and Amelia's son who burned to death on his rocking horse. How might our story have changed had he lived?

Thalhimers at Crabtree Valley Mall in Raleigh, NC, 1970s.

CHAPTER TWENTY-FIVE

THALHIMER DAY
1970 - 1977

"It's always good when a person recognizes what they can't do and what they can do," William Jr. said. "What they don't know, and what they do know." With this conviction, he surrounded himself with the most capable management team and work force he could muster. He acknowledged his strengths and brought in the most capable people to counterbalance his weaknesses.

While his brother Charles served as Executive Vice President, management staff included longtime Thalhimers employees Walter Fisher, Newt Hamblett, Dan Schiller, and Sherwood Michael. Beyond this tight-knit team, which stuck together for more than a decade, thousands of employees felt they belonged to the extended Thalhimer family. William Jr.'s enthusiasm and uplifting vision for The Store were contagious. Employees and customers alike were fiercely loyal.

William Jr. watched as Bank AmeriCard, a successful credit card company, put plastic chargeplates into the hands of tens of thousands of Americans. When Master Charge arrived on the scene, he decided to take a risk and pursue accepting bank credit cards at Thalhimers. Any shopper could use a bank credit card, versus a store credit card that was limited to local shoppers. Credit card money seemed just as good as currency because as soon as merchandise was sold, the cash appeared instantaneously. What wasn't intelligent about that kind of transaction?

Thalhimers put out bids to banks including First & Merchants, Central National Bank, State Planters, and Bank of Virginia, and each came back with a proposition of

Ken Roberts of Central National Bank and William Jr. promote Thalhimers' acceptance of bank credit cards. April 1973.

what percentage it would charge to enable Master Charge transactions.

Amidst negotiations, William Jr. was chatting with Dan Schiller in his office when the CEO of Central National Bank, Ken Roberts, walked in empty-handed.

Confused, William Jr. said, "Ken, where's your proposal?"

"I don't have one," he said, holding up two open palms.

"Well, what's the cost?"

"Nothing," Ken said, smiling. "There's no charge. We'll just do it."

Standing up to seal a gentleman's agreement with a firm handshake, William Jr. couldn't believe his good fortune.

"Now that's a deal," he said enthusiastically.

A few months later, the two executives realized they had overlooked one major blunder. Ken was a director of Thalhimers board and William Jr. served on the board of Central National Bank. The two men were quick to recognize and correct their error and establish an arm's length arrangement: Central National would charge Thalhimers a competitive price for Master Charge transactions. Now they had a deal.

The Wall Street Journal, Women's Wear Daily, The New York Times and other media outlets quickly reported the news about Thalhimers' accepting Master Charge. It caused a big stir among other retailers still profiting handsomely from their in-house credit cards and the benefit of having direct mail addresses for everyone on their credit list. The prospect of accepting bank credit cards sounded preposterous, and they were blindsided by Thalhimers' move. Dozens of merchants across the country read their newspapers then picked up the phone to have a stern word with William Jr.

Ralph Lazarus, of Lazarus and Federated, bawled him out. "What the hell do you think you're doing, Billy? We're gonna lose a lot of marbles on this."

"We need cash to grow our business, Ralph," William Jr. said in plain terms. "If we can collect cash immediately, we'll have rapid growth. We see it as cash flow we don't have to pile up on the books as accounts receivable."

Ed Hyde, the CEO of Miller & Rhoads, was so angry he wouldn't even speak to William Jr. Several weeks later, Mr. Hyde finally got himself together and called William Jr., blasting, "You pulled the rug out from under us and caused us all kinds of problems and embarrassment."

Seeing Thalhimers' sales increase and realizing the benefits of bank credit cards, other department stores – including Miller & Rhoads – couldn't jump on the bandwagon fast enough. Nearly every store in the country accepted Bank AmeriCard or Master Charge within the year.

1974 brought with it the worst recession in decades. Inflation soared to double digits. World oil prices quadrupled, triggering an energy crisis. Unemployment reached its highest level since the 1930s. Consumer confidence eroded. Despite all of the odds working against it, Thalhimers managed a nine percent sales increase.

When it became clear that Thalhimers was about to tip the one hundred million dollar mark, its executive team figured about what time of the day it would happen and assembled together in the boardroom with a cash register. At the appointed hour, William Jr. and his brother Charles rang up a package of hosiery on the cash register, pushing annual sales over one hundred million dollars for the first time in The Store's history.

To celebrate the team's success, William Jr. announced that every employee would receive an extra week of paid vacation. He never took credit for The Store's accomplishments, always heaping the praise upon Thalhimers' employees.

Charles Sr. buys a pair of stockings from William Jr., putting Thalhimers' annual sales over $100 million, 1976.

William Jr. announced at the next shareholders' meeting, "We did it, but let's focus on what's next. We're going to hit TWO HUNDRED FIFTY MILLION DOLLARS ten years from today."

A hush fell around the table. Had their fearless leader gone over the edge? However absurdly optimistic this number seemed, his dedicated team would achieve the quarter-of-a-billion mark only nine years later. Mission accomplished, Thalhimers continued to grow.

In 1976, distinguished members of the Associated Merchandising Corporation gathered from across the nation in Richmond for their annual meeting. They celebrated "Thalhimer Day" in the auditorium on the fifth floor where William Jr. and Charles beamed with pride as they spoke of their recent successes, giving due credit to their loyal employees and devoted customers.

William Jr. and his wife Barbara, with every ounce of graciousness and hospitality, hosted a reception for some of the America's most respected merchants at their home on Old Locke Lane. As more than a hundred well-starched businessmen emerged from buses, waiters approached with trays of mint juleps. The guests were ushered through the home's elegant foyer to the rolling hills of the backyard, where a specially built pavilion next to the rose garden emanated the melodic sounds of a full orchestra. The pavilion had air conditioning and heat to assure the comfort of the guests regardless of the weather, and had even been secured in the unlikely case of a hurricane. Ninety waiters, waitresses and cooks waited on the crowd, roughly a one-to-one ratio to the number of guests. Thalhimer Day, indeed, had arrived.

CHAPTER TWENTY-SIX

WATER SEEKS ITS LEVEL
2008

At Padow's Deli, I carry two tuna fish sandwiches to the table as Dad walks around and shakes hands, including those of some older men flocked around a long table in the back. I imagine a similar scene took place in the Men's Soup Bar at Thalhimers years ago.

"I'm going to interview you today," I announce to Dad when he makes his way over to our table.

"All right," he says, handing me an iced tea. "But I don't know what I can add. Grandpa pretty much covered everything."

"Yeah, but he's not you," I say. "Can I have your pickle?"

"Sure."

"See? This interview is already different from the ones with Grandpa. I never would have asked to have his pickle."

We laugh, knowing Grandpa's affinity for pickles.

"Did you ever think about working anywhere other than The Store?" I ask, pulling out a pen and notebook.

"I never thought about doing anything else. Thalhimers was my lifetime employer. That's just the way things worked in those days. I worked where my father and grandfather worked. I never dreamed it would go away. You don't consider that something that's been around for over a hundred years will ever go away. Want a potato chip?"

"No, thanks. You know, it's funny. I never thought Thalhimers would go away either. It seemed so permanent. At least I've got a few memories like crawling around the Bridal Salon looking for beads and playing on your secretary's typewriter. What do you remember from when you were little?"

"I think my earliest memories are of sitting at the telephone switchboards on Saturdays while Dad went to his office. I'd watch the ladies plug the extensions into the different lines. They were always so nice to me. We'd go change burned out flood lights at the Westmoreland warehouse. I loved to work with the warehouse guys, going out with the TV repairman to hold the mirror while he fixed people's TVs. We'd take merchandise out of boxes and install it. I'd go with Tommy the deliveryman all around Windsor Farms."

"When did you get your first paid job?" I ask, slowly taking his potato chips one by one.

"Bert Brent in Men's Furnishing hired me as a stock boy. I'd work during summers in high school. Little odds and ends jobs. After I got out of the Army, I went to San Francisco to live for the summer with Grandma Ro. I did the Junior Executive Training Program at Emporium. When the summer ended, I came back to Richmond in 1969 and interviewed at The Store."

"Were you guaranteed a job?"

"Well, I remember meeting with the Personnel Manager. He said, 'Young Bill, what position would you like to have?' I said, 'Yours.' He jumped back, and I laughed. I think he took it personally, and I realized he wasn't someone I could joke with."

I can imagine Dad's jokes being taken the wrong way by store employees, based on his father's intimidating sense of humor. On the odd occasion I thought Grandpa had told a joke, I would look around to see if anyone else in the room was laughing. It was hard to tell what he considered funny.

"I became an Assistant Buyer in Junior Sportswear. Grandpa wrote me a letter congratulating me, or at least his secretary did and he signed it. He always acknowledged everything with a typed letter as I went up through the business, but I came into very little contact with him. After you were born, when I became Executive Vice President and joined the board, I worked more closely with my father."

"Hey, what happened to my potato chips?"

"Sorry, Dad. I changed my mind."

"What kind of an interview is this?"

Bill III and his father William Jr. outside the Thalhimers store in Memphis, TN, 1983.

"I guess I'm just a chip off the old block."

"Ha ha."

"So, I remember sleeping in the bed with Mom a lot when I was little and you were away. Where did you go?"

"When I was a buyer, I traveled a lot. They sent me to the AMC offices in Hong Kong and I went up to New York about once a month. Most of our imports, from Shetland sweaters to basement merchandise, came from Hong Kong. For certain items, we had to travel to Europe to place orders directly with the vendors. Small leather goods like handbags came from Florence, Italy. Silk scarves from the Lake Como area. Aris gloves came from Paris."

"I can't imagine you as a fashion buyer. You've been wearing the same robe since I was in Middle School." Dad laughs, but I'm not kidding. I swear it's the same blue robe.

"The worst purchase I ever made as a handbag buyer was the Adolfo bag, the 'A' bag as they called it. It was a status bag selling like crazy in New York. I bought one hundred of them. Right when we first displayed them, the first little old lady hobbled up to me and said, 'don't you have anything with an R on it? My name starts with an R.' My mother felt so sorry for me that she bought four of them."

"That's hilarious," I laugh, never having heard the story before. "I can imagine Gram doing that."

"I always liked The Store and never wanted to do anything aside from work there, but I wasn't so much into merchandising. It wasn't my strength. Neither was finance. My strength was working with people."

"Did you ever want to run the business?" I ask, unable to imagine Dad as a hard-hitting executive like Grandpa.

"I never aspired to running the store, and I think Grandpa knew that. Water seeks its level. I had no interest in going any farther than I did. I was very happy where I was. Very happy. Are you ready to roll?"

"Sure," I tell him as we get up and walk to the register. "Thanks for the interview," I say in my most professional voice and reach out for a joking handshake. Dad grabs two Peppermint Patties from the jar and places them in my hand instead.

"It's a down-payment for this work you're doing," he says to me.

"Thanks for the advance," I tell him.

The saleswoman rings up our tab and gives Dad the receipt.

"You're not going to believe this," Dad says, handing me the receipt.

The receipt is for exactly $18.42, which we both recognize as the year William Thalhimer founded The Store.

"Serendipity," I tell him, smiling like Irma Marie from Virginia Stern's album.

CHAPTER TWENTY-SEVEN

GROWING UP THALHIMERS
1980 - 1992

Mom dressed Katherine, Christie and me in smocked dresses made by our grand-mother Mimi, shiny black Mary Janes, and woolen coats with velveteen collars to go downtown at Christmastime. During the chilly months, we didn't see Dad as often since it was the busiest time of the year for any retail executive. As Executive Vice President of Stores and Visual Presentation, he worked hard to keep the stores stocked with the right merchandise, keep employees' spirits up, and ensure that goods looked attractive and ready for sale.

Our adventure began when Figgus, a jovial parking attendant, parked our car in the garage at the corner of Grace and Sixth. Then we scurried over to the corral by the garage entrance to pat the noses of the majestic police horses eating hay in their stall. Mary Janes tapping the pavement as our white tights slowly slipped and bunched around our ankles, we paraded across the street like ducklings behind our mother. Shoppers with their Thalhimers and Miller & Rhoads bags lingered to admire the stores' animated Christmas windows. My sisters and I held hands in a chain as we crossed the busy street.

The minute we walked through Thalhimers' big glass entrance doors, breathing in the familiar, flowery smell of the fragrance department, we were showered with attention by smiling salesladies. Many of them knew our names and would pat us on our heads, telling us how much we had grown.

To our delight, we enjoyed munching on chocolate leaf-shaped cookies in the bakery

Snow Bear and (l to r): Katherine, me, Mom and baby
Christie, in Thalhimers' toy department. 1983.

even though we hadn't eaten lunch yet. We took the elevator up to LegoLand and the Toy Department to play for a bit, then continued up to the French Room. While the salesladies brought St. John's knit dresses for Mom to try on, Katherine and I crawled under the racks of wedding gowns to pick up beads and rhinestones that had fallen off so we could string bracelets with them later.

After singing songs and enjoying grits, scrambled eggs, and toast with jam at the Santa and Snow Bear Breakfast, we met Dad in his office on the fifth floor. If he still had work to do, we played with the Snow Bears and other stuffed animals he kept in his closet to entertain us. His secretary Val let us sit at her desk and use her typewriter, which made us feel very grown-up. When Dad was ready, we went to the auditorium to enjoy the magical world of Santaland, with its animated characters, snow-covered décor, and, of course, Santa Claus.

When The Store closed for the day and the security guards were locking up, we ran up the down escalators, providing a particularly rebellious thrill. I imagined myself being Corduroy the Bear, one of my favorite storybook characters, roaming around the department store after all the customers had gone home.

Thalhimers set the scene for much of my childhood, from birth through adolescence. It was where my father, a Men's Furnishings buyer, met my mother, working a brief stint as a salesgirl in the Menswear department after graduating from college. Many salespeople remember watching my sisters and me grow up; they gave us baby gifts, built our swing set, and arrived dressed as Snow Bear and different cartoon characters at our birthday parties. We owned every single piece of Snow Bear merchandise, from pajamas to placemats to dozens of stuffed bears.

In 1989, hundreds of employees cheered when I opened my first charge account before the ribbon-cutting ceremony opening the Colonial Heights' Thalhimers at SouthPark Mall. I loved running my fingers across the raised letters of my name on that rectangular piece of plastic.

My sister Christie modeled in a fashion show, I helped set up promotional displays at store openings, and Katherine and I spent hours in Loss Prevention watching all of the little black and white TVs with the security guards. Once we even helped nab a thief in the hosiery department.

I tagged along with Dad as he drove all over the South from store to store, checking up on management and operations. In preparation for the grand opening of the Charlotte, North Carolina, store, Katherine and I proudly organized a colorful display of plastic soap dispensers, toothbrush holders and cups in the Housewares department. I knew about SKU numbers before I knew what my Social Security number was.

I viewed Thalhimers as the past, present, and future of our family. Following five generations before me, I longed to be part of the next chapter of the story. Unfortunately, it was not to be.

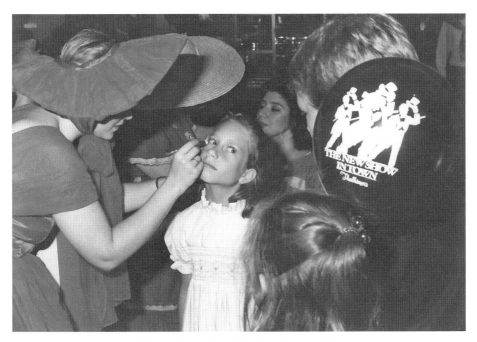

Me, age 8, at opening of the Memphis store, 1983.

Little sister Christie (center), in a fashion show rehearsal. Circa 1990.

Katherine and me at the Charlotte store opening (cousin Stanton in center),1988.

CHAPTER TWENTY-EIGHT

THE TIME IS RIGHT
1977 - 1990

Thalhimers' shoppers spent big money on popular clothing brands of the 1970s, including Polo and Izod for men, Esprit for juniors, and Liz Claiborne, Pendleton, Chaus, and Anne Klein for ladies. New Thalhimers stores opened in malls across Virginia and North Carolina at the rate of roughly one store per year: Petersburg, Norfolk, Raleigh, Durham, Fayetteville, Winston-Salem, Greensboro, High Point. Malls had become ubiquitous as downtown stores saw their customer base steadily shrinking.

Charles and William Jr. continued to make a point of visiting all Virginia locations at least once a week and the North Carolina stores every three months. During the holiday season, they attempted to greet every single one of their fifty-five hundred employees in person. Much to the delight of their staff, the Thalhimer brothers remembered an astonishing number of their employees' names.

Annual Old Timers meetings acknowledged employees with more than ten years service to the company, which included roughly a third of Thalhimers' workforce. Dozens of folks had spent as many as forty to fifty years working for The Store, including Jim Savage, who volunteered as a Christmastime salesman well into his nineties, and Sam Brown, who worked at Thalhimers for sixty years. Some of William Jr.'s happiest moments were at the Old Timer's parties chuckling at the silly songs and skits and leading the chorus of "Hail, Hail, the gang's all here!" just as his grandfather Isaac had done years prior.

When The Store made a staggering four million dollar profit and surpassed one hundred two million in sales, *Women's Wear Daily* announced that Thalhimers had achieved the top earnings percentage of any department store in the country. Overtures to acquire the one hundred thirty-three year old family business came flooding in. William Jr.'s phone rang off the hook. Allied called. Federated, too. Associated Dry Goods put in a bid. Dayton Hudson begged. May Company set up a meeting in New York. Marshall Fields made an attractive offer.

Of all of the offers, William Jr. thought Federated was the best match, but they were involved in litigation with Rich's and couldn't expand any further until they settled the case. It would probably take several years.

Federated's Ralph Lazarus said to William Jr., "Billy, we want Thalhimers in the worst kind of way to come be part of our system, but we don't want to stand in the way of any good opportunity that you may have if the timing isn't right for you."

"Ralph, it's mighty decent of you to call," said William Jr. "In fact, the time isn't right for us. I'm glad you understand."

William Jr. was a merchant, first and foremost, and business acumen coursed like lifeblood through his veins. He trusted his visceral instinct to sell when the time was right. Timing, as he said, was everything.

Over the course of the next year, William Jr. began to notice that ambitious goals similar to those he set for his team in the past were starting to seem unreachable. Discount retailers and "big box" stores continued to attract customers' attention and wallets. And, if Thalhimers remained a family business, who would take the reins? Bill III was coming up through the ranks, but he didn't possess the same fire as his father. Bobby showed no interest in the family business. Barbara and Ellen were women, so it was assumed they would never run the business. Charles' sons, Harry and Charles Jr., were enterprising but too young to gauge as potential leaders.

Then, in 1978, Carter Hawley Hale, a holding company based in Los Angeles, came calling. The venerable lineup of CHH stores included Bergdorf Goodman of New York, Neiman-Marcus of Dallas, Wanamaker's of Philadelphia, Holt Renfrew of Montreal, the Sunset House and The Broadway in Los Angeles, The Emporium in San Francisco, Capwell's in Oakland, Weinstock's in Sacramento, and the national bookseller Waldenbooks. They were collegial, and William Jr. thought their CEO Philip Hawley had the demeanor and drive of an old-school merchant.

CHH proposed a very attractive deal. Mr. Hawley offered a nearly one-to-one Thalhimers-for-CHH stock swap, plus he would allow Thalhimers to maintain their current management team under William Jr.'s leadership. Companies like Allied and Federated would most likely make sweeping management changes and alter The Store's atmosphere altogether.

William Jr. finally felt that the time was right.

On August 14, 1978, Thalhimers' Board of Directors approved a merger with CHH. In his office with its wood-grain wallpaper and worn draperies, William B. Thalhimer Jr. shook hands with Philip M. Hawley, officially ending Thalhimers' chain of family ownership spanning one hundred and thirty-six years. However, William Jr. was not upset. He saw the merger as a new beginning and only wished his father had been in the room when the deal was made.

"We think it's a great day," he told the press. "It's a happy day. I believe it's the most progressive move the company has ever made."

"You have achieved in your forty-five years what most people would think would require two or three lifetimes," Mr. Hawley told William Jr. "Not only have you built a

William Jr. (far right) congratulates President's Cup recipients at the annual "Old Timers" party, 1984.

great business, but more importantly you have done it with dignity, distinction, compassion, and humanity." CHH even invited William Jr. to join their board.

William Jr. beamed with pride, CHH was pleased with its newest acquisition, and Thalhimers' management team, Board of Directors, and employees celebrated. Shareholders benefited handsomely from the deal.

William Jr. continued setting impressive goals for Thalhimers, announcing at a rousing meeting in 1982, "I will apply absolute determination to lead our business to achieve our goal of being the number one department store in CHH on or before the end of the year… I will encourage higher levels of expectation and higher productivity. I WON'T STOP UNTIL WE SUCCEED." His enthusiasm continued, but his energy was waning. William Jr. was nearly seventy years old.

At an Old Timers' party in 1984, with more than a thousand longtime Thalhimers' employees present, Bill III requested, "Dad, will you please come forward." William Jr. approached the podium to stand beside his eldest son. "It is indeed my privilege to stand here with you to make this presentation of your fiftieth year service pin with Thalhimers."

Consistent with his charming personality, Bill III made the crowd smile with lighthearted jokes. "For those of you who know Dad's Richmond Room eating habits, fifty years represents twenty-six hundred bowls of Friday New England Clam Chowder and, figured at three times per week, seventy-eight hundred hearts of lettuce salads with Richmond Room dressing along with twenty-three thousand four-hundred pieces of melba toast *with garlic*." He knew his father's routines and quirks as well as anyone.

"On November 9, 1956, you presented your dad with his fiftieth year pin. Now I present you with yours," said the son to his father. Bill III pinned the golden charm to his father's lapel as the crowd rose to their feet and cheered. If only they could have seen a visual montage of every similar father and son exchange that had occurred in the business up to that point: William turning The Store over to Isaac and his brothers in the 1870s, Isaac welcoming William Sr. into the business, William Jr. presenting his father with his fifty and sixty year service pins, and now, the next generation of Thalhimers. It was a hopeful moment amidst the murky backdrop of an indefinite future.

When William Jr. started out as the Art and Needlework buyer in 1934, Thalhimers reported sales of nearly five million dollars. Fifty years later, in no small way due to his leadership, The Store was doing more than three hundred million in volume.

"We're not the greatest business in the world or the biggest business in the world,"

Bill III presents his father, William Jr., with a gold pin signifying 50 years of service at Thalhimers, 1984.

William Jr. said, "but we're still alive."

Later that year, William Jr. made another momentous decision. It was time for him to step down as President, ushering in Thalhimers' first non-family President, Stewart M. Kasen, as his successor. It too felt like the right decision and the best possible scenario for transitioning away from family leadership.

Mr. Kasen started working at Thalhimers right out of college as a shoe buyer in the Winston-Salem store and worked his way up the corporate ladder over the course of twenty years with the business. Employees, merchants, and customers already knew Mr. Kasen and felt he was already part of the Thalhimers' family. For many years, William Jr. had led the business but provided Mr. Kasen with on-the-job training as he groomed him

William Jr. congratulates his successor, Thalhimers' first non-family President and CEO, Stewart M. Kasen, 1984.

to take over. By the time Mr. Kasen got the title of President, he was already doing the job. William Jr. stayed on as Chairman of the Board and showed up to his office as often as he could, just as his father had done.

It was smooth sailing under CHH until 1984, when Leslie H. Wexner, the founder and chairman of The Limited, recognized CHH as "a sleeping giant" and made his first hostile takeover bid. Two years later, he did it again.

In between Wexner's takeover bids, Charles retired from his position as Vice Chairman after devoting thirty-eight years of service to Thalhimers. His sons Charles Jr. and Harry walked out the front door with their father, telling the press it was an amicable split. The time was right, they had decided, to break free from the family business.

William Jr. and Bill III knew that Charles had been displeased with the recent volatile activity at CHH, but were nonetheless blindsided by his dramatic departure with his sons. It formalized a rift between the families, who – needless to say – would no longer celebrate Thanksgiving together.

Suffering the combined impact of nearly two billion dollars in debt, Wexner's hostile takeover attempts, and an economic recession, CHH began selling off their empire one piece at a time. After spinning off Waldenbooks, Neiman-Marcus, Bergdorf Goodman, Contempo Casuals, Holt Renfrew, and Wanamakers, CHH sold Thalhimers to May Department Stores of St. Louis for three hundred twenty-five million dollars in cash. Thalhimers' sales at the time were nearly half a billion dollars and they were adding an average of one store per year, which had made them one of the crown jewels in CHH's collection of stores.

May, the nation's largest operator of department stores, announced that Thalhimers would keep its name and continue to be headquartered in Richmond. "The stores will have the same merchandise, the same salespeople, and the same general philosophy," said May's president. But things began to change immediately. Many of Thalhimers' departments and services were eliminated, including furs, area rugs, mattresses, shoe repair, the pharmacy, the optical department, and nearly all restaurants. May's preferred vendors replaced the popular brands customers had come to expect, and they changed the Thalhimers' logo and brand identity to match those of other May stores. To its loyal customers and employees, Thalhimers was barely recognizable as its old self.

Nationwide, the shopping scene had changed dramatically from prior decades. Americans no longer wanted to get dressed up and spend a whole day shopping, preferring convenience and low prices over personalized customer service and hand-selected merchandise. After twenty years in business, discount stores including Target, Walmart, and Kmart had grown to be major retail players. Mergers and acquisitions continued to gobble up department store chains and homogenize operations, many stores losing their character and homegrown appeal. Downtowns were dying as the word "sprawl" entered the American lexicon.

"Customers want rock bottom prices and shopping carts, and that's what they're getting," said William Jr.

After Mr. Kasen had left to run CHH's Emporium stores, a rapidfire succession of Thalhimers' CEOs included Mike Weisberg from Weinstock's followed by Robert Rieland, from the bankrupt Miller & Rhoads. When May Company took over in 1990 and put their own people in place, it didn't take a psychic to see that it was the beginning of the end for Thalhimers.

William Jr. announced his retirement in a fifty-two-word press release only days before Christmas in 1990. His retirement made front-page news in Richmond, and the community responded with an outburst of emotion. William Jr. received hundreds of letters from retailers, merchants, and employees from across the country.

O'Bryant "Dick" Ayscue, a Senior Vice President and longtime store employee, wrote, "It is almost impossible to express my appreciation for all you have contributed to the business, its associates, and personally to me. You truly made our job more meaningful by your direction and exemplary principles." Said Mrs. Emmie Waller, an Old Timer from the Credit Union, "Most of all, I thank you for your support over the years. You wrote me thirty-two letters regarding the operation of the Credit Union...I am very proud of them and I have them all in a book."

Asked by a reporter if he had any regrets upon his retirement, William Jr. responded, "I wish I were about forty years younger right now, so I could participate in the future growth of the company."

But, in his heart, he knew it was time to go. The time was right.

CHAPTER TWENTY-NINE

THE WORST VALENTINE'S DAY EVER
1991 - 1992

It's February 14, 1991, and Katherine and I are taking our backpacks off after school when Mom says, "I need to tell you something important. Let's sit down." She sounds serious, and my sister and I look at each other with raised eyebrows, hoping we're not in trouble. The three of us sit down to the dining room table.

"May Company laid-off hundreds of employees today," Mom says, "including Dad. So we need to be extra nice to him. He's had a really hard week."

My head floods with questions, but I can't make words come out. How can this be happening? The May Company promised they wouldn't change things at The Store when they bought it from Carter Hawley Hale. They even said it in the paper. Doesn't a promise mean *anything* to these people?

While we're eating breakfast the next day, we read an article entitled "Last of Thalhimers to leave company." It begins, "William B. Thalhimer III...confirmed today he will leave the company." They make it sound like it was *his* decision to leave Thalhimers after a twenty-five year career, after five generations of a family business, but I know the truth. Those jerks at May Company pushed him out, along with hundreds of other Thalhimers employees. It makes my blood boil.

Only months away from turning sixteen, when I would be old enough to start working at The Store, the business feels like it's crumbling around me. I wanted to be the first female president and prove to Grandpa that a woman can run the show just as well as any man. I'm even taking Economics to fully understand phrases like "return on investment" and "debt to equity ratio."

On Saturday morning, I stomp off to my desk, sit down in the hand-painted blue chair, and pull out the gold cardboard box of my best stationary. Taking out a single sheet of the baby blue paper embossed with ELIZABETH THALHIMER in navy upper-case letters, I tap my pen and wait for the words to come.

My letter to the CEO of May Company goes something like this: "You should be ashamed of your heartless, disrespectful behavior. You are ruining people's dreams and their families and their lives. This is not the way to run a business. You are destroying something more important than you know. Sincerely, Elizabeth Thalhimer."

I lick the envelope shut, slam a stamp on it, and march the letter up the driveway to the mailbox where I throw it in and flip up the red flag like a middle finger. Dad must have watched me from the dining room window because he intercepts the letter before the mailman comes.

With the opened, baby blue envelope in one hand and his other hand resting gently on my shoulder, Dad says, "Sit down, Elizabeth." I flop down in a dining room chair, propping my head on my hands. Dad sits next to me.

"I appreciate your concern," he says, softly but firmly, "But The Store is in different hands now. We can't do anything about it. It's over, sweetie."

I swallow back the tears as he rips my letter in half and throws it into the trashcan in the kitchen.

"I'm sorry, Bibbie," he says as I run off to my room, slamming the door.

That night, I sob hysterically into my pillow, my soul aching for reasons I can't understand. When something you've known and embraced every day of your life disappears, you have to redefine your whole reality – especially when you're only fifteen and thought you had it all figured out.

⚜   ⚜   ⚜

In January of 1992, twenty-six Thalhimers signs across the south disappear from their storefronts, many of them replaced by Hechts signs. Some stores, including the downtown Richmond store, are closed or sold off. The Richmond newspapers and local television channels report stories about the Thalhimers store closing only two years after the bankruptcy of its noble competitor, Miller & Rhoads. It makes me wish I had shopped there, even just once, and heard Eddie Weaver play the organ in the Tea Room.

Uncle Charles establishes a million-dollar United Way emergency fund to provide support for hundreds of Thalhimers' Old Timers fired by the May Company. Even though he and Grandpa aren't on speaking terms, he seems like an awfully nice guy to do such a generous thing. Maybe someday we can patch things up with him and his family. I have Thalhimer cousins living across town that I barely know.

One gray, February afternoon, Mom and Dad announce, "Everybody in the car. We're going to Regency."

Katherine, Christie and I zip up our jackets, all from Thalhimers of course, and pile into the backseat of the station wagon. We pull into a space in the empty parking lot outside the Regency Mall Thalhimers store, a place as familiar as our grandparents' houses, and get out in front of the entrance. Silently, we watch the workmen prepare to tear down the Thalhimers sign. Mom asks one of them if he'll take a picture of us and he says, "sure." Mom, Dad, Katherine, Christie and I force smiles as we pose awkwardly below the Thalhimers sign's last stand, my youngest sister clutching her beloved Snow Bear. She'll probably never remember Thalhimers.

(l to r) Katherine, me, Christie (and her Snow Bear), Dad and Mom outside Regency Mall Thalhimers before they removed the sign. 1992.

The Thalhimers Liquidation.
150 Years Of History Must Go!

Thalhimers is closed. The merchandise is gone. Nothing remains but a gold mine of store fixtures, mannequins, office equipment, display cases, Thalhimers memorabilia, and more. And now it all must go at huge liquidation sale prices.

Richmond Times-Dispatch ad announcing Thalhimers' liquidation. 1992.

CHAPTER THIRTY

DEMOLITION
2004

On the day they begin demolishing The Store, it's Grandpa's ninetieth birthday, but he's far too weak to attend. Assorted members of the Thalhimer family sit on a stage erected in the middle of Broad Street in front of the derelict downtown Thalhimers building. Throngs of children eat cotton candy as they gather around a juggler on a unicycle. Faces in the crowd tilt upwards to see the huge illustration plastered on the aluminum façade depicting the performing arts center to be built in its place.

I can sense Dad's emotions stirring as city government officials and performing arts foundation members pull a velvet sheath to reveal the massive clock that hung above Thalhimers' entrance at the corner of Sixth and Broad Street. The crowd claps as our family accepts the clock as a gift.

The clock looks lonely sitting on the street, its hands still and its pulse no longer ticking. I think of all of the events it has witnessed: the move from Fifth Street with the red rolling cartons, the Toy Parades and giant candlesticks at Christmastime, the Reynolds aluminum panels going up, the Civil Rights boycotts, the crowds gathered for Thalhimers' closing day. I wonder how we'll get the clock home; it's bigger than my car.

Dad said he could never go back to the downtown Thalhimers building after it closed because he didn't want to see it without customers. When I see the clock sitting there on the street corner, I understand what he means. Sometimes it's best to remember things at the peak of their glory.

The Thalhimer family accepts the clock as a gift (l to r): Dad, Mom, Ryan, me, Katherine, John Adamson, Harry and Marcia Thalhimer, Brad Armstrong, Jim Ukrop. 2003. *Ronald Carrington photo.*

I return to The Store about a week later to have one last look. No one in the family accepts the offer to join me, and Ryan says he's too busy to take a break from work.

It's a muggy summer day, and the workman who unlocks the delivery dock door looks puzzled at my request to go inside.

"It's over a hundred and five degrees in there. You sure you wanna go?" he asks.

"I'm sure," I tell him. "I just need to see it one more time."

Growing weary from the heavy heat, I slowly climb five flights of stairs to Dad's office where we used to play with Snow Bear and Val's typewriter. My mouth feels dry but my shirt sticks to my back, drenched with sweat. On the fifth floor landing, right where the old Thalhimers delivery wagon once stood, a large blue plastic tarp blocks the entrance to the executive offices.

"We're removing asbestos," the workman says. "It won't kill you just to walk through, but be quick." He lifts the plastic and I duck under.

Then I see it – the barely recognizable doorway to Dad's office. A few scattered plastic letters remain on an office sign in the hallway, but they don't spell anything. I don't know what I expected, but Dad's office is just an empty cinder-block room with sagging roof tiles, a box of nothingness unworthy of even a photograph.

I turn around and run up two flights of stairs to the roof of The Store, the bewildered workman following close behind. I step over a partially decomposed pigeon, a pile of skeletal remains and sticky feathers, before bursting out the door to the roof for fresh air. The air is heavy and hot, but I gulp it in and look around at Richmond's skyline.

I finally realize that the city will be more beautiful when this building is gone. It no longer has a purpose.

❧   ❧   ❧

Approaching the Medical College of Virginia Hospital where Grandpa awaits a blood transfusion, I stop at the intersection of Broad and Seventh Streets. The Store's windows are shattered or boarded up, and the few that remain have traces of the old checkerboard motif from the bakery. Down the building's side, the outline of the Thalhimers sign is barely visible. A tree grows from the roof on the seventh floor. How can this building possibly support life?

A car honks behind me; the light is green. I accelerate past the decrepit giant and make my way to the hospital.

On the ninth floor, in the elegant comfort of the Gumenick Suites, I find Grandpa's room. It smells sterile and foreign. Grandpa's eyes are closed so I quietly take a seat in the chair next to his bed. The skin on his hands looks almost translucent, exposing a fine network of purplish red veins. His thin grey hair, the hair that Isaac said should be messed up, has been uncharacteristically brushed straight across the top of his head. He doesn't look like himself without his glasses, shiny black wingtips, and gold chain and key dangling from his front belt loop.

He can't die, I think to myself. Grandpa is bigger than death. But I never thought Thalhimers would die, and it's been gone for more than a decade.

I reach out to gently touch his hand and his eyes open.

"Lizaboo," he says in his inimitable, throaty voice. "I'm glad you're here."

"I'm glad you're here too, Grandpa," I tell him.

He returns home from the hospital a few days later, but our interviews get shorter and shorter. Unable to answer the door himself, he sends Gram or one of his live-in nurses instead. He no longer cares if I'm late or wearing something unprofessional. Once I wore flannel pajama pants and he didn't even notice.

Grandpa sits awaiting my visit in his wicker chair on the sun porch, his thin legs wrapped in a blanket my sister Christie made for him. He can't remember if he's eaten lunch or not, but he can recall the most obscure details about The Store.

"Before the Odeon Theatre was torn down," he says, his eyes barely open, "we used the stage for men's alterations. Cleaning and pressing with a steam iron. Sam Brown and a boy named Pettus worked in there. Sam worked for us for more than sixty years."

"Tell me more, Grandpa," I plead, holding his hand until he falls asleep.

A few days after that, Gram, Dad, and Aunt Barbara drive Grandpa downtown to see the demolition. Although he had shown little emotion when May Company announced that the Thalhimers name would change to Hechts, he broke down into sobs when he saw the wrecking ball hit The Store.

"I spent my life building that store," he said. "I just can't watch. It makes me sick. Take me home." So they drove home.

Never again would William Jr. visit the corner of Sixth and Broad Streets in downtown Richmond.

Demolition of downtown Richmond Thalhimers, 2003.

After meeting with my graduate thesis advisor, I drive down Broad Street to see what has become of The Store since the painfully slow demolition began several months prior. I brace myself as I approach the hole in the sky where Thalhimers used to stand. Now it's just a huge sandbox; a whole block's worth of dirt. I continue driving west to Lockgreen, through the guard station, and up the driveway to Gram and Grandpa's house. Gram greets me at the door and takes my coat.

"Come on in," she says, giving me a kiss on the cheek. "Grandpa's not awake yet."

The late afternoon sun droops over the James River beyond the treeline. As Gram and I sit to chat about what's new, I sneak a few sesame sticks from the blue and white ginger jar.

Eventually I ask, "Even though he's asleep, can I go see him?"

"Of course," Gram says.

She leads me back to the master bedroom where Grandpa lies frail and motionless on his bed; his nurse Jo Ann stands beside him stroking his hand.

Grandpa opens his eyes briefly and says, "I don't feel so happy."

Gram turns to me, shaking her head, and whispers, "He says that every day now."

Grasping his other hand, I tell him, "Grandpa, it's me, Lizaboo. I just wanted you to know I'm almost finished writing my thesis about The Store."

He opens his eyes wider and says in his deep voice, "Bring it by. Read it to me."

I return the following week, a few pages in hand, and sit facing him and Gram in the sunroom. Jo Ann rubs Grandpa's legs, which no longer provide his body with sufficient circulation. He grumbles that he's cold and tired and not hungry for dinner. Gram welcomes me warmly and hands me a glass of red wine.

"Happy days," she says, clinking her glass with mine.

"Happy days, Gram."

"I brought an excerpt from my thesis," I tell them nervously after taking a gulp of wine. "Would it be okay for me to read it out loud?"

Grandpa rubs his eyes and looks agitated. Jo Ann leaves the room to allow us some privacy.

"Of course we would," Gram says.

Grandpa grunts "hmpf."

Timidly, I begin reading. After several paragraphs, Grandpa closes his eyes, grunts again, and raises his hand. Fully expecting him to say he's had enough and it's time for me to leave, he says instead, "Read louder."

The words come out loudly but fall gently, accumulating like snowflakes in the stillness between us. Finishing the last sentence, I take a deep breath and lift my head.

Gram smiles broadly, shaking her head.

Grandpa looks me directly in the eye, purses his lips, and says, "Beautiful. Wonderful. Bring me a copy tomorrow."

"Absolutely, Grandpa," I assure him with tears in my eyes. "I will." And I do.

Days later, Gram writes me an email telling me how much Grandpa loves the excerpt. "He reads it every night. It's become his bible," she says gratefully.

Grandpa passes away peacefully in his sleep on the morning of May 28, 2005. A *Richmond Times-Dispatch* editorial poignantly declares, "Billy Thalhimer – diminutive and self-effacing – strode with giants in Richmond and in retailing during the last half of the century past...Billy Thalhimer made his way with grace, charm, an infectious smile, and an overflowing heart. Professionally, he believed in 'honesty, quality, and service' – a credo his stores reflected the moment customers walked in. He lived by that credo in his personal life as well, through magnanimity to countless Richmond causes and philanthropies large and small. This was a gentleman – verily, a gentle man. Now, with his death Saturday at 90, surely Billy Thalhimer is trading stories in re honesty, quality, and service on the loftiest heights of all."

Uncle Bobby and I stand together on the sacred bimah of Temple Beth Ahabah to deliver our eulogies to Grandpa. I can see the light of Isaac's Yahrzeit plaque on the back wall, and William and Mary's stained glass window on the left. Hundreds of faces in the pews, from Thalhimers' shoe salesmen to Mayor Douglas Wilder, blend into a blurry sea as tears cloud my vision midway through my remarks. Uncle Bobby places a reassuring hand on my shoulder. I'm glad I practiced so many times that I can deliver the rest of the eulogy from memory. In my sweaty right palm, I squeeze a perfectly round, smooth stone Uncle Bobby gave me for strength and luck. Grandpa always searched for flawless round stones along the shore of Lake Tahoe, amassing a collection of them in his desk drawer.

After the funeral service, I walk down the empty hallway of the Barbara and William B. Thalhimer, Jr. Religious School, clutching the smooth stone so tightly that my fingernails dig into my palm. Photographs of past confirmation classes line the walls. I find the photograph of my class with Rabbi Spiro, wincing at my ridiculous 1980s bangs and enormous faux-pearl earrings. I find Christie, Katherine, Dad, Grandpa, and scores of cousins and friends in the other confirmation photographs.

Just before the exit, in the very last picture on the wall, a familiar smile catches my eye. It belongs to Irma Marie Thalhimer, leaning nonchalantly on the rabbi's arm at the very center of her class picture. She wears a huge bow in her hair and smiles mischievously, almost as if she knows me. It sends a shiver down the back of my neck.

I look around to make sure no one's watching, then whisper, "Thank you," and gently tap the smooth, circular stone to the glass, seeing my smile reflected in hers.

CHAPTER THIRTY-ONE

FINDING GÖETZ
2006 - 2007

Thumbing through the folders in Dad's grey file cabinet one afternoon, I come across the Göetz Lazarus note that fell out of Virginia Stern's scrapbook that summer ten years ago. I stare at it until it blurs.

"What ever happened to Virginia Stern?" I ask Dad, working at his desk. "Do you have her phone number?"

"Too late," he says, not even looking up from his Mac. "They didn't even call me when she died. She was such a lovely lady. I'm glad you got to meet her."

"Me too," I tell him. "I wish I could thank her."

"You could probably go thank that killer doorman, if he's not in jail," Dad says.

"What did you do with his album?"

"I sent it back to him."

"Dad, that's so weird. Why would he want it back?"

"I don't know. I guess he has a thing for Irma Marie. I made copies of the album before I mailed it back. They're in the closet."

I carry the Göetz paper over to Dad's storage closet, flip on the light, and poke around below the Kermit the Frog sleeping bag and a pink Vinyl box full of beat-up ballet shoes to find the copies of the doorman's album.

Distracted from the task at hand, I lift the lid of an archival box and sift through its perpetually fascinating contents: Isaac Thalhimer's prayer book; Amelia Thalhimer's scrapbook; Wolff Thalheimer's Visa for the Ship Lorena to New Orleans; and finally, a torn, yellowed letter from *Joshua son of Moses in the town of Thairenbach to Wolff Thalheimer in Amerika.*

Even if they couldn't read the writing, each generation of Dad's family has preserved this piece of paper and passed it down gingerly from hand to hand. I'm surprised it was saved at all since the Thalhimer family has a genetic predisposition for throwing things away. We like to keep our desks clean.

For many years, no one even knew what this scrap of a letter said because it's hand-written in Judendeutch script and large pieces of it are missing. In the early 1990s, Dad had Mrs. Windmueller, a German Jewish neighbor and friend from Beth Ahabah, trans-late the still-legible parts into English. He laminated the old letter and the new translation so they won't continue to deteriorate.

Down the side of the letter's translation, in Mrs. Windmueller's handwriting, it says, "Your father died the 27th of April 1844." I glance at Virginia's note in my other hand, which says Göetz Lazarus died April 27th 1844.

Holy bingo. I can't believe I never thought to crosscheck these dates before.

I'm going to find you, Göetz Lazarus. I'm going to prove you were our first Thalhim-er ancestor, just like Virginia Stern said.

⚜   ⚜   ⚜

While juggling grad school, a part-time job at a creative consultancy, and freelance naming projects, I spend my spare moments researching the Thalhimer family and store history. One day, I Google "Thairenbach" and a website pops up. Aha! The reason Dad couldn't find it before is because the spelling has changed to "Tairnbach." It didn't show up on the atlas he found at the Library of Congress years ago because it is a very, very small town.

Modern-day Tairnbach lies nestled in a valley about a half-hour's drive from Heidel-berg. Its population hovers around sixteen hundred people – about the size of my old prep school Collegiate. Photographs show a main street lined by traditional half-timbered Ger-man houses, a small castle in the middle of town called the Schloss, a restaurant that only serves dinner, and a stone church with a hillside cemetery. The bird's-eye photographs of Tairnbach make it seem even more magical and mysterious. I imagine walking down its main street towards the church and leaning down to smell the red and white flowers planted in the barrel outside the Schloss.

I order two books about Tairnbach's history from the town's website and pay extra to have them shipped to the United States. When *250 Jahre Schloss Tairnbach* and *Historische Streiflichter aus Tairnbach* arrive a week later, I sit by the front door and tear open the packaging, reading every word of every page even though I don't speak German.

As my pointer finger traces each line, I pause occasionally as my brain catches up. Halfway through the first book, I find the words "Jüdische" then "synagoge." Then the name "Dahlheimer."

"Holy bingo," I say out loud to Rocky, cocking his head quizzically and flipping his ears backwards. "These are my people."

⚜   ⚜   ⚜

"I'm positive that Tairnbach exists," I practically shout at Dad, frustrated by his cool reception of my dramatic discovery. "I know you think it's gone because it wasn't in that atlas or whatever, but it's *still there*. In a valley. In Germany. Where there were *Dahlheimers*, for Lord's sake. Why don't you want to go there? Aren't you curious? Don't you want to find Göetz?"

"Maybe there are goats grazing there that look like us," Dad says. "If they saw you they'd say 'ba-a-a-ad luck, there are no Tha-a-a-lhimers here.'"

"Dad, don't you get it? Dahlheimer is Thalhimer. Göetz is Gustav. Thairenbach is Tairnbach. *These are our people.*"

"I don't know, Elizabeth. It's a stretch. You get these ideas in your head, like that doorman mailing us a bomb," he says. "Plus, even if you're right, even if we're from there, the Holocaust probably destroyed any evidence of them. You know there aren't any Jews there now. You'd just be disappointed. Why don't you just do more research here? The file cabinet is full of stuff."

"How can I tell our story if I don't know where it begins?" I ask him dramatically, closing my eyes as my head falls into my hands.

As the months pass and we continue going about our busy lives, the topic of Tairnbach does not have time to arise. Occasionally, I think about the German books gathering dust on the bookshelves and wonder if I should hire someone to translate them into English. The name Dahlheimer is bound to be ours.

One day while checking email after work, the familiar glass bell sound dings indicating that I have a new message. I click on it. It's an email from Dad to my two sisters and me that says, "Mom and I are going to Germany for two weeks starting June 10. You are welcome to join us. It's our treat, so just let us know. Love, Dad"

A smug, satisfied smile crosses my lips as I infer the subtext: Dad has changed his mind. He wants to visit Tairnbach after all. He believes me. He wants to find Goëtz.

The glass bell sound dings again. It's an immediate reply from my youngest sister Christie, who is still single, living in Nashville, and always up for an adventure. "I'm totally in," she says.

Our middle sister Katherine declines since she and her husband are busy caring for their two-month-old baby Katie. "Wish we could go," Katherine laments. "Take lots of pictures."

I hesitate in front of a blank email, my fingers hovering above the keyboard. Although I'm obsessed with finding Thalhimers, our recent lives have been consumed with something much more important. Ryan and I are desperately trying to start a family of our own.

Realizing something wasn't right, we started seeing a fertility doctor back in December. Our first two in-vitro fertilization procedures were failures, and seven precious embryos slipped away from us. Covered with bruises from a barrage of daily injections and a sore abdomen from having eggs surgically extracted, I began losing hope as the emotional and physical stress grew almost unbearable. I announced my resignation to my co-workers and gave two months notice to wrap up some projects I was working on.

Our next in-vitro procedure was scheduled for the first of June. If we chose to go on the Germany trip, we would depart nine days after that.

"You know, we could really use a vacation," I say to Ryan over a filet of poached salmon with dill sauce. "Just some time to be together. Maybe in-vitro would work better if we didn't think about it so much. Plus, it's Tairnbach. I mean, when will I ever get this opportunity again?"

Ryan says nothing, but I know he's listening. He wants to have a baby as much as I do, maybe even more. He pokes at the salmon with his fork.

"I only have five vacation days left this year," Ryan says. "And with the procedure a few days before the trip? I just don't know."

"I don't know either. I don't know anything anymore."

We both sip our wine in silence.

"The fresh dill is nice. So much better than the dried stuff," I say in a feeble attempt to ease the tension.

Ryan looks up with a sudden burst of optimism and says, "You know what? I think we should go. Maybe not for the whole two weeks, since I can't get that much time off. Maybe just for a week. We could celebrate our anniversary in Germany."

"But what about flying right after in-vitro?"

He reaches across the table, squeezes my hand, and says, "I think this will be our baby's first trip."

"Our baby," I repeat, squeezing his hand again, my eyes welling up with tears.

Wiping my eyes with my sleeve, I reach over and pick up the kitchen phone to call Dad.

"Hi, Dad. It's Bibbie. We're in."

⚜   ⚜   ⚜

A month before leaving for Germany, I'm sitting at my computer, eating a bowl of Brunswick stew as Rocky snores loudly in my lap. I Google "Gustav Thalheimer," just for fun. Maybe Dad's right. Maybe my ideas about Goëtz are too far-fetched. Maybe I've jumped to easy conclusions. Ever since that evening with Virginia Stern, I've never even bothered to look for "Gustav Thalhimer."

In sifting through the hits that pop up, I find an archival record for a document housed at the Leo Baeck Institute, a New York library specializing in the history of German-speaking American Jews. The record says that this document contains the family tree of a German Jew named "Gustav Thalheimer" from the mid-nineteenth century.

"Oh my gosh," I say outloud, jarring Rocky, who starts barking and automatically

runs toward the front door. Could it be? Could this be our Gustav Thalheimer, errone-
ously known by Virginia Stern as Göetz Lazarus?

Several phone calls later, I realize that no one working in the Leo Baeck library is going to take the time read this document aloud to a frantic stranger. It doesn't help that it's
written entirely in German. I simply must see it with my own eyes.

I call Dad.

"Dad, this document could be the beginning of our story. *I have to know the beginning of our story.* Can't you feel how important this is?" I get impatient, knowing he's
going to tell me to calm down.

"Elizabeth," he says, "Calm down. What happened to Göetz Lazarus? I thought he
was our guy. You get these ideas in your head…"

"I know," I whine back to him childishly. "But maybe I was wrong. It's happened
before."

Then, after a brief silence, Dad says, "Where did you say we have to go again?"

⚜   ⚜   ⚜

Taking off from the Richmond airport a few days later, I watch the ground become
hazy and distant. I hate flying but accept it in exchange for the momentous discovery I
imagine is about to take place.

Walking out of the airport to the cab line, I shiver, remembering how much I dislike
the frigid, colorless days of early spring in New York City. The whole city, minus maybe
Central Park, feels gray and dismal and overly paved. To me, it's nothing like the fresh,
fragrant splendor of Richmond as it emerges from winter.

We get out of the taxi at Union Square and start looking for the Leo Baeck Institute,
our suitcases bumping down the sidewalk behind us. In my haste to leave, I forgot to
write down the address.

After a few blocks, we locate the right building and walk through the metal detectors.
Once upstairs, Dad and I quickly find the correct microfiche tape and pull two chairs up
to a film reader. Dad puts on his glasses and looks more serious than usual.

"Do you think it'll be him?" I ask.

"It'd better be. He's why we're here."

As the microfiche pages zip past on the monitor, my palms start to sweat.

Finally, the name "Gustav Thalheimer" rushes past on the top of the screen. Toggling the wheel, I skip slowly backwards until I see the name again: Gustav Thalheimer. There he is.

"Dad," I say, grabbing his arm. "It's him."

Our eyes scan the German text carefully. The only words I recognize are "Gustav Thalheimer" and "Jüdische." Several pages into the document, there's a family tree. Dad and I turn our heads sideways and strain to read all of the names. As we do, the air feels like it's being sucked out of the room. Not a single name is familiar. This "Gustav Thalheimer" is not ours. He's a character in someone else's story.

Completely deflated, I shrug and act like it's no big deal. I don't want Dad to be disappointed in me. I suddenly realize that he trusts me very much, otherwise he wouldn't have agreed to this impulsive adventure. I hope I haven't jeopardized that trust.

"So, what now?" Dad asks me, handing the microfiche tape to the librarian and leaning on the front desk, looking at his watch.

I pause, gazing past him into the atrium of the two-story Leo Baeck library. Surely there is something else in there for us. Some missing piece we can have the satisfaction of pressing into the puzzle.

"This is a world-renowned Jewish library," I say with false confidence. "We just need to broaden our search parameters. Let's look up the German towns from the family tree starting with Tairnbach."

Invigorated by our new mission, we open a few archival boxes containing information about the towns of Tairnbach, Hagenbach, Leutershausen and Schreisheim. Nothing in the boxes mentions any family names. They mostly contain general information, vital records, and information about synagogues destroyed and Jews killed in the Holocaust. I make photocopies of our findings and put them in a manila folder blandly labeled "Germany Research."

As the clock ticks through the afternoon hours, I decide to apologize to Dad and admit my mistake.

"I'm really sorry I wasn't more thorough in my research before we came," I say, struggling to find the right words. "I thought I was onto something. I guess sometimes I can be impulsive."

"It's ok," says Dad. "Let's just enjoy the day. We're in New York!"

I take a deep breath and smile. I love my Dad.

On a final whim, I suggest that we find an employee named Karen Franklin whom I'd read about online. Once I submitted a genealogical research form to her but never heard back. It's not a great lead, but it gives us something to do before the library closes.

"Is Karen Franklin here?" I ask the librarian at the front desk.

"Karen is unavailable," he says brusquely.

Dad continues to chat up Mr. Unfriendly Librarian as I wander back into the stacks where a young woman on a stepstool re-shelves books from a cart.

"Excuse me," I ask her. "Do you happen to know Karen Franklin?"

"Of course," she says in a German accent, stepping down from the stool.

"Because my Dad and I are here for the day, trying to find our German ancestors, and I think she can help us. Do you know if she's around?"

The young woman smiles and responds, "I'll go look for her. Just wait right here."

Moments later, she returns and says, "Karen will be out shortly. She'll meet you by the information desk."

"Thank you so, so much," I tell her. "You have no idea how much I appreciate it."

"It's really not a problem," she says, returning to her stepstool.

I go back to the desk to tell Dad what's going on. Only minutes before the library is scheduled to close, Karen Franklin emerges to meet us. We exchange niceties, then she, Dad and I sit at a long table beneath a window.

"How can I help you?" she asks.

"We're going to Germany," I tell Karen clumsily, "to visit our hometown."

Dad can tell I'm tired and can't find the right words, so he takes it from there.

"We're going to Heidelberg, specifically to visit the town of Tairnbach. I've been do-ing genealogy on our family for about ten years now, but we haven't found much on our German ancestry. We'd like to know if any information exists on our first ancestor from Tairnbach, known either as Goëtz Lazarus or Gustav Thalheimer."

I'm proud of Dad for mentioning Goëtz. I think we're finally on the same page.

Karen says, "Sure. What, specifically, would be most helpful to you?"

"We need to find someone in the Baden region of Germany who can assist us with our research," I chime in. "Someone who knows their way around archives. Someone who speaks fluent German and English. Preferably someone who knows about German Jews." It's a stretch, but I might as well aim for the best-case scenario.

Without a moment's hesitation, our new friend Karen smiles and says, "Dr. Roland Flade. Tell him I sent you."

As Karen writes Roland's name and email address into my notebook, my eyes shift to the window behind her. It's snowing, which seems odd for April, even in New York.

❖   ❖   ❖

After returning to Richmond the next day, I email Roland in Würzburg, Germany. He writes back almost immediately, saying, "Thanks for your e-mail. I love the kind of work you are asking me to do, so please feel free to send me whatever material you have and to tell me what else you want to know…I can join you during your stay in June: I work as a newspaper editor, but June 14 and June 15 are my days off. We could use those days for visits to archives, your ancestral towns, cemeteries etc. I can get into contact with the relevant people in advance. We can use my car, an old Volkswagen van."

Roland and I email back and forth for the next few weeks, piecing together clues about the early history of the Thalheimer family based on documentation in Dad's file cabinet. I mail him the books about Tairnbach I ordered from the Internet and a pile of other research, including the note about Goëtz.

Roland reads the Tairnbach books and translates the relevant parts. They reveal that Napoleon did, in fact, mandate that all Jews in Tairnbach either adopt or purchase surnames in 1809, and the most common Jewish names adopted in the town were Dahlheimer, a variation of Thalheimer, and Flegenheimer. The town used to have a synagogue but it has long since been torn down and a barn-like house stands in its place. The Judenschulweg, the "synagogue path," still exists.

Sadly, Roland conveys, the books report that the registers of Jewish births, marriages and deaths from the town of Tairnbach have been lost. But he challenges this information, suspecting that maybe no one has ever taken the time to properly search for the records. Roland phones the book's author, Gerhard Höflin.

"To my knowledge, Tairnbach's Jewish records have, in fact, been lost," says the elderly Herr Höflin, Tairnbach's ex-pastor and historian. "But," he says, "as a last resort, you should ask the Catholic priest of Mühlhausen. He has access to the old church records from the area."

Roland phones the priest of Mühlhausen, the town right next to Tairnbach. The priest promises to go through his records when he has time.

The following day, the priest calls Roland back.

"I have found a record mentioning the birth of a daughter to a Göetz Thalheimer in 1814 in Tairnbach," the priest says in German. "I might add that I recently heard a rumor that the other Jewish records of Tairnbach were not in fact lost. They were hidden by the Catholic Church during the Holocaust and are currently housed in the Karlsruhe archives. You might want to check."

When Roland contacts the Karlsruhe archives in search of the "lost" records of Tairnbach, the archivist responds, "How could anyone think these records were lost? I have them right here." There, housed in nearby Karlsruhe all along, are six huge volumes of Tairnbach's Jewish history.

Roland hits the road for Karlsruhe the next day in his Volkswagen van. I am wild with anticipation, checking my Blackberry every few minutes at work. Sure enough, a message from Roland arrives to my inbox. I sneak out of a conference call to read it.

Swiftly scanning the text, my pulse quickens. The Karlsruhe records confirm that Goëtz Lazarus Dahlheimer and his wife Malke lived in Tairnbach with five daughters and one son, Wolff. Goëtz had a brother named Isaak Lazarus Dahlheimer, who lived with his wife and two daughters in Tairnbach. Goëtz and Isaak both took the name Dahlheimer in 1809.

Then comes the biggest surprise of all: Goëtz and Malke's gravestones still stand in the Jewish cemetery of Waibstadt.

The conference call suddenly feels distant and trivial; I don't even remember what it was about. My legs refuse to walk, so I slide my back down the wall and sit on the floor. I read the email again then dial Dad's number.

"Dad," I say, sniffing back tears. "I found him. I found Goëtz Lazarus."

Dad listens as I read Roland's email outloud.

"Congratulations," he says. "I guess we are 'goats' after all."

Then he laughs, and I laugh, sniffing back tears and wiping my nose with my sleeve. Someone leans out of the conference room to see what's going on.

"I just found my people," I say, sitting cross-legged on the floor with mascara-stained cheeks.

Of course Irma Marie Thalhimer was right when she told her daughter Virginia that Goëtz Lazarus was the first Thalhimer. Of course she knew. He was her great-grandfather.

※　　※　　※

An excerpt from my diary:

June 14, 2006. 8:30am. Heidelberg, Germany. Today we go to Tairn-bach. I am so excited to finally set foot on the ground where my ancestors walked. I'm a little nervous for some reason. I want something special to happen. I know that's a big expectation, but the poetic side of me wants to write about some sort of coincidence. A sign. If you want a sign, will it come?

※　　※　　※

In the lobby of our hotel, I approach an attractive, middle-aged man with grayish hair and glasses standing by the front stairs.

"Roland?" I ask hesitantly.

"Yes," he says. "Elizabeth?"

"I am. It's so nice to finally meet you."

"I expected you to be much older," Roland says as he shakes my hand. "People your age aren't usually interested in their ancestry."

"I guess I should have described myself," I laugh. "I'm thirty years old, five feet tall, and look younger than I am."

"Yes, I see that now!"

After a round of introductions, Mom, Dad, my sister Christie, Ryan and I follow Roland into the blinding morning sunlight and pile into his un-air-conditioned Volkswagen van. Leaving the busy streets of Heidelberg behind, we meander through the hazy German countryside, lush with grapevines, asparagus fields, and apple trees. The rolling hills and fields with hay bales remind me of the familiar drive through the Virginia piedmont on our way to the Blue Ridge Mountains. While Mom and Dad chat with Roland, I lean my head back as the sun warms my face, cooled only slightly by the breeze from a small window.

After driving for an hour or so, we enter the tiny hamlet of Tairnbach. Roland parks the van across the street from a stately yellow building and turns off the ignition.

I squeeze Ryan's hand.

"We're here," he whispers.

"I'm so excited," I tell him. "I can't believe this. I'm nervous."

"Don't be," he says. "Just enjoy it."

Roland takes my hand to help me out of the van as I look around, absorbing every detail. Nothing seems very modern aside from a few cars and the occasional television satellite dish clamped to a patio railing or fence. About twenty buildings, mostly homes, line the quiet main street. A picturesque stone church with a clock tower sits at the top of the lane, literally on the edge of town. On my left, I recognize the wooden barrel planter full of red and white flowers from the Tairnbach website.

Two smiling men walk towards us, their right hands outstretched to greet us with handshakes.

"Welcome!" says the first man, a portly, affable-looking fellow. The second man is elderly and thin, but not frail.

Roland says, "This is Rüdiger Egenlauf, Tairnbach's supervisor, and this is Gerhard Höflin, the author of the history books about Tairnbach. I contacted them in advance to tell them you were coming."

"Welcome to Tairnbach! We are so pleased you are here," the men say, treating us like foreign dignitaries. I photograph them shaking hands with Dad, which reminds me of the Thalhimers' openings I attended as a child.

Egenlauf and Höflin welcome us into the Schloss and we all take seats around a big conference table with pitchers of water. It feels like we're about to call a board meeting to order. Herr Egenlauf stands, clears his throat, and, in German, gives us a brief history of the Schloss, where Tairnbach's nobility once lived. He pauses after each sentence so Roland can translate into English for us.

Upon finishing his presentation, Herr Egenlauf ceremoniously presents Dad with a stained glass sculpture of the town's coat-of-arms with blue, green and gold grapes, symbolizing the town's winemaking history. Herr Höflin presents me with his newest volume on the history of Tairnbach.

"Danke schoen," I say to him, nodding my head and saying a silent prayer of thanks to Wayne Newton. Aside from "Jüdische" and "synagoge," it's the only German I know.

My mother smiles and graciously gives both gentlemen coffee table books about Richmond and Virginia, spiral notebooks with the Thalhimers store depicted on the cover, and personalized copies of *Our Snow Bear Scrapbook: Memories and Recipes from Thalhimers.* The men look confused but grateful for these unusual gifts from their American visitors.

Reiterating how happy we are to be in Tairnbach, Roland translates our statements as we explain why we have come to visit. Herr Höflin responds that, to his knowledge, only one other Jewish family has visited the town seeking their roots.

Heading outside into the increasingly hot morning, we walk uphill to the opposite end of town, which takes the better part of five minutes. A weathered-looking man with a long face and unusually large ears spots us, a herd of strangers accompanied by the town's supervisor and ex-pastor, headed up the hill past his house.

He hears us speaking English and rightly assumes that we are American. Walking towards us, he shouts, "Hello, friends! I am Ewald Filsinger. I have relatives in American."

Each of us introduces ourselves to him and shakes his hand, complimenting him on his attractive home. Roland steps aside to have a brief conversation with Herr Filsinger in German, then turns back to us and says, "Herr Filsinger wants you to know that his wine cellar was built in 1605. He has invited us to step inside and see it."

Herr Filsinger opens the wooden door to the cellar, and one at a time we walk down into the cool underground room. As I step down the sagging stairs, it occurs to me that they are almost twice as old as our country.

Filsinger explains slowly, "I am the seventh generation of Filsingers to live in Tairnbach. We make our own wine." He walks to the corner of the cellar and picks up several green bottles, naturally chilled from the coolness of the stone room. He offers them to Dad and says, "Please take this wine. It is from my family to your family. My house to your house. A special gift for you from Tairnbach."

"Danke," Dad says to him, shaking his hand. Then, like the quintessential American tourists, we gather around and smile and take pictures with Herr Filsinger and our green wine bottles. As we do, I imagine that the subtext to our chance meeting runs much

Ewald Filsinger's wine cellar, Tairnbach, Germany. (l to r): Rüdiger Egenlauf, Mom, Christie, Gerhard Höflin, me, Ryan, Roland Flade, Herr Filsinger. 2006.

deeper. His ancestors knew ours, I think to myself. In such a small town there's no way they didn't, even if separated by religious differences and laws.

Ryan whispers to me, "Herr Filsinger looks like Grandpa," and I wonder if somehow we could be cousins.

Saying goodbye to Herr Filsinger, our little tour group walks diagonally across the street to the church and cemetery overlooking the town of Tairnbach. The church was built in 1823, so Göetz and his family must have walked past it many times.

Standing at the edge of the cemetery, gazing over the rooftops of the old houses towards more modern houses in the distance, I inhale deeply. The warm air is sweet with the scent of the flowering white vines encircling the cemetery. A summer haze surrounds us and falls like a veil over the town.

Christie walks over and grabs my hand. "I'm so glad you found this place," she says. "It feels like Virginia here, you know?"

And it does, except that we are most likely some of the only Jews to have ever set foot in this cemetery. Our relatives couldn't be buried here in this picturesque resting place where lovely, manicured gardens grow atop the gravesites. Jews like the Thalheimers had to be buried far away in the town of Waibstadt, miles away from home. Jewish burials might be allowed there today except that Tairnbach hasn't had a single Jewish resident for over a hundred years. They left long ago, decades before the Holocaust, and never returned.

Thinking aloud, I ask Herr Höflin, "So why aren't there any Jews living here today?"

He replies with an honest curtness, "Would you want to come back and live here as a Jew?"

Despite the town's quaint charm, my silent answer is "no."

We leave the cemetery and walk in the opposite direction down the lane. Having made our way to the other side of town within minutes, we arrive at the last house before a clearing on the edge of a forest. The house is built in the traditional German half-timbered style. In the front yard, there's an old water pump and a rectangular fountain where water from the underground Tairnbächl stream flows. I put my hand under the faucet, feeling the water's coolness.

Roland says, "This may have been what your ancestors' first home looked like. It's the right age and the right size – much smaller than the others. It is now two stories tall, but it would have been only one story during their time."

This modest half-timbered house and garden paint as romantic a picture as any I could have invented. It feels hauntingly familiar, like an early childhood memory or a déjà vu. Is it possible to remember something you've never seen? I want to stand and stare longer to see if there are any ghosts, but the rest of the group has already moved on.

Following Herr Egenlauf, we weave back down the main street to an alleyway. There, a tiny bridge arches over weeds and dirt instead of the stream that once flowed beneath it. Beside the bridge stands a sign that reads "Judenschulweg." Town records roughly indicate that Göetz and Malke's one-story home once stood beside this path, but there's nothing there now aside from trashcans, a pile of firewood, and a chain-link fence.

Nearby stands a primitive, barn-like stone building, which Roland says was built on the site of the old synagogue in the 1880s. The synagogue was torn down so the stones could be used to build a cigar factory, also long gone. Herr Höflin says that the elderly woman currently living in the barn-house remembers her father telling her it used to be a synagogue. What did she think about that story, I wonder? Are Jews like unicorns to the people of this town, something you hear stories about but never see?

Each of us takes a few steps down the very short Judenschulweg. We stop for several touristy pictures huddled together in front of the path, walking down the path, behind the path, and looking back at the path.

Then I turn around and walk it again alone.

Here the little shoes of William Thalhimer – called Wolff at the time – and his sisters paddled off to school and back home. I can imagine the sounds of their footsteps, pitter-pattering down the path.

Mom, Dad and Christie walk ahead of me and disappear around the corner of a stucco house. Ryan waits as I bend down to pick up three stones.

"I'm keeping this one," I tell him. "This one's for Emily. And this one's going to Hebrew Cemetery. William needs to know we were here."

Up on the hillside of the Fluhr Eben overlooking Tairnbach, we visit a plot of land once owned by Isaak Thalheimer, Goëtz' brother. It was probably the first land our family ever owned. I pick a couple stems of wheatgrass, and Dad and I pose for a picture.

"I'm so glad we did this, Dad," I tell him.

"Me too," he says, giving me a kiss on the cheek.

After stopping for lunch in a neighboring town, we climb back into the oppressive heat of Roland's van and drive a short distance to the town of Waibstadt. We stop at the local town hall to pick up a secretary named Anni Wagenblass, who told Roland she has a map of the Jewish cemetery and can help us find the gravestones of Goëtz and Malke Thalheimer. Anni speaks very little English.

Our windows rolled all the way down with the midday sun blazing, we follow Anni's car into the shadows of a thick forest. We weave our way down a winding gravel road through the woods until we arrive at a mausoleum. Our caravan stops in a clearing, where we get out and climb the stairs into the strange building.

Built by a wealthy Jewish citizen by the name of Weil, the mausoleum is modeled after a mosque in Jerusalem. Its interior mostly desecrated by the Nazis, the ceiling remains lined with resplendent blue and gold mosaic stones shimmering in the form of a night sky. Ryan finds a golf ball on the floor and puts it in his pocket. A few candles lay about along with some empty beer bottles, and a small bird chirps and flits around above us. I am surprised the mausoleum exists at all, but equally surprised that no one seems to be taking care of it.

We follow Anni down a small trail leading to a vast, wooded cemetery of more than a thousand gravestones overgrown with foliage and vines. Although some stones look recent, they date back to 1940 at the very latest.

Anni tells Roland something in German, then he turns to us and says, "Look for plot numbers 3-0-3 and 4-4-2. The numbers should be etched on the backs of the gravestones.

Waibstadt Cemetery in Germany, 2006.

The headstone of Goëtz also has the carving of a flower symbol."

Brushing aside the ivy and leaves, I find plot numbers etched on the backs of a few. Most of the numbers have rubbed off entirely from the elements and the passage of time. Some graves bear the etched flower symbol.

We shuffle through the underbrush, sometimes in pairs and sometimes alone, up and down the lines of gravestones. Sunlight beams through the canopy of trees as sweat drips down the back of my neck. Increasingly disillusioned and dizzy, I squint to scan row after row for the magic numbers. Feeling like I might pass out, I squeeze my eyes shut, hoping that I'll open them to see the lucky numbers or flower symbol.

Since our arrival at the Waibstadt cemetery, I've been squeezing ten stones from Hebrew Cemetery in my hands. I had hoped to put five stones, representing the family members who have come to visit, on Goëtz and Malke's gravestones. Suddenly, one of the stones slips from my sweaty grip and gets lost in the thick foliage at my feet. I curse, shuffling the leaves and vines at my feet to find it, then give up and look up at the gravestone in front of me. At the top, it has a carving of a flower. I run around and look at the other side – all Hebrew. Then I notice the vague outline of a number carved into the stone. Is it 303? Maybe. It could also be 202. Or 505. Or 282. Or 838. My mind plays tricks on me.

"Hey, y'all," I shout into the woods. "Come here. I think I've found something."

Mom, Dad, Christie, Ryan, Roland and Anni shuffle through the woods from every direction and gather around the stone, trying to make out the numbers and decipher the German and Hebrew epitaph.

We all look to Roland for his evaluation. Silence. Crouching down, he takes a moment to read and analyze the etchings, his finger running over the stone.

"The flower symbol is right," he says, "but this is not the right stone. It's for someone of a different town." My heart sinks when he says, "I think we'll have to come back another day."

We don't have another day, I think to myself. *This is our day.*

As Mom, Dad, and Anni give up on the search and head back towards the van, I turn to Christie, still standing next to me. Ryan and Roland continue to wander around the nearby graves, taking a final look around.

"This grave belongs to someone, even if it's not one of our people," I tell Christie. "I think we should say a prayer or something."

"Me, too. Let's just have a moment of silence." She holds my hand and we close our eyes.

Gripping my youngest sister's hand, I think about the thousands of Jews laid to rest in this eerie, sun-dappled cemetery full of ivy and ticks and vines and scorching heat. Whether their families survived the Holocaust or not, whether they have descendents or not, whether they are related to me by blood or not, they are all my people. I squeeze Christie's hand tighter, opening my eyes, and she nods her head. Without talking, I give her a stone from Hebrew Cemetery, and she places it on top of the unidentified grave. Ryan holds a piece of rice paper against the epitaph so I can do a charcoal rubbing to take back home as a souvenir.

"It's like honoring the unknown soldier," says Roland. "It is symbolic."

"It seems like the right thing to do," I concede.

Trudging silently back through the woods, I wipe streams of sweat from my forehead with the sleeve of my shirt. As Roland closes and latches the cemetery gate, I place the remaining stones from Hebrew Cemetery on one of its posts. Waiting until Roland walks away, I touch the stones and whisper, "Goodbye, Goëtz and Malke. I know you're in there."

Back at the van, I thank Anni as graciously as I can and give her a hardbound book about Richmond. I later confess to my parents that I didn't want to give Anni anything, but Mom said it was the proper thing to do. After all, she had taken time off work to wander around a Jewish cemetery with strangers on a hot day.

Exhausted and emotionally drained, I rest my head on Ryan's shoulder as Roland drives us back through Waibstadt, past the asparagus fields and vineyards, and drops us off at our hotel in Heidelberg.

⚜   ⚜   ⚜

Whether by coincidence or divine intervention, I received the sign I had asked for in my diary on the morning of June 14, 2006, the day we visited Tairnbach. A pregnancy test Ryan bought from the local pharmacy revealed that I was "schwanger." With the aid of a dictionary, we realized this amusing German word meant we were finally expecting a baby. As Ryan held me tightly in his arms, I could hardly believe the timing of this extraordinary news. Timing is everything.

"Danke schoen, Goëtz and Malke," I whispered into my pillow that night in Heidelberg, rubbing my belly.

⚜   ⚜   ⚜

Five months later, balancing my computer on my huge and still-growing belly, the glass bell dings indicating an incoming email. I'm shocked to see that the email is from Anni Wagenblass back in Waibstadt. She writes, "Dear family Thalhimer Smartt, I write this letter in English, but you know that my English is not so good. First I thank you for your nice letter – I was glad of it. The book from Richmond is very interesting – thank you for it. Now I found a person who can help me to find the graves you searched when you were at the cemetery. He has a plan from the cemetery. I told it also Dr. Flade. I will make photos and send you also the inscriptions from the gravestones. So you can give it to someone who can translate it for you and you see that this are the right graves from the family Thalheimer. Good luck and warm regards from Anni Wagenblass."

Upon receiving this email, Roland drives several hours to the Waibstadt cemetery and locates the final resting places of Goëtz and Malke Thalheimer. As it turns out, we hadn't been far off the first time around. Their graves stand quite close to the random one where Christie and I held hands and offered our silent prayers.

Roland photographs the gravesites from every angle, rubs charcoal across rice paper to copy the epitaphs, and, unable to find any loose stones nearby, gathers two bags of dirt. He places five stones each on Goëtz and Malke's headstones, representing Mom, Dad, Christie, Ryan and me. He seals the photographs, charcoal rubbings, and bags of dirt into an overnight shipping package and mails it across the sea to me.

On the morning of my thirty-first birthday, Dad shows up at the front door and says, "Does the birthday girl have a lunch date?"

"I'd love to have lunch," I tell him, picking up the package from the front table and holding it up. "But look what we got from Roland. We have to go visit William first." Dad knows exactly what I mean.

"Well, let's go."

Dad hoists me up into the Suburban and we drive straight to Hebrew Cemetery. Ever protective of his unborn grandchild, he holds my arm as I wobble up the cemetery hill to William Thalhimer's grave.

"Here, Dad," I say, handing him my camera. "You take a picture of me pouring dirt on William's grave, then I'll do the same for you."

As I scatter the dirt from Goëtz and Malke's graves atop their only son's resting place, I can't help but think that they are all there with me. Like stars forming a constellation, I imagine lines connecting all of us across time and space – Goëtz, Malke, William, Mary, Isaac, Amelia, William Sr., Annette, Gram, Grandpa, Dad, me, my unborn baby. Are we part of a story that's already been written or are we the ones writing it? It's not an original question, but it's the first time the question has ever really seemed relevant to me.

"You know," I say, tracing the carved lettering of William Thalhimer's name with my finger, "as weird as it is to be pregnant and dumping bags of German dirt in a cemetery, I think this is the best birthday I've ever had."

"Happy birthday, Bibbie," Dad says to me, taking my arm in his. "I think they would be as proud of you as I am."

Dad and I take turns pouring dirt from Goëtz and Malke Thalheimer's gravesites on William Thalhimer's grave in Hebrew Cemetery, Richmond, VA, 2006.

Me holding baby Lyla in front of the portrait of her great-great-great-great grandfather, William Thalhimer, 2007.

Chapter Thirty-Two

Malka Lilah bat Elisheva
2007

Lyla's first cries are the sweetest, most exquisite sounds I have ever heard, nothing like the frantic wails of babies born in movies. Hearing our daughter's voice for the first time, Ryan and I look at each other with tear-filled eyes. Suddenly, we are parents, and we are elated.

After celebrating her birth with the family, all gathered at St. Mary's Hospital, I call Emily and ask if she will be Lyla's godmother. "I'd be honored," she says. "Now you're really part of our family," I tell her, and think about how much William Thalhimer would have appreciated the significance of this gesture. Now Emily can share William's story with Lyla, her goddaughter.

On a resplendent spring day, the yard of our yellow cottage bursting with camellias and azaleas, Lyla's grandparents, great-grandparents, aunts, uncles, and cousins gather around our living room. We call Christie by speakerphone, since she still lives in Nashville, and leave the receiver on the mantel.

Holding Lyla in my arms, I stand next to Ryan and Rabbi Beifield from Temple Beth Ahabah. Lyla's eyes stay open long enough to pose for a few pictures then flutter shut as she falls into an uncharacteristically blissful sleep. On most days she fusses in the afternoons, and I had worried she would cry through the whole ceremony.

Ryan and I light the candles on the mantel as we say a prayer together, then each relative reads a blessing at the Rabbi's cue. The poignant simplicity of their prescribed words makes me wish I had written them: "Fortunate the woman who knows the pangs of birth, for she has held a star. Fortunate the man who fathers a child, for he has held eternity in his arms. Hidden in birth and death and in gentle voices of loved ones lies the harmony of existence."

Then, in hushed voices, we join together in reciting that most holy and familiar of Jewish prayers, the Shema. Even my mother, raised Methodist, knows its words by heart.

Rabbi Beifield blesses our daughter with the Hebrew name we have chosen for her: Malka Lilah bat Elisheva. We chose Malka in memory of Malke Thalheimer, the first known woman in my father's family. Lilah bat Elisheva means Lyla, daughter of Elizabeth. I like the graceful cadence of the name as I whisper it into Lyla's ear then kiss her gently on the forehead.

With the Rabbi's blessing, Ryan and I pop the cork and pour Herr Filsinger's wine from Tairnbach into William Thalhimer's sterling silver Kiddush cup. Our fingers intertwined around the stem of the cup, we read the closing words of the ceremony together, "May Lyla's life know security and trust, May Lyla's life shine with dignity and freedom, May Lyla's life know the creative harmony of peace."

We wish these blessings upon our baby girl just as Malke and Goëtz once wished them upon baby Wolff. I hope Lyla will understand that these are not things to be taken for granted. They are hard-won opportunities we have inherited from our ancestors.

As the coolness of my great-great-great grandfather's sterling cup presses against my lips and the German wine sweeps deliciously across my tongue, Ryan squeezes my hand. I hand him the cup and he takes a sip. Together we gaze down at Malka Lilah bat Elisheva, bathed in a beam of sunlight and sleeping peacefully. A huge framed photograph of the downtown Thalhimers store hangs on the wall to our right, its glass reflecting the whole family gathered around its newest member.

I've often wondered how I could possibly honor the extraordinary legacy my paternal ancestors left behind, but watching Lyla's tiny chest rise and fall with each breath, I finally know. I'm the one who's supposed to tell their story.

Dementi Studios, 1955

We have always believed that a store should be part of the lives and hopes, part of the growth and future of the people who share its fortunes. For that reason we have always endeavored to contribute more than our function of supplying goods and services.

We have built, and we intend to keep on building, a store that will make the vast area we serve a better place in which to live by our earnest effort to add to the pleasures, the accomplishments, the cultural achievements, the education, the higher standards of living of every person who crosses our threshold.

Thalhimers

ACKNOWLEDGEMENTS

First, my most heartfelt thanks go to my husband Ryan for his tireless patience and overwhelming support as I've worked on this project for the entirety of our relationship. My daughter Lyla has been patient with Mommy as well; when I recently overheard her telling her babysitter, "Mommy is writing a book for me," it nearly melted my heart! Gracious thanks to my parents, Billy and Sallie Thalhimer, for everything they've done for me throughout my life. I'd especially like to thank Dad for sparking my interest in studying Thalhimers and his side of the family many years ago. His meticulous and painstaking genealogy research laid the groundwork for this project, and I couldn't have done it without him.

All of my friends and family, including Mimi and Pop Brush, Katherine and John Adamson, Christie Thalhimer, Jerry (my very first editor!) and Dan Smartt, Jeremy and Sara Smartt, and Jason and Jamie Smartt, have supported and tolerated me throughout this long process. A special thanks to Aunt Lisa and Uncle Bobby Thalhimer for editing early drafts of the book and providing much-needed advice and words of encouragement along the way. I never expected to lose Aunt Lisa, one of my biggest cheerleaders, during the writing of this book; I miss her incredibly, but know she's smiling down on me from the highest heaven. I also didn't expect to lose Rocky, my furry companion, rest his soul.

So many researchers and writers provided significant help, including Emily Rusk, whose careful research on the Thalhimers story continues to amaze me; Alexandra Levit, who skillfully guided me through early drafts of my thesis before it grew into a book; Bob Gillette, whose recent research on Hyde Farmlands will soon result in his own book; and Karen Franklin at Leo Baeck Institute, who led me to Roland Flade, the expert genealogist and journalist without whom our trip to Germany would have been just a vacation.

Grandpa said that he put together the best possible team to run his business, and that's what I attempted to do with this book. I am ever-grateful to my magnificent "book team" of Wayne Dementi, whose photography skills, publishing prowess, and fatherly guidance ushered this book into being; Jayne Hushen, who stayed up until all hours of the night designing page layouts; Noah Scalin of Another Limited Rebellion for the übercool book cover; and editor Erin Niumata, an extraordinary editor with a talent for multitasking in times of personal chaos.

To Charlotte Morgan and all of the Nimrod Hall writer women (especially Jenny Block and Denny Stein): thanks to each of you for your edits, suggestions, late night conversations over wine, and writerly inspiration. I only recently realized that the "healing baths" we go to in Bath County every summer are the same ones that my great-great-great-grandmother once visited in the 1800s. What an opportune place to have written significant portions of this book.

Many thanks to Charles G. Thalhimer, Rev. Leroy Bray, Elizabeth "Betty" Bauder, Elizabeth "Big E" Johnson Rice, Dr. Allix B. James, the late Aline Thalhimer Livingstone Williams, Hans George Hirsch, the late Ernst Cramer, George Landecker, and Kenneth Gassman for their personal interviews. I'd also like to thank my four thesis committee members at Virginia Commonwealth University: Dr. Catherine Ingrassia, Dr. James Kinney, Dr. Elizabeth Hodges, and Dr. John Kneebone. Without their guidance, I wouldn't have had the confidence to grow my thesis, just a seedling of this story, into a full-fledged book.

Dad's, Emily's and my research would not have been possible without the help of staff members at the Virginia Historical Society, Beth Ahabah Museum and Archives, *Richmond Times-Dispatch*, Valentine Richmond History Center, Dementi Studios, Library of Virginia, James Branch Cabell Library at VCU, Baker Library at Harvard Business School, The Leo Baeck Institute, and the John F. Kennedy Presidential Library and Museum.

Thanks to Virginia Stern, although she never had any idea of the impact she had on my life; Elizabeth Jamerson for her early research with Dad; Gerhard Höflin for his scholarship on Tairnbach; and the late Otti Windmueller for translating all of our Judendeutch and German documents into English.

Many thanks to Mr. John Stewart Bryan III for such a lovely foreword. Our families maintained a symbiotic business relationship as well as personal friendships through the generations. Additional thanks to Shane Harris and Lisa Tracy for their kind endorsements.

Finally, I am ever grateful to Gram and Grandpa Thalhimer. In so many respects, they are the reason why this project exists. Gram taught each of us to choose optimism, to live in the moment and for the moment, to share good fortune with others, and that we can't spoil our children with too much love. Grandpa taught me to live within my means, never spend my principal, keep a clean desk, and commit myself wholeheartedly to building my own success. Writing this book gave me a special chance to say goodbye to both of them and honor their contributions to our community, our store, and our family. Thanksgiving will never be the same without them, but at least I have the privilege of this final opportunity to express my everlasting gratitude. I love you, Gram and Grandpa.

Elizabeth Thalhimer Smartt

1   Flade, Dr. Roland. "The Thalheimer Family of Tairnbach." Würzburg, Germany. 4 June 2006.

2   Lange, Johann Gottfried. "The Changed Name or the Shoemaker in the Old and the New World: Thirty Years in Europe and Thirty years in America" Original journal entries written in German. Richmond, Virginia. 1844. Translated into English by Ida S. Windmueller. Virginia Historical Society Manuscripts Collection. p. 61.

3   ibid.

4   Oral history tells that William Thalhimer traveled with Kaufmann, Rosenstock and Stern, who went on to found department stores bearing their names in Pittsburgh, Petersberg, and New York respectively. These stores, however, were started much later than 1842. Surely there is some truth to the oral history, especially since it was passed down through several lines of the Thalhimer family.

5   Again, this story is based on oral tradition. It also appears in a letter written by Morton G. Thalhimer Sr.

6   Muhlhauser, Mariane. Letter to her parents Akiva and Meiline Heller Muhlhauser in Hagenbach, Germany. 3 Oct 1841.

7   Kethubah of William Thalhimer and Mary Milheiser. 9 Sept 1845. Beth Ahabah Museum & Archives. Richmond, VA.

8   The name Gustavus continues to be passed through the Morton G. Thalhimer family, who operated movie theaters and sold real estate in the state of Virginia in the latter part of the 1900s. The middle initial "G" stands for Gustavus.

9   Virginia. Vol. 44 p. 226. R.G. Dun & Co. Collection. Baker Library Historical Collections. Harvard Business School.

10 Advertisement in *Richmonder Anzeiger*. 25 Aug 1855.

11 Gutmann, Joseph and Stanley F. Chyet, eds. *Moses Jacob Ezekiel: Memoirs from the Baths of Diocletian*. Wayne State University Press, Detroit: 1975.

12 Lange, Johann Gottfried. "The Changed Name or the Shoemaker in the Old and the New World: Thirty Years in Europe and Thirty years in America" Original journal entries written in German. Richmond, Virginia. 1844. Translated into English by Ida S. Windmueller. Virginia Historical Society Manuscripts Collection.

13 Virginia. Vol. 44 p. 304. R.G. Dun & Co. Collection. Baker Library Historical Collections. Harvard Business School.

14 Whitlock, Philip. "The Life of Philip Whitlock, Written by Himself." Beth Ahabah Museum and Archives Trust. Richmond, VA.

15 Advertisement. "J. Millhiser & Bro. at 193 Broad Street." *Richmond Daily Dispatch*. 12 May 1862.

16 Boyd's Directory of Richmond. 1869. Listings for William, Gus, and Charles Thalhimer at 1519 E. Main and 315 E. Broad.

17 Virginia. Vol. 44 p. 201. R.G. Dun & Co. Collection. Baker Library Historical Collections. Harvard Business School.

18 *Richmond Daily Dispatch*. 4 Jan 1870. p2, c5.

19 Lange, Johann Gottfried. "The Changed Name or the Shoemaker in the Old and the New World: Thirty Years in Europe and Thirty years in America" Original journal entries written in German. Richmond, Virginia. 1844. Translated into English by Ida S. Windmueller. Virginia Historical Society Manuscripts Collection.

20 U.S. District Court, Eastern District of Virginia, Richmond Division, Bankruptcy Act of 1867 involuntary case file #186: Paton v. Thalhimer. Feb 1873 - Apr 1874.

21 Virginia. Vol. 45 p. 141. R.G. Dun & Co. Collection. Baker Library Historical Collections. Harvard Business School.

22 J.R.K. "Mr. Thalhimer" (Letter to the Editor). *Richmond Daily Dispatch*. 25 March 1883.

23 Thalhimer, William. "Death of This Old and Prominent Merchant and Leading Citizen of Israelitish Faith." *Richmond Daily Dispatch*. 25 Mar 1882.

24   "William B. Thalhimer is Admitted to Firm." Unknown print date and publication. In private collection of William B. Thalhimer III.

25   Rathbone, Patricia. " 'Dean of Merchants' Recalls Early Days in Virginia Capital." *Richmond Times-Dispatch*. 22 Sept 1929.

26   "Isaac Thalhimer's Birthday" editorial. *Richmond Times-Dispatch*. 19 Feb 1925.

27   Jennings, H.L.D. "A Romance of Richmond and Richmond Business." *Richmond Magazine*. Nov 1929. p. 25 and 32.

28   Freeman, Douglas S. "Isaac Thalhimer" (Editorial) Richmond News Leader. 3 Nov 1930.

29   Ashe, Arthur and Arnold Rampersad. *Days of Grace: A Memoir*. New York: Alfred A. Knopf, 1993. p.180.

30   Angress, Werner. "Auswandererlehrgut Gross-Breesen." Yearbook 10. London: Leo Baeck Institute, 1965. p. 179.

31   "Rumors about Thalhimers." *Richmond News Leader*. 21 Sept 1938.

32   Hall, Larry. "Woman's stand brought businesses to their knees." *Richmond Times-Dispatch*. 1 Feb 2006.

33   Kennedy, President John F. to William B. Thalhimer, Jr. Western Union Telegram. 29 May 1963.

34   Knight, Rev. H.G. "Presentation Speech to Mr. William B. Thalhimer, Jr. on Race Relations Sunday." 21 Feb 1965. Private collection of William B. Thalhimer III.

35   *Womens' Wear Daily*. 2 Nov 1967. p.1.

"Passenger lists of vessels arriving at New Orleans, 1820-1945; index to passenger lists of vessels arriving in New Orleans, 1853-1952." National Archives microcopy T527, T618, M259, and T905. NARA record group M259. LDS film # 200150, 1 Jul 1840 - 20 Oct 1841.

"5-Story Drop Kills Veteran Woman Clerk." *Richmond Times-Dispatch*. 5 June 1943.

"92 Years of Thalhimer Store's Progress Here Directed by 3 Generations of Family: Record for Intra-family Control in State; Few Firms in Nation Older." *Richmond Times-Dispatch*. 29 April 1934.

"A Father's Awful Revenge: J.E. Wimmer, A Blacksmith, Stabs Young S. G. Thalhimer to Death." *Richmond Times*. 8 Sept 1896.

"After Eighty-Three Years" (Editorial). *Richmond News Leader*. 18 Feb 1925.

"Arrest of a Skillful Robber." *Richmond Daily Dispatch*. 1 July 1868.

"Basic Programs Initiated During Past 22 Years and/or Concluded by William B. Thalhimer, Jr." Undated. Private collection of William B. Thalhimer III.

"Bathrobe Cord is Used as Means of Suicide; Louis Thalheimer [sic] Hangs Self on Hotel Room Door." *Richmond Times-Dispatch*. 11 June 1931.

"Brotherhood Week: William B. Thalhimer Jr. Honored." *Richmond News Leader*. 22 Feb 1965.

"Building up Background." 7 Nov 1931. Publication unknown. Private collection of William B. Thalhimer III.

"Closing Shop: Retail giant shuts his register." *Richmond News Leader*. Metro Business section B-18. 17 Dec 1990.

"Counterfeiting." *Richmond Daily Dispatch*. 31 Oct 1861.

"Dear Book" No. XVIII. Congregation Beth Ahabah. President's report by Isaac Thalhimer. 12 Sept 1926.

"Federated Completes Merger with May Company." Federated Department Stores, Inc. – May 30 Aug. 2005. 22 Oct. 2005 <http://www.federated-fds.com/ir/maymerger/template/pressrelease.asp?item_id=750420>.

"FINDS SOUTH RECOVERING. Better Feeling Among People There, William Thalhimer Declares." *The New York Times*. 12 May 1935.

"Fined." *Richmond Daily Dispatch*. 20 July 1854.

"Gathered to His Fathers – A Merited Tribute of Respect." *Richmond Daily Dispatch*. 25 Mar 1883.

"Il Capo del Cerimoniale Diplomatico della Repubblica." Order of merit ("Cavaliere Ufficiale") bestowed by President Saragat of the Italian Republic upon William B. Thalhimer Jr. for Thalhimers' "Bravissima Italia" promotional celebration in 1964. 22 Jan 1968. Private collection of William B. Thalhimer III.

"In Memoriam" (obituary for Mary Millhiser Thalhimer). *Richmond Dispatch*. 15 Jan 1876.

"Isaac Thalhimer's Birthday Brings Gathering of Friends to his Store: Has Won Warm Place in Employes' Hearts." *Richmond News Leader*. 18 Feb 1925.

"Isaac Thalhimer's Birthday"(editorial). *Richmond Times-Dispatch*. 19 Feb 1925.

"Jewish Worship from Richmond's Foundation." *Richmond News Leader* (Saturday supplement). 19 Jan 1901.

"JFK Sales Pitch is Successful." *The Washington Daily News*. 5 June 1963.

"Modern Humanitarianism in the 'Old Dominion'." *Department Store Buyer*. Vol. 1 No. 6. April 1939.

"No. 3 Div. of Jackson Hospital, bot of W.Thalhimer "(Receipt). Richmond. 20 June 1864. Private collection of William B. Thalhimer III.

"J. Millhiser & Bro. at 193 Broad street"(Notice). *Richmond Daily Dispatch*. 28 Nov 1860.

"Prelude." A poem written for Isaac by his children and grandchildren on the occasion of his 70th birthday, 1925. Private collection of Charles Williams, son of Aline Thalhimer Livingstone Williams.

"Races: The Inexorable Process." *TIME Magazine*. Vol 81 No 24. 14 June 1963.

"Racial Foes of '61 Embrace at a Ceremony in Richmond." *The New York Times*. 21 Feb 1965.

"Radio Free Europe's Aims Told." *Richmond News Leader*. 1 April 1963.

"Ran a Slot Machine." *Richmond Dispatch*. 5 Oct 1902.

"Re: Thalhimers History Outline and Slides." Memo to Betty Bauder from L. Bruce. 19 Jan 1981. Private collection of William B. Thalhimer III.

"Retail Stores." *Richmond Daily Dispatch*. 29 Jun 1858.

"Rumors about Thalhimers." *Richmond News Leader*. 21 Sept 1938.

"Some Hit and Miss Chat; Stray Bits of Gossip from an Observer's Notebook. Stories of A.T. Stewart and the Oldtime Dry Goods Business Recalled by the Death of H. B. Claflin." *The New York Times*. 29 Nov 1885.

"Strange Affair." *Richmond Daily Dispatch*. 19 July 1854.

"Thalhimer Bros. chairman will step down." *Richmond News Leader*. 1 Dec 1990.

"Thalhimer Fined for Running Gambling Game." *Richmond News*. 29 Oct 1902.

"Thalhimer Share Offering Is Made by Underwriter." *The New York Times*. 16 June 1966.

"Thalhimer, Jr., New President of Thalhimer's." *Women's Wear Daily*. 12 Dec 1950.

"Thalhimer's Has Business Study." *Richmond Times-Dispatch*. 1 Feb 1926.

"Thalhimers Store Closing Confirmed." *Richmond Times-Dispatch*. 31 Jan 1980.

"Thalhimers Welcomes You." Richmond, VA: Thalhimer Brothers, 1956. Private collection of William B. Thalhimer III.

"The Management of a Family Enterprise." 17 June 1968. Private collection of William B. Thalhimer III.

"The Nation." *TIME Magazine*. 14 June 1963.

"The Race Crisis: Coming to a head." *Business Week*. No. 1762. 8 June 1963.

"Three Thalhimers Quit Family Firm." *Richmond Times-Dispatch*. 24 Dec 1985.

"William B. Thalhimer Jr." (Editorial). *Richmond Times-Dispatch*. 29 May 2005.

"William B. Thalhimer, Jr." (Editorial). *Richmond Times-Dispatch*. 1 June 2005.

"William B. Thalhimer." (Editorial). *Richmond Times-Dispatch*. 3 Dec 1969.

"Woman Dies in Fall in 6th St.; Miss Esther Thalhimer is Instantly Killed in Drop from Roof." *Richmond News Leader*. 27 Mar 1930.

1860 Richmond City Business Directory. Civil War Richmond website. http://www.mdgorman.com.

Adelson, Andrea. "COMPANY NEWS; Retirement Set at Carter Hawley Hale." *The New York Times*. 10 Oct 1992.

Advertisement (in German) for "William Thalheimer's Dry Good and Clothing Store." *Richmonder Anzeiger*. 25 Aug. 1855.

Advertisement for "Thalhimers Fall Fashion Show." *Richmond Times-Dispatch*. 22 Sept 1935.

Advertisement for Thalhimer Brothers. *Richmond Dispatch*. 2 Jan 1883.

Advertisement for Thalhimer Brothers. *Richmond Dispatch*. 26 Apr 1883.

Advertisements for Thalhimer Brothers. *Richmond Dispatch*. 1884 - 1903.

Advertisement for Thalhimer Brothers. *Richmond News Leader*. 3 Nov 1930.

Andrews, Robert M. "Here at Maymont: Ground Broken for Wildlife Refuge." *Richmond Times-Dispatch*. 5 June 1958.

Angress, Werner T. "Auswandererlehrgut Gross-Breesen." *Yearbook 10*. New London: Leo Baeck Institute. 1965.

Angress, Werner T. *Between Fear and Hope*. New York: Columbia University Press, 1988.

Appel, Joseph H. *The Business Biography of John Wanamaker: Founder and Builder*. New York: Macmillan, 1930.

Ashe, Arthur and Arnold Rampersad. *Days of Grace: A Memoir*. New York: Alfred A. Knopf, 1993.

Auditor of Public Accounts, Personal Property Tax Lists, Richmond City, 1836-50 (microfilm). Library of Virginia. Richmond, VA.

Ayres, B. Drummond Jr. "Unlike Most of the Country, Richmond is Thriving." *The New York Times*. 12 Jan 1975.

Ayscue, O'Brient R. "Dick." Personal letter to William B. Thalhimer III in memory of William B. Thalhimer Jr. 25 May, 2005.

Baker, Henry Givens. *Rich's of Atlanta: The Story of a Store Since 1867*. Atlanta: University of Georgia School of Business Administration, 1953.

Barker, John H. Jr. Email to the author. 13 Nov. 2002.

Barmash, Isadore. "All About Retailers; Down the Scale With the Major Store Chains." *The New York Times*. 2 Feb 1992.

Barmash, Isadore. "Big Retail Chain In South Will Use Bank Credit Cards." *The New York Times*. 4 Jan 1973.

Barmash, Isadore. "Carter Hawley Bid By Limited." *The New York Times*. 3 Apr 1984.

Barmash, Isadore. "COMPANY NEWS; Carter Hawley to Sell Thalhimer's" *The New York Times*. 10 Oct 1990.

Barth, Gunther. "The Department Store." *City People: The Rise of Modern City Culture in Nineteenth-Century America*. New York: Oxford University Press, 1980.

Bauder, Elizabeth B. Interviews with the author. Oct. 2002.

Benson, Susan Porter. *Counter Culture: Saleswomen, Managers and Customers in American Department Stores, 1890-1940*. Urbana, IL: University of Illinois Press, 1988.

Bien, William. "Thalhimer Sets Hard-driving Example." *Richmond News Leader*. 22 Feb 1954.

Birmingham, Nan Tillson. *Store*. New York: Putnam, 1978.

Blatt, Warren. "Jewish Given Names in Eastern Europe and the U.S." *Avotaynu*. Vol. XIV, No. 3. Fall 1998.

Boyd's Directory of Richmond City. Richmond: West and Johnston, 1869.

Bray, Leroy. Interview with the author. Richmond, Virginia. 30 July 2004.

Brown, Aubrey Neblett Jr. Papers. 1944-1995. Series 2: Richmond Sit Ins 1960. Virginia Historical Society Manuscripts Collection.

Bryant, James. *Department Store Disease*. Toronto: McClelland and Stewart, 1977.

Bryson, George and Earle Dunford. *Under the Clock: The Story of Miller & Rhoads*. Charleston, SC: The History Press, 2008.

Burge, Michael. "Descendant fights to regain piece of family archive." Quoting Severin Hochberg, Senior Historian at the United States Holocaust Memorial Museum. *The San Diego Union-Tribune*. 22 Jan 2007.

Carter Hawley Hale annual report. 1982. Private collection of William B. Thalhimer III.

Chaney, David. "The Department Store as a Cultural Form." *Theory, Culture and Society*. Vol. 1 No. 3. London: Sage Publications, 1983.

Auditor of Public Accounts. License Returns. Richmond City. 1842, 1843, 1844, 1845, 1846, 1847, 1848, 1849. Library of Virginia.

Congregation Beth Shalome Marriage Register. Congregation Beth Ahabah, Richmond, VA Collection. MS 298. Jacob Rader Marcus Center of the American Jewish Archives, Cincinnati Campus, Hebrew Union College Jewish Institute of Religion.

Covington, Howard E. Jr. *Belk: A Century of Retail Leadership*. Chapel Hill: U of North Carolina Press, 1988.

Cramer, Ernst. Letter to the author. 3 Jun 2008. Private collection of Elizabeth Thalhimer Smartt.

Cuff, Daniel F. "BUSINESS PEOPLE; Chairman of Thalhimers Is Named by May Stores." *The New York Times*. 21 Dec 1990.

Cutchins, John A. *Memories of Old Richmond (1881-1944)*. Verona, Virginia: McClure Printing Co., 1974.

Doherty, Jim. *In Praise of Givers*. Self published. 2005.

Doubman, J. Russell and John R. Whitaker. *The Organization and Operation of Department Stores*. New York: John Wiley & Sons, 1927.

Downtown Richmond Memories. Narr. Charley McDowell and Harvey Hudson. Writ. Judith Warrington. Prod. Paul Roberts. PBS/WCVW Richmond. Mar 2002.

Dunford, Earle. *Richmond Times-Dispatch: The Story of a Newspaper*. Richmond, VA: Cadmus Publishing, 1995.

Ellyson, H.K. *Ellyson's Business Directory and Almanac for the year 1845*. Richmond, VA: Ellyson. 1844.

Ezekiel, Herbert T. and Gaston Lichtenstein. *The History of the Jews of Richmond from 1769 to 1917*. Richmond, Virginia: Herbert T. Ezekiel, 1917.

Ferry, John William. *A History of the Department Store*. New York: Macmillan, 1960.

Flade, Dr. Roland. "Thalheimer Report #2." Würzburg, Germany. 7 Sept 2006.

Flade, Dr. Roland. "The Jewish Congregation of Hagenbach." Würzburg, Germany. Undated and unpublished.

Flade, Dr. Roland. "The Thalheimer Family of Tairnbach." Würzburg, Germany. 4 June 2006.

Flegenheimer, William. "BIOGRAPHY OF WILLIAM FLEGENHEIMER: A short biography of his family and relatives written by himself November 1905." Private collection of William B. Thalhimer III.

Freeman, Douglas S. "Isaac Thalhimer" (Editorial) Richmond News Leader. 3 Nov 1930.

Gatins, Joseph. "Stockholders Approve Merger by Thalhimers." *Richmond Times-Dispatch*. 15 Aug 1978.

Gilligan, Gregory J. "Retailer's Ex-workers to Reunite: Thalhimers 'Family' Missed Camaraderie." *Richmond Times-Dispatch*. 1 May 1993.

Goodman, David H. "A Mishpocheh of Yid." Jan 1972. Beth Ahabah Museum & Archives. Richmond, VA.

Groner, Alex, ed., *The American Heritage History of American Business and Industry*. New York: American Heritage, 1972.

Grossman, Robert. "Saving Souls." *The Richmond Jewish News*. 6 Feb 1998.

Gutmann, Joseph and Stanley F. Chyet, eds. *Moses Jacob Ezekiel: Memoirs from the Baths of Diocletian*. Wayne State University Press, Detroit: 1975.

Hall, Larry. "Woman's stand brought businesses to their knees." *Richmond Times-Dispatch*. 1 Feb 2006.

Hallman, Randy. "Closing Shop: Retail giant shuts his register." *Richmond News Leader*. 17 Dec. 1990.

Hallman, Randy. "May Co. plans to buy Thalhimers store chain." *Richmond News Leader*. 9 Oct 1990.

Harris, Leon. *Merchant Princes: An Intimate History of Jewish Families Who Built Great Department Stores*. New York: Harper & Row, 1979.

Hawley, Philip M. to William B. Thalhimer Jr. Letter written 23 Mar 1979.

Heinze, Andrew R. *Adapting to Abundance: Jewish Immigrants, Mass Consumption, and the Search for American Identity*. New York: Columbia UP, 1990.

Held, Louis I. Jr. *Held Family History: From Antiquity to the Generation of Irving I. Held*. 1990. Virginia Historical Society Manuscripts Collection.

Hendrickson, Robert. *The Grand Emporiums: The Illustrated History of America's Great Department Stores*. New York: Stein and Day, 1979.

Herring, Mary Pollard Darracott and Alferd Sumner Winston III, ed. *My Silent Friend: A Church Hill Journal 1882-1884*. Westminster, MD: Willow Bend Books, 2003.

Höflin, Gerhard. *Historische Streiflichter aus Tairnbach*. Heimatbuch, Vol 1, Mühlhausen, 1995.

Höflin, Gerhard. *Historische Streiflichter aus Tairnbach*. Heimatbuch, Vol 2, Mühlhausen, 2005

Holmberg, Mark. "Will council agree it's 'put-up or shut-up time' for center?" *Richmond Times-Dispatch*. 22 May 2005.

Hower, Ralph M. *History of Macy's of New York 1858-1919*. Cambridge, Massachusetts: Harvard UP, 1946.

Hutzler, Charles. Personal 34-page letter to Isaac, Charles, Gus and Moses Thalhimer. 15 Aug 1883. Private collection of William B. Thalhimer III.

Hyde Farmlands brochure. 1938. Beth Ahabah Museum & Archives. Richmond, VA.

Iarocci, Louisa M. "Spaces of Desire: The Department Store in America." (Dissertation). Boston University, 2003.

J.R.K. "Mr. Thalhimer" (Letter to the editor). *Richmond Daily Dispatch*. 25 March 1883.

Jackson, Estelle. "Thalhimers: The Memories Come Rushing to Mind." *Richmond Times-Dispatch*. 24 Nov 1991.

Jacob, Charles Richmond. "I remember Mr. Ike." Essay written for William B. Thalhimer III. Private collection of William B. Thalhimer III.

James, Dr. Allix. Interview with the author. Richmond, Virginia. 28 Oct. 2005.

Jennings, H.L.D. "A Romance of Richmond and Richmond Business." *Richmond Magazine*. Nov 1929.

John F. Kennedy White House Central Files; White House Subject File Box 365; Human Rights; HU 2/MC – Executive. Proposed press release on meeting with business leaders plus guest list. John F. Kennedy Presidential Library and Museum. Boston, MA.

John F. Kennedy White House Staff Files: Lee C. White Box 23; Civil Rights File, 1961 - 1963, undated: Meeting with the President, Miscellaneous, 1963: 5 June 5 - 19 June : Suggested Schedule and Notes for Civil Rights Meeting, May 21, 1963. John F. Kennedy Presidential Library and Museum. Boston, MA.

Kaplan, Marion A. ed. *Jewish Daily Life in Germany: 1618-1945*. New York: Oxford University Press, 2005.

Kelley, Jeffrey G. "A 'bittersweet' end: Downtown makes room for planned performing-arts center." *Richmond Times-Dispatch*. 13 June 2004.

Kennedy, Pres. John F. to William B. Thalhimer, Jr. Western Union Telefax. 29 May1963. Private collection of William B. Thalhimer III.

Kennedy, Robert F. to William B. Thalhimer, Jr. Western Union Telegram. 28 May 1963. Private collection of William B. Thalhimer III.

Kethubah of Abraham Smith and Henrietta Thalheimer. Beth Ahabah Museum & Archives. Richmond, VA.

Kethubah of William Thalhimer and Mary Milheiser. 9 Sept 1845. Beth Ahabah Museum & Archives. Richmond, VA.

Kimball, Gregg D. *American City, Southern Place: A Cultural History of Antebellum Richmond*. Athens, GA: University of Georgia Press, 2000.

Knight, Rev. H.G. "Presentation Speech to Mr. William B. Thalhimer, Jr. on Race Relations Sunday." 21 Feb 1965. Private collection of William B. Thalhimer III.

Kollatz, Harry Jr. "Stones Against Forgetting." *Richmond Magazine*. May 1999.

Koshetz, Herbert. "Thalhimer to Buy Norfolk Building" *The New York Times*. 27 Dec 1975.

Lanahan, Rosemary. "FEATURES." *Women's Wear Daily*. 2 Nov 1967.

Lancaster, William. *The Department Store: A Social History*. London: Leicester UP, 1995.

Lange, Johann Gottfried. "The Changed Name or the Shoemaker in the Old and the New World: Thirty Years in Europe and Thirty years in America" Original journal entries written in German. Richmond, Virginia. 1844. Translated into English by Ida S. Windmueller. Virginia Historical Society Manuscripts Collection.

Leach, William. *Land of Desire: Merchants, Power, and the Rise of a New American Culture*. New York: Pantheon, 1993.

Leeser, Isaac ed. *The Occident and American Jewish Advocate*. Vol VII, No. 7. October 1849.

Livingstone, Emma and Sally Cox. "Thalhimers' Soup Bar 'Liberated' by Women." *Richmond Times-Dispatch*. 27 Aug 1970.

Mahoney, Tom and Leonard Sloane. *The Great Merchants: America's Foremost Retail Institutions and the People Who Made Them Great*. New York: Harper & Row, 1966.

Marcus, Jacob Rader. *Memoirs of American Jews 1775-1865, Volume Two*. Philadelphia: The Jewish Publication Society of America, 1955.

May, Irving. Letter to William B. Thalhimer Jr. 8 Sep 1934. Private collection of William B. Thalhimer III.

Mayfield, Frank M. *The Department Store Story*. New York: Fairchild Publications, 1949.

Mayhew, Melanie. "A bittersweet farewell: New era set to begin as Thalhimers demolition gets under way." *Richmond Times-Dispatch*. 24 Oct 2004.

McAllister, Jane M. *Thalhimers: A Family, A Tradition, A Business*. Unpublished. 1988. Private collection of Elizabeth Thalhimer Smartt.

McCown, Virginia. "Thalhimer's List: Saved from the Nazis, Holocaust." *The News Journal* (Amelia, Virginia). Vol 5, No 1. Dec 1997.

Michael, Sherwood. Speech written on the occasion of William B. Thalhimer Jr.'s 80th birthday. June 1994.

Millhiser, Claire. *Universal and Particular Obligations*. Richmond, VA: Beth Ahabah Museum and Archives Trust, 1988.

Millhiser, Mary. Letter to her parents in Hagenbach sent from Trieste, Italy. 3 Oct 1841. Private collection of William B. Thalhimer III.

Mordecai, Emma. Personal journal. 1864-1865. Virginia Historical Society.

Mordecai, Samuel. *Virginia, Especially Richmond, in By-Gone Days*. 2nd ed. Richmond, VA: West and Johnston, 1860.

Munford, William Tayloe. *Fond Memories*. Richmond, VA: Dietz Press, 1992.

Munford, William Tayloe. "Thalhimers' Centurama." *Display World*. March 1942.

Mutual Assurance Society of Virginia Papers. Declarations and Revaluations of Assurance, 1796-1867. Library of Virginia. Richmond, VA.

NCR advertisement. *TIME Magazine*. 1967. Private collection of William B. Thalhimer III.

"New Orleans, Louisiana." *Encyclopedia of Southern Jewish Communities*. The Goldring/Woldenberg Institute of Southern Jewish Life. www.isjl.org/history/archive/la/new_orleans.htm

November, Neil. "I Remember When…" *Richmond Times-Dispatch*. 1 May 1949.

O'Neil, Paul. "A Little Gift from Your Friendly Banker." *LIFE Magazine*. 27 March 1970.

Pasdermadjian, H. *The Department Store: Its Origins, Evolution and Economics*. London: Newman Books, 1954.

Personal correspondence between William B. Thalhimer Jr. and Webster S. Rhoads, Jr. 1953-1967. Private collection of William B. Thalhimer III.

Phillips, Wanda L. Email to the author. 20 Nov 2002.

Pittman, Ray. "Leader of Flight from Nazis to Revisit Germany." *Richmond Times-Dispatch*. 16 June 1948.

Powers, William Dudley. "A Family Sketch for Thomas Underwood Dudley." Flint, MI, 1904. Unpublished essay written for his cousin. Virginia Historical Society Manuscript Collection.

Price, Kimball W. Sr. "Thalhimers Cloverleaf Store Case Study." *Production/Operations Management: Concepts and Situations*. ed. Roger W. Schmenner. New York: Macmillan, 1990.

Quarles, Anne Winston. Letter to her brother. Richmond, VA. 27 Apr 1865. Courtesy of Kent Bennett.

Randolph, Lewis A. and Gayle T. Tate. *Rights for a Season: The Politics of Race, Class, and Gender in Richmond. Virginia*. Knoxville, TN: University of Tennessee Press, 2003.

Rathbone, Patricia. " 'Dean of Merchants' Recalls Early Days in Virginia Capital." *Richmond Times-Dispatch*. 22 Sept 1929.

Reilly, Philip J. *Old Masters of Retailing*. New York: Fairchild Publications, 1966.

Rice, Elizabeth Johnson. Interviews with the author in-person, by phone, and by email. 2004-2009.

Richmond City, Hustings Court Deed Books, 1840-60 (microfilm). Library of Virginia. Richmond, VA.

Richmond City, Hustings Court Will Books, 1840-60 (microfilm). Library of Virginia. Richmond, VA.

Richmond History Vertical Files. Valentine Richmond History Center. Richmond, VA.

Richmond Jewish Community Council award presentation speech to William B. Thalhimer Sr. Undated. Private collection of William B. Thalhimer III.

Rorrer, Mollie. "William Thalhimer Jr. retires as 26-store chain's chairman: Executive wins praise as leader." *Richmond Times-Dispatch*. 1 Dec 1990.

Rosenthal, Berthold. "The Genealogical Table of the Children of Loesermann Mayer of Seeheim." 1952. Berthold Rosenthal Family Collection. AR 25248. Leo Baeck Institute.

Row, Steve. "Former Thalhimers chairman saddened at end of 'institution'." *Richmond News Leader*. 12 Nov 1991.

Sauder, Rick. "Bobb Lashes May Co. for Heartless Decision." *Richmond News Leader*. 12 Nov 1991.

Sibley, Celestine. *Dear Store: An Affectionate Portrait of Rich's*. Atlanta: Peachtree, 1967.

Silas Omohundro Business and Estate Records, Richmond 1842-1882. Library of Virginia. Richmond, VA.

Sinclair, Melissa Scott. "Thalhimers Treasures Unearthed." *Style Weekly*. 28 Sept. 2005.

Slipek, Edward Jr. "Life During Wartime." *Style Weekly*. 26 June 2002.

Slipek, Edwin Jr. "William B. Thalhimer Jr., 1914-2005." *Style Weekly*. 8 June 2005.

TBI Talks (employee newsletter). William B. Thalhimer, Jr. Corporate and Family Archives: 1862-1992. Virginia Historical Society Manuscripts Collection.

Thalheimer, Carola. Personal letter to William B. Thalhimer Sr. 2 Aug 1938. Private collection of William B. Thalhimer III.

Thalheimer, Wolff. Passport documents. Germany, 1840. Private collection of William B. Thalhimer III.

Thalhimer Brothers, Inc. Accounting Ledgers: 1924-1946. Private collection of William B. Thalhimer III.

Thalhimer, Barbara. Email to the author. 17 Nov 2009.

Thalhimer, Charles G. Sr. Interviews with the author. 2007-2009.

Thalhimer, Elizabeth. *Our Snow Bear Scrapbook: Memories and Recipes from Thalhimers*. Richmond, Virginia: Dietz Press, 2000.

Thalhimer, Isaac to Amelia Blum. Personal correspondence. April 1877. Private collection of William B. Thalhimer III.

Thalhimer, Jacob. "A Biography of My Mother Mary Thalhimer." 12 Jan. 1933. Private collection of William B. Thalhimer III.

Thalhimer, Jacob. "Copy of the Biography of William Thalhimer written by his son, Jacob, and presented by him to his Nephew William B. Thalhimer." 5 Dec 1930. New York. Private collection of William B. Thalhimer III.

Thalhimer, Morton G. to Dr. Stanley F. Chyet, American Jewish Archives. Personal letter. 4 May 1973. Private collection of William B. Thalhimer III.

Thalhimer, Robert L. Interviews with the author. By phone, 31 July 2009, and by email.

Thalhimer, William B. III. Interviews with the author. 1997-2009.

Thalhimer, William B. Jr. "Satisfy ALL your customers." *Piece Goods Merchandiser*. Sept-Nov 1960.

Thalhimer, William B. Jr. "The Thalhimer Story as of April 1976 updated to October 1978." Presented by William B. Thalhimer Jr. to AMC store principals at The Greenbrier resort. Apr 1976. Private collection of William B. Thalhimer III.

Thalhimer, William B. Jr. Cassette tape of interview. Interviewer unknown (possibly a *Richmond Times-Dispatch* or News Leader reporter). Thalhimers executives Betty Bauder and Marion Horseley also present. 26 Feb. 1986. Private collection of Elizabeth Thalhimer Smartt.

Thalhimer, William B. Jr. Corporate and Family Archives: 1862-1992. Virginia Historical Society.

Thalhimer, William B. Jr. Correspondence regarding serving as Virginia State Chairman for Radio Free Europe. 1963-71. Private collection of William B. Thalhimer III.

Thalhimer, William B. Jr. Interviews with the author. 1997-2005.

Thalhimer, William B. Jr. to his children and grandchildren. Personal letter. 5 Jan 1979. Private collection of William B. Thalhimer Jr.

Thalhimer, William B. Jr. to Isaac Thalhimer. Letter written in 1930. Private collection of William B. Thalhimer III.

Thalhimer, William B. Sr. "Vocational Column." Tabasco. Vol. 11, no. 3. 14 June 1927.

Thalhimer, William B. Sr. Resume. 13 Oct 1954. Private collection of William B. Thalhimer III.

Thalhimer, William B. Sr. Speech delivered on occasion of portrait unveiling. 1942. Private collection of William B. Thalhimer III.

Thalhimer, William B. Sr. to Annette Goldsmith. Personal correspondence. 1912-1915.

Thalhimer, William B. Sr. to Philip J. Reilly. Letter and essay about Thalhimers' history. 27 July 1959. Private collection of William B. Thalhimer III.

Thalhimer, William B. Sr. to William B. Thalhimer Jr. Letter written 15 Sept 1954. Private collection of William B. Thalhimer III.

Thalhimer, William B. Sr. to William B. Thalhimer Jr. Letter written 5 May 1965. Private collection of William B. Thalhimer III.

Thalhimer, William. "Death of This Old and Prominent Merchant and Leading Citizen of Israelitish Faith." *Richmond Daily Dispatch*. 25 Mar 1882.

The City Intelligencer, or, Stranger's Guide by V. & C. Richmond, VA: Macfarlane & Fergusson, 1862. Library of Virginia.

The Richmond Virginian. 15 Apr. 1917.

The Southern Bank. Shinplaster for 10 cents in Dry Goods, Clothing, Shoes & c. Signed W. Thalhimer President and G. Thalhimer Cashier. Richmond, VA. 25 Mar 1862. Private collection of William B. Thalhimer III.

Thomas, Louise. "Whatever Happened to the Grand Emporiums?" Unpublished, undated essay. Private collection of William B. Thalhimer III.

Traub, Marvin and Tom Teicholz. *Like No Other Store…The Bloomingdale's Legend and the Revolution in American Marketing.* New York: Times Books, 1993.

Twitchell, James B. *Lead Us Into Temptation: The Triumph of American Materialism.* New York: Columbia UP, 1999.

Tyler-McGraw, Marie. *At the Falls: Richmond, Virginia, and Its People.* Chapel Hill, NC: University of North Carolina Press, 1994.

U.S. Bureau of the Census. 1850, 1860, 1870, 1880, 1890, 1900, 1910, 1920, 1930.

U.S. District Court, Eastern District of VA, Richmond Division, Bankruptcy Act of 1867 Involuntary Case File, #186: Paton v. Thalheimer. Feb 1873 – Apr 1874.

Urofsky, Melvin I. *Commonwealth and Community: The Jewish Experience in Virginia.* Richmond, VA: Virginia Historical Society, 1997.

Valentine Family Papers, 1786-1920. Valentine Richmond History Center. Richmond, VA.

Virginia Business Directory and Gazetteer and Richmond City Directory. Compiled and published by Chataigne and Gillis. Richmond, VA: J.W. Randolph & English. 1877-78. Library of Virginia.

Virginia. Volumes 43-45. R.G. Dun & Co. Collection. Baker Library Historical Collections. Harvard Business School.

Waller, Emmie S. Letter to William B. Thalhimer Jr. 17 Nov 2002.

Weekley, Larry. "$500,000 Computer System Is Installed by Thalhimers." *Richmond Times-Dispatch.* 6 May 1962.

Weidenfeld, Rose Goodman. "Thalhimer Family Is Richmond Institution." (Letter to the editor). *Richmond News Leader.* 28 June 1978.

Wendt, Lloyd and Herman Kogan. *Give the Lady What She Wants!* Chicago: Rand McNally, 1952.

Whitaker, Jan. *Service and Style: How the American Department Store Fashioned the Middle Class.* New York: St. Martin's Press, 2006.

Whitlock, Philip. "The Life of Philip Whitlock, Written by Himself." Beth Ahabah Museum and Archives Trust. Richmond, VA.

Winslow, Olivia. "Fund set up for Ex-Thalhimers Staff." *Richmond Times-Dispatch.* 24 Jan 1992.

William B. Thalhimer Jr. Letter to Isaac Thalhimer written in 1930. Private collection of William B. Thalhimer III.

William B. Thalhimer Jr.'s scrapbook of 1934 Europe trip with William Flatow, Jr. Private collection of William B. Thalhimer III.

Williams, Aline Thalhimer Livingstone. Interview with the author. Rydal, PA . 28 Jan. 2003.

Williams, Michael Paul. "Thalhimers sit-in remembered." *Richmond Times-Dispatch.* 21 Feb 2004.

Williams, Winston. "The Holiday Season, 1985: A Tale of Three Towns." *The New York Times.* 22 Dec 1985.

Williamson, Harriet. "William B. Thalhimer Marks 50th Year with Family Store." *Women's Wear Daily.* 15 Aug 1956.

Womens' Wear Daily. 2 Nov 1967.

Wood, James M. *Halle's Memoirs of a Family Department Store 1891-1982.* Cleveland: Geranium Press, 1987.

Zukin, Sharon. *Point of Purchase: How Shopping Changed American Culture.* New York: Routledge, 2004.

Zulker, William Allen. *John Wanamaker: King of Merchants.* Wayne, PA: Eaglecrest Press, 1993.

Dr. Roland Flade cites the following additional sources in his research on the Thalheimer family of Tairnbach:

Printed Sources

Bloch, Heinrich. *Israelitischer Verbands-Friedhof Waibstadt.* Gräber-Verzeichnis, Bad Rappenau, 1914.

Flade, Dr. Roland. *The Lehmans: From Rimpar to the New World, A Family History.* Würzburg (second enlarged edition), 1999.

Gutjahr, Rainer. *Der israelitische Elementarunterricht im badischen Leutershausen an der Bergstraße zwischen dem "Judenedikt" von 1809 und der Einführung der Simultanschule 1876.* In: Gerhard Fritz (Ed.): Landesgeschichte und Geschichtsdidaktik. Festschrift für Rainer Jooß (Gmünder Hochschulreihe Nr. 24). Schwäbisch Gmünd, 2004, p. 53-71.

Israelitischer Verbandsfriedhof Waibstadt. *Nachtrag zum Gräberverzeichnis.* Fortgeführt bis zum 27. Oktober 1936 (Grab Nr. 339) durch Lehrer Jakob Bloch, Neckarbischofsheim. Mannheim, 1936.

Burgert, Annette Kunselmann. *Eighteenth Century Emigrants from German-Speaking Lands to North America, Vol. 1: The Northern Kraichgau.* Breiningsville, PA: The Pennsylvania German Society, 1983.

Lewin, Adolf. *Geschichte der badischen Juden seit der Regierung Karl Friedrichs, 1738-1909.*

Ramon, Esther. "Geschichte der jüdischen Erziehung in Karlsruhe von 1730-1933", in: Heinz Schmitt (ed.), *Juden in Karlsruhe.* Beiträge zu ihrer Geschichte bis zur nationalsozialistischen. Machtergreifung, Karlruhe, no year, p. 301-310.

Wikipedia, entries for "Pestalozzi" and "Karlsruhe."

Allemannia Judaica website entries for "Feudenheim" and "Karlsruhe."

Strehlen, Martina. Der jüdische Friedhof von Waibstadt. Unveröffentlichte Grunddokumentation des Landesdenkmalamtes, 2004 (on CD ROM).

Unpublished documents from the Gemeindearchiv Mühlhausen:

Darnbacher Güterbuch, 1784

Tairnbacher Bann- und Fluhrbuch, 1828/30
    Generallandesarchiv Karlsruhe:

Abt. 229 Tairnbach, 104175, Verwaltungssachen Thairnbach

236/970, Die Organisation der Juden, 1819

313/1262, Familiennamen der Juden, 1809-1810

6065, Standesbuch, 1804-1806, 1810-1823

6066, Standesbuch, 1824-1839

6067, Standesbuch, 1840-1850

6068, Standesbuch, 1851-1860

6069, Standesbuch, 1861-1869

Katholisches Pfarrarchiv Mühlhausen:

Israeliten zu Tairnbach: Geburts- und Totenscheine, 1814

From the Generallandesarchiv Karlsruhe:

390/5907 Standesbuch Großsachsen

390/2954 Standesbuch Schriesheim

390/560 and 390/559 Standesbuch Flehingen

313/1262 Familiennamen der Juden betreffend (Flehingen, Schriesheim, Leutershausen)

236/970 Die Organisation der Juden, 1819

362/572 Errichtung einer öffentlichen Schule für die Israelitische Gemeinde Feudenheim, 1838-1879

299/104200 Tabellarisches Verzeichnis, 1806

229/104195 Kriegssteuer, Einstufung nach Haus- und Grundbesitz, March 3, 1807

229/2411 Tairnbach, Bürgergelder 1825